SPECIAL EDUCATION SERIES
Peter Knoblock, Editor

Achieving the Complete School:
Strategies for Effective Mainstreaming
Douglas Biklen
with Robert Bogdan, Dianne L. Ferguson,
Stanford J. Searl, Jr., and Steven J. Taylor

Classic Readings in Autism
Anne M. Donnellan, Editor

Stress in Childhood:
An Intervention Model for Teachers
and Other Professionals
Gaston E. Blom, Bruce D. Cheney,
and James E. Snoddy

Curriculum Decision Making
for Students with Severe Handicaps:
Policy and Practice
Dianne L. Ferguson

Community Integration for People
with Severe Disabilities
Steven J. Taylor, Douglas Biklen,
and James Knoll, Editors

Community Integration for People with Severe Disabilities

Steven J. Taylor
Douglas Biklen
James Knoll

Editors

Teachers College, Columbia University
New York and London

Preparation of Chapters 1, 2, 3, 7, 9, and 11 was supported in part by the Community Integration Project and the Research and Training Center on Community Integration, through Contract No. 300-85-0076 and Cooperative Agreement No. G0085C03503 between the National Institute on Handicapped Research, U.S. Department of Education, and the Center on Human Policy at Syracuse University. Opinions expressed therein are solely those of the authors and no official endorsement by the U.S. Department of Education should be inferred.

Partial support for Chapter 9 was also provided through Preparing Leadership Personnel in the Area of Transitions from School to Employment and Community Living, Cooperative Agreement No. G008430063, and Post-Secondary Nonsheltered Vocational Training and Continuing Education for Severely Handicapped Young Adults, Agreement No. G008430043.

Support for Chapter 10 was provided in part through a grant from the C. S. Mott Foundation.

Published by Teachers College Press, 1234 Amsterdam Avenue,
New York, NY 10027

Library of Congress Cataloging-in-Publication Data

Community integration for people with severe disabilities.

(Special education series)
Includes bibliographies and index.
1. Developmentally disabled—United States.
2. Community life. 3. Social integration—United States. I. Taylor, Steven J., 1949– . II. Biklen, Douglas. III. Knoll, James. IV. Series: Special education series (New York, N.Y.)
HV3006.A4C646 1987 362.1'968 87-6465
ISBN 0-8077-2847-0
ISBN 0-8077-2846-2 (pbk.)

Manufactured in the United States of America

92 91 90 89 88 87 1 2 3 4 5 6

To
Burton Blatt,
a colleague, mentor, and friend

Contents

Foreword *by Gunnar Dybwad* ix

Preface xi

Acknowledgments xiii

Introduction *by Steven J. Taylor* xv

PART I: Policy, Principles, and Practices

1 The Disabled Minority 3
Douglas Biklen and *James Knoll*

2 Continuum Traps 25
Steven J. Taylor

3 Down Home: Community Integration for People with the Most Severe Disabilities 36
Steven J. Taylor, Julie Racino, James Knoll, and *Zana Lutfiyya*

PART II: Leadership

4 Culturing Commitment 67
Gerald Provencal

5 Embracing Ignorance, Error, and Fallibility: Competencies for Leadership of Effective Services 85
John O'Brien

6 A Difference You Can See: One Example of Services to Persons with Severe Mental Retardation in the Community 109
Lyn Rucker

PART III: With the People

7 Beyond Caregiving: A Reconceptualization of the Role of the Residential Service Provider 129
James Knoll and *Alison Ford*

8 Gentle Teaching: An Alternative to Punishment for People with Challenging Behaviors 147
John J. McGee, *Paul E. Menousek*, and *Daniel Hobbs*

9 Achieving Success in Integrated Workplaces: Critical Elements in Assisting Persons with Severe Disabilities 184
Jan Nisbet and *Michael Callahan*

10 Living in the Community: Speaking for Yourself 202
Michael Kennedy and *Patricia Killius*, with Deborah Olson

11 Conclusion: The Next Wave 209
Robert Bogdan and *Steven J. Taylor*

Author Index 221

Subject Index 227

Foreword

At a memorial service at Boston University at the time of Burton Blatt's death, I suggested that out of the tremendous wealth of his writings and activities one might well select as his most significant contribution the creation in 1971 of the Center on Human Policy. He planned, initiated, and directed the Center while he was Director of the Division of Special Education and Rehabilitation in the School of Education at Syracuse University, where he served as Dean at the time of his death. I said: "It is through this Center and the staff he selected and guided, and to whom he entrusted its future, that Burton Blatt will continue to be heard—will continue to challenge us to move forward on the road he so clearly outlined for us."

This book fulfills this prediction. It demonstrates that Burton Blatt's goal of community integration for all is not merely realizable, but that it is being realized in countless, carefully planned and carefully monitored community projects which long since have ceased to be "experiments." Most persuasive are the accounts of steady achievements in Macomb Oakland in Michigan and Region V in Nebraska, both of which have made steady and solid progress for more than a decade.

But with equal clarity, the authors of this volume show that in many states and on the federal level strong forces are at work resisting the ideas put forth cogently by Burton Blatt, and they are pursuing practices that put into question the pious and pompous pronouncements of the political leadership.

For example: It is just 20 years ago that Burton Blatt, then serving as Assistant Commissioner for Mental Retardation in the Massachusetts Department of Mental Health, addressed a special session of the Massachusetts legislature. He said on that occasion:

> It is my hope that our governor, our legislature, and commissioners . . . will encourage us to develop a network of small community-centered residential facilities, interrelated with a total community program of preservice and inservice training and research, collaborating with our best universities where students in medicine, nursing, social work, education, and psychology may be employed during the course of their training, and may devote to our common need and common good their idealism, service, and professional skills. . . . Without such approaches, we will continue to fund new curtains and paint jobs and, once or twice in a century, we will demolish old buildings.

Several months later he issued a state document entitled *A Plan for Reformation of Services for the Mentally Retarded in Massachusetts*. In it he declared: "There is explicit recognition that in the past, the larger the size of a residential facility, the poorer the services within the facility, the less there is of community awareness and responsibility, and the greater the likelihood that more and bigger facilities will be built."

His premonition has been borne out: On December 31, 1986 the Governor of Massachusetts boasted that since 1974 the Commonwealth of Massachusetts had spent $240 million to improve the buildings at the state's five mental retardation "schools" serving 3,150 individuals. This equaled $76,000 for each resident, merely for building improvement and for "new curtains and paint jobs," at a time when placement in ordinary cost-effective community residences was kept to a bare minimum. The "refurbished" Walter E. Fernell School housed over 900 residents with a staff of 2,500, at a cost of $65,000 per resident, even though a comprehensive report submitted to the governor 21 years earlier by Commissioners of Mental Health and of Public Health, entitled *Massachusetts' Plan for its Retarded—A 10-Year Plan*, clearly stated: "All future residential facilities should house no more than 500 retarded persons. Plans should be developed to reduce the capacity of existing institutions to this size" (p. 1). The example of Massachusetts and of other states that persist in the institutional model is indeed most unfortunate.

Yet recent federal legislation significantly extending programs for the education in the public schools of children with handicaps, as well as the growing development of "after 22" services and opportunities, clearly support the affirmative view toward community integration which is the theme of this volume. Furthermore, the voices of self-advocacy in the community, state, nation, and indeed throughout the world, are assuming a more militant tone and slowly but surely are gaining a more meaningful participatory role. It is fitting, therefore, that this book ends with a powerful chapter written by self-advocates broadcasting the new view of the self-image and stance of liberated persons with disabilities and their growing potential for participation in effecting change.

Gunnar Dybwad
Waltham, Massachusetts
January, 1987

Preface

Throughout the 1970s and early 1980s, the issue of deinstitutionalization dominated the attention of the field of developmental disabilities. Spurred by lawsuits; exposés; federal initiatives; and parent, consumer, and professional activism, there has been an accelerated decline in the populations of public institutions. State representatives, agency administrators, parents and consumers, and professionals have devoted considerable discussion to the issue of institutionalization versus community living. Do community services cost less than institutions? Do people learn more in institutional or community settings? Are smaller facilities better than larger ones? The issue of deinstitutionalization will continue to command attention for the foreseeable future.

It is time, however, to devote equal attention to the quality of life in the community. The challenge today is not simply to open the doors of the institution. The challenge is to help people with developmental disabilities, including those with the most challenging needs, to become part of the community.

We have recently completed an examination of the "state of the art" in community integration for people with the most severe disabilities—people with multiple disabilities, severe and profound mental retardation, challenging behaviors, and medical involvements. We have reviewed manuals, books, and articles on community living, vocational services, family supports, and other services. We have conducted an in-depth phone survey with over 40 innovative programs across the country. We have visited over 12 community service systems or agencies in 7 states, and we have talked to dozens of people.

The state of the art in community integration is moving rapidly. Blink, and you might miss it. If you are not careful, you might get the impression that the major issues dominating the field have to do with whether people with severe disabilities are better off in institutions or in less restrictive community environments or in large or small facilities. Yet these are yesterday's issues. To be sure, these issues are still real. With roughly 100,000 people with developmental disabilities living in public institutions and thousands of others living in other kinds of institutions, it would be foolish to suggest that such issues have gone away. But the state of the art has moved beyond these issues. That people with the most severe disabilities can live in the community is not just an idea; it is a reality at a growing number of places across the country. The issues today have to do with how these people should be served in the community and what arrangements foster the greatest degree of integration.

In this book, we try to capture the direction in which the state of the art is moving and, together with colleagues, give our readers a sense of the issues today.

Steven J. Taylor
Douglas Biklen
James Knoll

Acknowledgments

Many people contributed to this book directly or indirectly. The staff of the Center on Human Policy and the faculty in the Division of Special Education at Syracuse University—especially Julie Racino, Alison Ford, Peter Knoblock, Luanna Meyer, Bob Bogdan, Jan Nisbet, Jo Scro, Frank Laski, Bonnie Shoultz, Hank Bersani, Pam Walker, Hillery Schneiderman, and Zana Lutfiyya—contributed many of the ideas found in this book. Friends and colleagues from around the country also offered numerous suggestions and ideas. Special thanks to Bob Perske, Gunnar Dybwad, Charlie Lakin, John McGee, Bill McCord, Lou Brown, John O'Brien, Jeff Strully, Gail Jacob, Jerry Provencal, Harvey Zuckerberg, Lyn Rucker, Mike Morris, Marilyn Wilson, Dianne Ferguson, Kathy Schwaniger, Charlie Galloway, Wade Hitzing, Nancy Rosenau, Mark Maxwell, Tom Nerney, Sheryl Dicker, and Mike Callahan for their ideas. We also want to thank the many people involved with innovative programs who took the time to talk with us, open their homes, and provide us with information about what they are doing. Thanks also to Helen Timmins for her ongoing support and Cyndy Colavita and Rachael Zubal for typing the manuscript.

Many of the chapters in this book were prepared with support from the U.S. Department of Education, Office of Special Education and Rehabilitative Services, National Institute on Handicapped Research. This support was awarded to the Center on Human Policy, Division of Special Education and Rehabilitation, Syracuse University (Contract No. 300-85-0076 and Cooperative Agreement No. G0085C03503), for the Community Integration Project and the Research and Training Center on Community Integration. Of course, the opinions expressed herein do not necessarily reflect the position or the policy of the U.S. Department of Education, and no official endorsement by the Department of Education should be inferred. We owe a special debt of gratitude to Naomi Karp of NIHR for her continuing support of our efforts.

We also want to thank Betsy Edinger, Betty H. Taylor, Sari Biklen, and Lois Knoll for their personal support of our work.

Finally, we want to acknowledge the contribution of the late Burton Blatt to this book and to all of our efforts. This book is dedicated to Burt and the values for which he stood.

Introduction

STEVEN J. TAYLOR

Is community integration a good idea? We can find excellent examples of community integration. As some researchers, policy makers, and professionals have been debating the institution-versus-community issue, others have been working to integrate people with the most severe disabilities into the community. Throughout the country, people with the most challenging needs—people with severe and profound mental retardation, medical involvements, multiple disabilities, and challenging behaviors—are living decent lives in the community.

We can also find some bad examples of community integration. Indeed, some practices associated with deinstitutionalization do not represent community integration at all. In some states, units constructed on the grounds of state institutions are referred to as "community residences." In many states, deinstitutionalization has meant "transinstitutionalization"; that is, the transfer of people from large public institutions to smaller, but just as segregated, private ones, including nursing homes. Even in some relatively small facilities, life is just as segregated, isolated, and devoid of caring relationships as in larger institutions. For some families, the trend toward the community means keeping their children at home without any support.

How can we make community integration work? That is what this book is about: what community integration means, how to think about it, and how to make it happen for people with severe disabilities.

Laying the Groundwork: Common Principles

It is difficult to make any book hang together. This is especially true in edited texts, with chapters written by different contributors. What unites the chapters in this book is a set of principles, deeply held beliefs and values about people with developmental disabilities. Like themes running through a novel, these principles appear and reappear, albeit sometimes in different forms. Taken together, the following six principles tell us what community integration means.

1. *All people with developmental disabilities belong in the community.* This book is not about the "least restrictive environment," the "residential continuum," or "normalization." It is about living in the community. All people, regardless of severity of disability, belong in the community. As the authors suggest, community integration can work only if people believe in it, cherish it, and embrace it. Lyn Rucker (Chapter 6) writes, "Put simply, if decision makers believe that *everyone* will be served and integrated in the community, half the struggle is over. In systems where that attitude is not embraced, I have seen every conceivable artificial barrier thrown up as a block to providing appropriate, integrated services for everyone."

As a corollary to this principle, no one belongs in an institution because of mental retardation or any other disability. One after another, the contributors to this book reject institutions that, in the words of John O'Brien (Chapter 5), "exclude ordinary relationships by design." Biklen and Knoll (Chapter 1) and then Provencal (Chapter 4) liken institutionalization to forms of discrimination practiced against other minority groups. For Biklen and Knoll, institutions represent "handicapism writ large." In poetic terms, Provencal tells us what he stands for:

> Always want them out, out of institutions, out of nursing homes, out of variations on these themes. It must become an anthem of sorts, a deep roll-over-everything lyrical dirge in folk opera voice: Our people do not belong in institutions of any size, shape, color, or creed.

2. *People with developmental disabilities should be integrated into typical neighborhoods, work environments, and community settings.* Community integration does not just mean physical placement in the community, but participation in community life. Some people living in group homes, community ICF/MRs (Medicaid-funded Intermediate Care Facilities for the Mentally Retarded), and other facilities are cut off from their communities. They live in a facility with six, eight, or ten or more people; board a van in the morning; go to a sheltered workshop or day activity center; return to the facility in mid-afternoon; and perhaps go on field trips as a group in the evening or on weekends.

Running throughout this book is the belief that people with developmental disabilities should have the same opportunities as other people. Biklen and Knoll (Chapter 1) write, "We must design schools, homes, workplaces, health care systems, transportation, and other social environments in such a way that they take in everyone. Our communities and our services must be pluralistic, rather than exclusionary." In Chapter 6, Rucker explains that we must view quality of life for people with disabilities in the same way we view the quality of our own lives. She goes on to describe how people with developmental disabilities are integrated into community life in the rural town of Fairbury, Nebraska. In Chapter 7, Knoll and Ford explain how residential staff can help people to become involved in their communities. Nisbet and Callahan argue in Chapter 9 that people with severe disabilities should be integrated into typical places in the community:

> Integration means working alongside and sharing responsibilities with nondisabled co-workers; taking breaks, having lunch and attending a happy hour with their nondisabled peers; receiving instructions from the company supervisors; learning from nondisabled co-workers; and being valued employees of the company.

3. *Support should be given to people with developmental disabilities in families and typical homes in the community.* The field of developmental disabilities has been successful in developing facilities, first large ones and now smaller and more "homelike" ones. Like other people, however, people with developmental disabilities need homes. For children, this means living with a family. For adults, this means living alone or with others they choose to live with or happen to get along with.

In Chapter 2, Taylor presents a critical analysis of the concept of a "continuum" between the most restrictive and the least restrictive environments. Building on this, in Chapter 3 Taylor, Racino, Knoll, and Lutfiyya describe how service systems and agencies across the country are supporting children in natural, adoptive, and foster families and adults in their own homes.

4. *We should encourage the development of relationships between people with developmental disabilities and other people.* "Community" is not only a place to be. It is a feeling of belonging among human beings. If there has been one thing lacking in the lives of people with developmental disabilities, and especially those with severe disabilities, it is the opportunity for close, mutual, and ongoing relationships with other people.

As O'Brien points out in Chapter 5, professional services cannot fulfill people's needs for friendship and companionship. O'Brien writes, "Personal relationships, including relationships with extended family members and unpaid, nonhandicapped people, fulfill the desires of people's hearts and strengthen people's sense of their own interests. But it seems difficult to make room for these relationships in professionally dominated environments." Similarly, in describing a new role for residential services workers, Knoll and Ford in Chapter 7 underline the importance of helping to build connections between people with developmental disabilities and other members of the community.

5. *We should give people with developmental disabilities opportunities to learn.* We are opposed to the custodialism of institutional warehousing or the senseless "make-work" of many programs today. People with severe disabilities should have the opportunity to learn practical, useful skills for living in the community, for example, using public transportation, ordering in restaurants, grocery shopping, cooking, cleaning, and many other home and community skills.

Chapter 7 by Knoll and Ford; Chapter 8 by McGee, Menousek, and Hobbs; and Chapter 9 by Nisbet and Callahan all deal with helping people to learn. Focusing on people with severe disabilities, Knoll and Ford explore ways in which residential caregivers can help people learn practical life skills. McGee, Menousek, and Hobbs present "gentle teaching" as an alternative to punishment for people with severely challenging behavior: "Gentle teaching . . . is a posture that refuses to punish, but one that focuses on teaching the value of reward, human presence, and participation." Nisbet and Callahan describe instructional approaches for teaching people with severe disabilities to work in typical jobs.

6. *Consumers and parents should be involved in the design, operation, and monitoring of services.* Throughout the chapters in this book, there is a deep respect for parents and people with developmental disabilities themselves. Consumers and parents should not be viewed as passive recipients of services, but as equal partners.

While many chapters in this book touch upon the importance of active consumer and parent involvement, Chapter 10 by Kennedy and Killius, with Olson, makes the strongest case for "speaking for yourself." Building on their experiences living in institutions, Kennedy and Killius explain what self-advocacy is and why it is important: "Self-advocacy, or speaking for yourself, is a big part of living in the community. People with disabilities who live in the community should have the right to make their own decisions, just like anyone else."

Perspectives on the Issues

The remainder of this book is divided into three parts, with a total of 11 chapters. Part I, entitled "Policy, Principles, and Practices," contains three chapters that address broad issues related to community integration. In Chapter 1, "The Disabled Minority," Biklen and Knoll characterize people with disabilities as a "discriminated-against minority" and trace the cultural roots of prejudice toward the disabled, which, in turn, act as barriers to community integration. In conclusion, they outline some of the crucial elements in the development of a system of truly integrated community services.

Chapter 2 by Taylor and Chapter 3 by Taylor, Racino, Knoll, and Lutfiyya are companion pieces. The first, "Continuum Traps," critiques the principle of the "least restrictive environment" and the closely aligned "continuum" concept. As an alternative to a continuum of placements ranging from the most to the least restrictive, he argues that everyone needs a home. This leads to the next chapter, "Down Home," in which the state of the art in community integration for people with the most severe disabilities is described. Based on site visits and phone interviews, this chapter looks at how innovative agencies are supporting adults and children with severe disabilities in families and community homes.

Part II, entitled "Leadership," takes the place of pieces on management and administration found in many books. Chapters 4, 5, and 6 offer different perspectives on designing and operating services for people with developmental disabilities. As each of these authors argues, it is leadership and commitment, not bureaucratic or technical expertise, that make programs effective and responsive. In Chapter 4, "Culturing Commitment," Provencal, writing personally and soulfully from the experience at Macomb Oakland in Michigan, gives an upbeat review of how to maintain commitment in human services. In Chapter 5, "Embracing Ignorance, Error and Fallibility: Competencies for Leadership of Effective Services," O'Brien, drawing on case studies of small, responsive agencies, writes about the limits of what service systems and agencies can accomplish for people with disabilities and underscores the importance of learning from mistakes and accepting imperfection. In Chapter 6, "A Difference You Can See," Rucker shows how services at Nebraska's Region V Mental Retardation Services are rooted in fundamental values such as "common sense" and "taking care of our own."

Part III, "With the People," contains 4 chapters that look at different slices of community life. In Chapter 7, Knoll and Ford present an alternative conceptualization of the role of staff members who work directly with people with severe disabilities. As they indicate, the role of residential caregiver is a demanding one, requiring a careful balance between teaching new skills, maintaining a home atmosphere, and helping people develop relationships with other members of the community.

In Chapter 8, "Gentle Teaching: An Alternative to Punishment for People with Challenging Behaviors," McGee, Menousek, and Hobbs present a positive approach to dealing with people who are viewed as the "most difficult to serve" in the community, people with severe behavior problems. Decrying the widespread use of punishment and dehumanizing behavioral interventions, they stress the importance of an affectionate and respectful posture toward people with challenging behavior and describe practical strategies for dealing with the most annoying and troublesome habits.

Chapter 9, by Nisbet and Callahan, provides an overview of the elements of successful integrated job placements for people with severe disabilities. After listing 14 elements, they present a case study that brings these elements to life.

Chapter 10, "Living in the Community: Speaking for Yourself," by Kennedy and Killius, with Olson, looks at community integration from the consumer's point of view. Based on their experiences living in institutions and in the community, the authors discuss the importance of self-advocacy.

Chapter 11, "Conclusion: The Next Wave," is written by Bogdan and Taylor. These authors pick up on themes introduced in earlier chapters, especially Chapter 1 by Biklen and Knoll and Chapter 2 by Taylor, and they review some of the lessons learned over the past 15 years, taking a look at some of the emerging and future issues in community integration.

This is a book on community integration for those committed, or at least open, to community integration, that is, to helping all people with developmental disabilities become part of the community. The chapters in this book get at the heart and soul of the community integration movement. Starting with a common philosophy, the authors give their own perspectives on the issues of the day. To be sure, they each see some things differently and take on different challenges. But there is much to be learned from all of the contributors to this book.

Enjoy!

Community Integration for People with Severe Disabilities

Part I

POLICY, PRINCIPLES, AND PRACTICES

1

The Disabled Minority

DOUGLAS BIKLEN
JAMES KNOLL

Issues in Disability

It was a crisp February morning in Wisconsin when we arrived at Maywood Manor (a pseudonym). This nursing home was like dozens of others around the state. Its residents were primarily older people; a third were people with intellectual disabilities (i.e., retardation). A common sitting room; signs indicating the director's and nurse's offices; a glass-enclosed nursing station; a cart filled with medicine; long corridors with rooms for one, two, and three people off to each side; and a television tuned to a game show announced that this was a nursing home like any other. As we walked through the main corridor, our guide, a community services specialist, explained that the people labeled "retarded" live in a separate section, beyond the set of steel doors at the end of the hall. We proceeded down the corridor, through the doors, and into another dayroom and set of hallways. This was the retardation unit. Here we encountered many of the same signs of institutional life that we had noted upon entering the front part of the nursing home, except that here everything seemed more austere, more controlled. A television hung from a brace high on the dayroom wall, individual rooms lacked personal decorations, adult "patients" had made valentine decorations of the sort usually constructed by school children, and one large plastic-covered mural brightened the hallway. Unlike the first section of the nursing home, this area had no carpeting. Large mirrors of the sort one sometimes sees along the aisles of supermarkets were positioned at the ends of the hallways, near the nursing station, making it possible for staff to monitor the wings from a single location. We learned that the residents of this retardation unit come and go (e.g., to or from day programs, on group outings, or home visits) through the back door, thus avoiding regular contact with the older people in the other part of the nursing home.

State officials count this nursing home as a "community placement" for the 30 people with retardation whom it houses. The majority are considered severely disabled. Some have recently been transferred from large state institutions. Others were placed into the nursing home by a family member or a community service agency, almost always because there had been a death or illness in the family and there was no alternative community placement. Once placed in the nursing home, these people are cut off from community life. One woman told us she would like to go shopping, and a young man told us he would like to go to a Milwaukee Brewers baseball game, but the staff do not have time or the opportunity to take them. Typically, the only opportunities for residents to leave the facility are large group outings.

No amount of rationalization could transform this nursing home into our image of typical community living. It is not a home. It is an institution.

Our visit to Maywood on that cold February morning raised a whole host of questions about community integration. For example, why has community integration been so difficult to achieve in the several decades since deinstitutionalization became a national policy? Why have counties and states allowed nursing home placements for literally thousands of people who have no medical (i.e., nursing) needs or whose needs could easily be addressed outside of nursing homes? Why has less than 7 percent of the federal funds for community living gone to support homes for fewer than 15 people each? Why have large state institutions been seen as the legitimate placements for more than 100,000 retarded people, most of whom have severe and multiple disabilities, especially when these same people have been shown to benefit most from community placement? Why have many states recently constructed large congregate residences for 50 and 100 retarded people each, when at the same time they profess a commitment to deinstitutionalization? Why have local, state, and federal government agencies been so reluctant to create supported apartment programs for one, two, and three people each, or to find homes in which people with severe intellectual disabilities will be accepted as family members? Why are nursing homes still considered a legitimate "community" placement? How can we foster community integration for people with severe disabilities?

Minority Status

The answers to these questions are not technical. In other words, the problem has not been our ignorance about how to make community integration work. Rather, the difficulties with community integration reflect the fact that, in the course of their lives, people with disabilities, particularly people with severe intellectual disabilities, regularly encounter discrimination. Ironically, disability discrimination surfaces even in human service agencies and their policies.

In this chapter we present the view that change will occur more rapidly toward community integration if we recognize people with disabilities as a discriminated-against minority (Gleidman & Roth, 1980; Hahn, 1984). This viewpoint has many ramifications, central among them the following:

1. All people, no matter how severely disabled, are entitled to basic constitutional rights, namely, equality, liberty, property, and the pursuit of happiness. The presence of an intellectual disability does not justify wholesale or even partial abrogation of rights.
2. Access to basic rights is not dependent upon a person's ability to pass an admissions test, whether to school, to transportation, to recreation and leisure, to medical treatment, or to community living.
3. The burden of proof in any debate over integration and segregation, whether for schooling, community living, or other basic rights, is on those who would justify segregation.
4. The role of professionals, far from acting as gatekeepers who decide who should be integrated or segregated, is to use their skills and talents to help people with disabilities achieve the fullest possible integration.
5. The experience of people with severe disabilities in community living will always be connected to and dependent on their experience with other aspects of society. These include, for example, societal attitudes, education and work, opportunities to make friends, and support available to their families.

Stereotypes. Nearly every aspect of the disabled person's life speaks of minority status. Only by changing this fact can we hope truly to accomplish the goal of community integration. While a disability is but one of many personal qualities—such as stature, hair color, geographic origin, race, and sex—it is frequently a basis for negative evaluation. People with disabilities find themselves given labels such as mentally retarded, brain injured, deaf, blind, emotionally disturbed, mentally ill, autistic, or learning disabled. Occasionally, these labels become epithets: "What are you, blind?" "It's like the blind leading the blind." "Retard." "What are you, deaf?" For severely disabled people, there is the term "vegetable." While professionals will sometimes make the case for the social utility of classifications and labeling—for example, to decide who needs special school or clinic services or economic subsidies—we cannot help wondering why such services cannot be provided without subjecting people to disability labels.

To some, disability, particularly retardation, conjures up an imagery of uncontrollable, violent people, perhaps someone like Steinbeck's (1937) retarded Lennie in *Of Mice and Men*. Ironically, perhaps it is this perceived threat or perhaps it is simply prejudice that seems to spark community opposition to group homes and other community living arrangements. In its ugliest form, such resistance has included bomb threats, vandalism, violence, and phone threats in what Keating (1979) has called "the war against the mentally retarded" (p. 87).

On the opposite end of the stereotype continuum, disabled people have been viewed as deserving recipients of charity and pity. However well intentioned, even these seemingly benevolent attitudes continue the invidious denial of dignity, respect, and, ultimately, equality. The Kennedy Foundation's Special Olympics typifies the charity approach. While these games offer a chance for disabled athletes to compete in sports, they are portrayed in the media and revealed in the public's minds as heart-rending events, filled with imagery of big hearts, love, circus entertainment, and a "see-what-they-can-do" motif. Through the lens of charity a severely retarded person is seen as essentially different and certainly not as a peer of the nondisabled person.

At one time in society's not-so-distant past—indeed, as recently as the 1930s—it was commonplace, everyday practice to display people with disabilities as human oddities (Bogdan, 1986). Being on stage was a legitimate, if bizarre way of making a living. Such sideshows are far less common now; they have been moved from the circus center to the back of the midway, almost as if they had become an embarrassment in today's professional, treatment-oriented society. Yet, in everyday life, many people with disabilities (e.g., Asch 1984) speak of being on display, on stage as it were, unable to gain full acceptance as ordinary, fully integrated members of the society.

Discrimination. Whether because of bureaucratic intransigence, societal neglect and indifference, or institutionally planned social control, being disabled also means having more limited choices about nearly everything, from where one gets an education (at the special school or in a regular school), to how one travels, to where one can enter (accessible or inaccessible restaurants and other public buildings), to where one lives (being sent to a nursing home or the "only available option"). Career options are perceived as limited and usually *are* limited. People with disabilities are twice as unlikely as nondisabled persons to work. The rate of unemployment among severely disabled people is well over 75 percent.

A natural byproduct of society's penchant to view people with disabilities as unusual has been the persistently espoused or implied notion that social policies and programs to accommodate people with disabilities are "add-ons," an extra expense, and possibly beyond society's ability to pay (*New York Times,* 1978; Starr, 1982). Indeed the costs *are* high for specialized transportation services ($40,000 for a bus lift, for example), for separate education systems (as high as $12,000 to $20,000 per student per year), for institutions (as high as between $60,000 and $100,000 per person per year) and group home apartments, and for the services of personal aides. But clearly, the primary reason that costs have escalated so dramatically is that people with disabilities have traditionally been closed out of cheaper, generic services (e.g., mass transit, small typical housing in the community, home support services, and regular schools). Furthermore, the critics fail to compare the costs of disability equity with other social costs. To make all of America accessible, for example, would cost less than 1.5 percent of the annual national debt; the cost of a year of federal support for special education is about the same cost as a tailfin of a nuclear submarine; the trillion-dollar cost for the Strategic Defense Initiative (popularly called "Star Wars") could fund the federal share of special education services for a thousand years.

It is a predictable irony of minority existence that disabled people find themselves at once the objects of resentment (as in the case of perceived high cost of service) on the one hand and forgotten on the other. In the early 1980s, one major educational reform report after another examined the state of public education (Goodlad, 1984; National Commission on Excellence in Education, 1983; Sizer, 1984), but none paid any serious attention to students with disabilities or to their education. It was as if these students did not exist. Their education, what we call special education or mainstreaming, had afforded public education its most significant reform in the preceding decade, yet the education reports of the 1980s failed to acknowledge disabled students or the enormous effects of the Education for All Handicapped Children Act (1975). Mainstreaming/integration, related services, functional curricula, IEPs, parental involvement, and due process had dramatically changed the educational prospects of disabled children and youth. Indeed, they had begun to change the face of public education (Biklen, 1985). For the first time, autistic students, multihandicapped students, deaf students, and many others found their way into public schools. Large numbers of disabled students still remain segregated, yet, because integration is emerging as the policy of preference, nondisabled students have been learning about severe disabilities and their peers who have them. But to read the national reports is to be left with the impression that disabled children have simply not yet made it into the consciousness of mainstream educational reformers.

At a more personal level, in the recent rise of autobiographical accounts, people with disabilities consistently remark on the public's lack of awareness about disabilities and society's part in making the disabled person's life more difficult (Bogdan & Taylor, 1983; Brightman, 1984; Jones, 1983; Roth, 1981). Parents of children with disabilities express similar frustration at society's ignorance and indifference about disabilities (Featherstone, 1982).

Institutions: Handicapism Writ Large

All people with a disability find themselves subject to prejudice and discrimination. Unfortunately, people with severe and multiple disabilities, who are the least able to demand their own rights, are the most likely to suffer the extreme forms of discrimination by being forgotten, unserved, or segregated in an institution. Thousands of severely disabled adults await a chance to work, to be part of social and recreational life, to go shopping in public, to attend integrated educational programs, to live in typical neighborhoods in typical homes. Thousands of multiply and severely disabled people await support services, aides, functional training, homemaker services, and quality health care. Families that cannot find help eventually grow tired of trying to provide all such services themselves. Even today these families must often resort to institutional placement to get services for their sons and daughters. Listen to the words of a father in a family that has asked for institutionalization of a severely disabled family member:

> You got no choice really. [We could] bring him home, Laura could watch him and take care of him all day, [and] I could take care of him when I got home from work, but who is going to see [to] him on the third shift? And Medicaid won't pay for a nurse. And I'm not going to get a nurse in here seven days a week for less than $300 takehome, and I don't make much more in my paycheck. And so we got no choice. (Foster, 1983, p. 126)

Thus it is that some families come to view the institution as a kind of damnable salvation, a safety valve or final resort. In their own minds they know that no amount of rationalizing can ever fully justify institutional placement. For most parents, the institution signifies giving up, a personal/family defeat of sorts, yet they also know that implied in the placement is a recognition that society has failed them, that they were not given sufficient support, that society required them to wage a lonely, too-difficult struggle. Sadly though, the institution offers no salvation at all. True, it shifts the burden of personal, day-to-day responsibility from the family to the state, but for the severely disabled person, the institution intensifies and exaggerates discrimination's most debilitating aspects.

Decades of careful research reveal the bleak history of institutions where dehumanization has been altogether predictable and routine. As we have previously reported, through observational studies, autobiographical accounts of families and formerly institutionalized people, legal briefs, and comparative studies of institutions and community programs, we see a veritable indictment of the institutional model (see Biklen & Knoll, in press; Center on Human Policy, 1979, for an overview of this literature). Some of the worst offenses are as follows:

- Despite promises of economies of scale, institutions are the most costly way of providing residential or any other services to retarded people (Braddock, Hemp, & Howes, 1985).
- Institutional architecture reveals that the old institutions could have doubled as zoos, the newer ones as austere nursing homes (see, for example, Blatt & Kaplan, 1966; Blatt, Ozolins, & McNally, 1979).

- Labeling is nowhere diminished. Terms such as "low-grades," "high-grades," "the medically fragile," and "the severely and profoundly retarded" flourish (Center on Human Policy, 1979).
- By keeping people away, out of circulation, institutions perpetuate and enforce the image of severely disabled people as oddities (Biklen & Knoll, in press).
- By definition, institutions deny people community living experiences, and so the skills needed for community life wither away or are never learned (Biklen & Knoll, in press).
- Holidays become times of loneliness or of stilted events orchestrated by civic groups that have no long-term connection to the people to whom they would bring happiness.
- An ideology of custodialism pervades the institution.
- Personal possessions (e.g., clothes and shoes) are quickly lost or destroyed (Blatt & Kaplan, 1966).
- Toxic medications fill the void of boredom left by a nearly total absence of meaningful programs (Center on Human Policy, 1979).
- Congregation ensures the worst effects of modeling, with one "maladaptive behavior" yielding another. It is as if bizarre behavior springs naturally from the unnatural limits of institutional living (Biklen & Knoll, in press; Center on Human Policy, 1979).
- Incidents of physical abuse reach epidemic proportions, as do communicable diseases such as hepatitis and scabies (Rothman & Rothman, 1984).
- Residents learn to eat meals in record speed, typically under five minutes, on wards and in austere cafeterias (Center on Human Policy, 1979).
- Hours upon hours of each day are spent waiting for activities (Blatt & Kaplan, 1966).
- Interaction with families diminishes rapidly the longer residents remain institutionalized (Center on Human Policy, 1979).
- In the worst cases, abuse takes the form of residents being forced to live in isolation cells, showers, and barren dayrooms; being washed down with hoses as if they were cattle in a slaughterhouse; being tied to benches and chairs or constrained in straitjackets; being forced to endure toilets without seats, toilet paper, or stall walls, and with broken plumbing and cockroaches; being kept unclothed and as a consequence being burned by floor detergent and overheated radiators; having ears bitten off by other residents; eating with hands or spoons rather than with a full complement of flatware; being burned intentionally with cigarette butts or beaten with keys by staff; and crowded into bedrooms filled wall to wall with beds (Center on Human Policy, 1979).
- Even the most modern, newest institutions fail to create homelike, individualized living quarters.

Unfortunately, many people review the reams of data on the deleterious effects of institutional placement through lenses that are distorted by the same fundamental prejudices that made institutions a viable option in the first place. From this perspective the abuses of institutions are attributed to myriad secondary causes, all of which are supposedly remediable in renovated institutions. Those who advocate for "new, quality facilities" fail to appreciate that the fundamental flaw, in an institutional system of services, lies not in failure to control a few discrete characteristics of the environment such as size, staffing pattern, and per diem rate of reimbursement, but in the exclusionary (i.e., discriminatory) ideology that undergirds institutions.

Many who started out as advocates of institutional reform have realized that the problems with institutions are anything but superficial. The problem of these places is in their very nature, in their existence, and in their perpetuation. In the words of this century's leading student and critic of institutions, Burton Blatt, the time has come to close the door on institutions:

> We must evacuate the institutions for the mentally retarded. . . . The quicker we get about converting our ideologies and resources to a community model, the quicker we will learn how to forget what we perpetrated in the name of humanity. . . . To live with our retarded children, our handicapped friends, our aging parents does place burdens on us. What we must learn from the nightmares of institutions is that these are burdens that cannot be avoided or delegated: to have a decent society we must behave as decent individuals (Blatt et al., 1979, pp. 143–144).

Barriers to Integration

A failure to understand the roots of institutional abuse has sometimes led to an unfocused approach to the development of a community-based service system. This has given community models of service a bad name, under the label of "deinstitutionalization." In the popular mind this neologism translates to the "dumping" of severely disabled people, with no supports other than a Supplemental Security Income (SSI) check and a ready supply of psychotropic drugs, onto the streets of many large cities. Even somewhat more sophisticated observers (including some who work in the service system) frequently define conversion as little more than moving people out of institutions and into group homes and sheltered workshops. In neither instance is any thought given to the fact that *community integration is vastly more complex than just deinstitutionalizing people*. A lack of awareness of this distinction has led to the adoption of an essentially passive policy of deinstitutionalization which is supported by arguments of cost effectiveness. This in turn has perpetuated the perverse logic of segregation in settings that are located in the community (cf. Bercovici, 1983).

When we regard people with disabilities as a disenfranchised minority, and not merely as "clients," the difference between deinstitutionalization and true community integration becomes even more clearly drawn. The practice of developing a system of services based solely on the push to decrease the inpatient population of state institutions changes nothing. Services located in the community but not truly integrated transmit the same message that the people they serve are intrinsically different. A superficial transfer of services that is not based on an effort to change underlying attitudes will merely create a new type of asylum, one that will require the attention of the next generation of reformers. On the other hand, if the service system fosters *active* integration of all disabled people into community homes, job sites, and neighborhoods, and facilitates enduring relationships, it will also eventually effect an end to the *handicapist*[1] attitudes that fostered and perpetuated segregated services.

Unfortunately, the pervasive nature of discriminatory attitudes predicated on the presence of a disability have led to the construction of a number of barriers that hinder social integration.

Community Resistance. Many of the arguments mustered by those who oppose community residences for people with severe multiple disabilities (cf. Keating, 1979) are a recycling of familiar demagoguery. The loss of property value, the threat from strange new infections, and the potential danger to women and children have been used throughout our history to rally opposition to the latest "alien" threat to the American way of life. The latest improvisation on this theme merely has a few variations on the lyrics—the chorus, as always, remains the same.

Research on community attitudes toward people classified as mentally retarded and on opposition to community residences reveals a strange pattern that makes sense only when analyzed through a filter that is sensitive to indicators of prejudice. When people are asked about the rights of disabled or mentally retarded people *in general,* they tend to be highly supportive of the right to live in the community (Gallup Organization, 1976; Krastner, Reppucci, & Pezzoli, 1979; Roth & Smith, 1983). However, when the question focuses on the particular and it appears that mentally retarded people are actually moving in next door, neighborhood enthusiasm quickly wanes (Krastner et al., 1979). Somewhere between one-third and one-half of all community residences meet active opposition (Seltzer, 1984). Ironically, the greatest amount of opposition appears to surface when the opening of a residence is directly preceded by a high-profile program of public education, which was intended to quell opposition (Seltzer, 1984). On the other hand, those homes that begin quietly are least likely to meet resistance.

---

[1] *Handicapism and handicapist* were defined by Bogdan and Biklen (1977, p. 14) as "a set of assumptions and practices that promote the differential and unequal treatment of people because of apparent or assumed physical, mental, or behavioral differences."

Zoning and Site-Selection Laws. Opposition to community residences for disabled individuals and the possible contribution of community education efforts to this opposition are intimately connected to local zoning regulations and various state site-selection laws. As the briefs filed in a zoning case before the U.S. Supreme Court (*City of Cleburne* v. *Cleburne Living Center,* 1984a, 1984b) clearly demonstrate, restrictions on the rights of people labeled mentally retarded abound in the laws of nearly every state. The briefs correctly link these laws to the eugenics movement and its efforts to institutionalize, sterilize, euthanasize, or otherwise control all disabled people. These archaic laws, with their restriction on facilities for people with mental retardation, make it necessary for a service agency to "sell" a community on the premise that disabled people make good neighbors. The "Catch 22" has been mentioned earlier: Public education, which is necessary to obtain a zoning waiver, may then in turn actually stimulate neighborhood opposition.

Some states (e.g., New York) have rewritten their laws to give special consideration to community residences for disabled people. Unfortunately, not much has changed. While the new laws are usually more flexible and allow for a right of appeal beyond the local zoning board, few of them are simple, straightforward statements on the right of disabled people to live anywhere housing is available. Most often, a special procedure is outlined that codifies the places where disabled people live. Often, such legislation creates long, drawn-out administrative procedures for appealing site selection, thus limiting the speed with which settings (even very small ones) can be established. This tedious process presumes that large numbers of people must continue living in institutions or are only able to move out of their family home if a crisis forces the service system to respond to their need ahead of others'.

Entrenched Institutional Interests. In many states the agency that determines whether policy will foster integration or merely push deinstitutionalization is administered by individuals who (1) after years in the agency bureaucracy have come to regard services to people labeled mentally retarded as synonymous with institutions and/or (2) have a background in public administration with no broader perspective on the needs of disabled people (cf. Rothman & Rothman, 1984). In both of these cases decisions made in the budget departments are likely to have the greatest effect on the nature of services. For example, from the accountant's point of view, the need to recoup expenditures for the construction of institutions forces states to keep newly constructed facilities filled (Biklen & Knoll, in press). Of course, there are numerous exceptions where dynamic leadership and innovative problem solving have pointed beyond limited administrative horizons and fostered integrated services.

At the highest levels of the bureaucracy that administers programs for people with developmental disabilities, the people who receive services are usually the least visible presence. Top administrators in most state departments are political appointees whose primary concerns are balancing the budget and making sure no major issues crop up that may cause the governor or the legislature a political problem. Given the political clout of institutions' investors (i.e., bond holders), institutional suppliers, and public employee unions, it is little wonder that the interests of disabled people and the voices of their advocates count for little.

At this level people with disabilities encounter a subtle and nefarious form of dehumanization. The disabled person becomes a commodity, a mere conduit for funds that serve the interests of others (Scull, 1981). A glaring example of this can be seen in the way funds from Title XIX of the Social Security Act, Medicaid, have been used to finance institutions (Taylor, Brown, et al., 1981) and vastly inflate the cost of community services in large, segregated, and highly medicalized ICF/MRs (Biklen & Knoll, in press), all in the name of saving the state tax money. Residents of the settings affected by these funding formulas become pawns in a national shell game that transfers the exorbitant bills for construction and service to the federal government. In the end, this process becomes an economic disincentive for smaller community residences. It does not matter that smaller settings are "more effective (as operationally defined) and less expensive to society," for they place "a greater burden upon the state tax base" (Jones, Conroy, Feinstein, & Lemanowicz, 1984, p. 311) and are therefore less favored in state policy circles.

The indiscriminate use of ICF funds and the failure to base state policy on a coherent vision of what the lives of people with severe disabilities should look like are both directly related to the services' dependence on political contingencies. As one state director explained, "Long-term planning is determined by how long it is until the next election." Within such a narrow time frame, the expediency of "capturing" federal Medicaid dollars through a process of reconstructing institutional facilities mortgages the lives and rights of retarded people for future decades.

Parental Fears. These same bureaucracies frequently cite parental pressure as a major rationale for the continued existence of state institutions. To be sure, public officials are confronted with the emotion-packed plea of parents who are afraid that their children will get lost in an uncontrolled and unmonitored move into the community (cf. U.S. Senate, 1982). It is true that parents who followed the best available professional opinion and placed their children in institutions are some of the leading advocates for institutions (e.g., Kupfner, 1982). However, when the position of public officials—who appeal to the fears of these parents—is carefully examined, their argument emerges as self-serving and more than a little cynical. We must ask, How many parents have been given a fair choice between quality personal-scale homes and institutionalization? Many parents have observed and have been told of inadequate or absent community services. Families report being told that to get early access to community programs (i.e., a group home or apartment) they must first institutionalize their son or daughter. A recent study of circumstances under which parents institutionalize their sons and daughters (Foster, 1983) reveals that parents make this decision under the pressure of insufficient or nonexistent community support or options. Yet, the families of those who have been deinstitutionalized for one year or more, whether the families feared or favored community placement at the outset, support it in the final analysis (Conroy & Bradley, 1985).

The Existing Community Service System. One vision of the future residential service system for severely disabled people foresees chains of group homes all across America, most of them ICF/MRs and many of them privately owned (Fiorelli, 1982). An examination of the most recent national data on residential services reveals that if current trends continue, this vision may well materialize.

Hauber and her colleagues (Hauber et al., 1984) report a consistent figure of approximately 250,000 people classified as mentally retarded residing in some type of supervised setting outside their family home. Of this number, 58% live in settings for 64 or more people and 72% in settings for 16 or more; 115,032 of the people in the system live in private facilities. The smallest settings (size: 1 to 5 people), including foster care, are growing at the fastest rate but serve only 10.5% of all residents. When these data are examined with an eye to level of disability, it becomes evident that people with the most extensive service needs tend to live in the larger, more segregated settings. Nearly half (46.8%) of the residents of facilities of 16 or more were profoundly retarded. Ironically, people with the most severe disabilities have been shown to benefit the most from placement in small community residences (Raynes, 1980). Of course, the selection of the number 16 as the cutoff point for a "small" setting appears arbitrary and highly questionable. In fact, it is an artifact of Medicaid legislation. When judged against the common-sense criteria of a typical home in modern America, the best that can be said, based on these data, is that 10.5% of the people who receive residential services *may* be living in what we would define as a "homelike" setting for any other segment of the population.

The development of a system of large group homes to provide for the residential needs of severely disabled people continues to impede community integration. Although most of the research shows that life in group homes represents a dramatic improvement over even the "best" institutions, the tacit acceptance of group homes as the "answer" sows the seeds of the new asylum. Choice, individualization, and real integration are ignored, as people are required to fit into whatever "beds" are available in this service system.

Even under the best of circumstances, systems of large group homes erect often subtle barriers to integration.

- As the size of a setting increases, residents are more likely to decrease their involvement in the outside community, since they find their social needs met within their place of residence (Willer & Intagliata, 1983).
- As size and complexity of duties increase, staff become more concerned with facility management and maintaining control of the group (Berry, 1975).
- Group homes impose difficult work schedules and provide few opportunities for career advancement, thereby leading to high staff turnover, even among dedicated workers (McCord, 1981). This creates difficulties for staff recruitment, training, and retention (Bruininks, Kudla, Wieck, & Hauber, 1980). In turn, these staffing problems interfere with consistency and maintenance of a clear focus on the need for residents to develop relationships in the community.
- Much of the public opposition voiced against group homes might be best characterized as the "sore thumb effect." The potential neighbors object to unusual renovations of existing buildings to accommodate large numbers of residents and staff, and to the impact of a staff parking lot on the residential character of the neighborhood.
- The multitude of regulations associated with group homes in general, and ICFs in particular, requires the development of a hierarchical management structure. This stands in sharp contradiction to the experience that a horizontal model of shared responsibility is best suited for the management of dispersed community programs (cf. Cherniss, 1981; Goldenberg, 1971).
- Not surprisingly, service systems have created large group homes and a focus on staff training that emphasizes the smooth running of facilities and concern for potential sources of liability (e.g., McCarthy, 1980; Youngblood & Bensberg, 1983) rather than quality programming. Few states have any staff training related to the promotion of community integration. In New York, for example, there is no significant difference between the training required for institutional employees and for community residential workers.

The point is, a truly integrated system of community services will be radically different from anything now in existence. As it stands now we have merely witnessed an incremental growth away from the institutional model that has defined services for over a century. This old system was based on the need to separate society from a potentially dangerous group (cf. Goddard, 1912; Terman, 1916). Such a system impedes and will continue to impede full social integration, for it remains grounded in a regressive vision of the people it serves. A system of services that is primarily focused on integration must be based on meeting the specific needs of *individuals* with severe disabilities to live in concert with their nondisabled peers. Such a system of services, rooted in the acceptance of the full humanity of disabled people, must form its own beginnings. It cannot be a simple reformation of what has been.

Clinical Judgment. One of the most pervasive barriers to integration and the hardest one for committed professionals to accept is the traditional clinical relationship. To those working within this paradigm it is incomprehensible that an approach that they have been trained to see as ideally suited to providing the best possible service to the client may at times contradict the liberty interest of those they seek to help.

The archetype of the clinical method is the relationship between physician and patient. Traditionally, professionals possess the specialized knowledge needed to remediate the patient's difficulty. This special knowledge places the professional in a position of almost complete authority vis-à-vis the patient, at least as it relates to the presenting problem. However, when the "problem" is a severe disability, which our society sees as life defining, clients are likely to lose all control over their lives when they enter the service system.

The roots of special education and many other human services, which have adopted the clinical model of service provision, lie in the principle of individualization. For example, in general education, at the turn of the century, standard practice emphasized the most efficient mode of instruction for the largest group of students. When the new compulsory educational system found itself confronted with increasing numbers of students who were perceived as not profiting from this model of education or who were seen as disrupting it, its response was to exclude them. This allowed the mainstream education of the majority to continue unchanged. The teachers who were asssigned to the "supervision" of excluded students had to look outside of education for a methodology for dealing with their pupils. From the beginning, the close association of these students' learning problems with real and supposed medical difficulties suggested the clinical (diagnostic/prescriptive) method as a useful model for structuring an approach to instruction. Also, since professionalization was a dominant goal in all of education, the medical model connection became a convenient avenue to professional legitimacy for the field of special education. (For a detailed discussion of this trend toward professionalism/medicalization, see Tomlinson, 1982.)

While this approach at first glance appears to be an individualized way of meeting specialized needs, in practice it has been distorted by narrowly focusing on the individual in isolation from other social forces. Historically, the seemingly endless queue of those in need of individualized services has subtly transformed the clinical endeavor. This clinical press has forced a shift in the focus of professional practice, away from a holistic approach to the person and toward a narrow focus on remediating *the problem*. Once this refocusing of the clinical relationship takes place, the larger context within which people live disappears as a relevant factor in the decision-making process. The priority becomes treating the problem in a controlled fashion. The obvious drawback of this approach is that natural life settings present far greater complexity than the controlled treatment context. So, unless a clinician views what she or he does in a critical manner and makes a conscious effort to see the whole person receiving services, this process runs the risk of becoming a restraint on the client. For example, from this perspective a segregated facility can be justified as a valid intervention if it alleviates the presenting problem. In the final analysis, a model of service that was founded on an attempt to prevent the individual from getting lost in the crowd can lead to the person's getting lost in the problem.

At its extreme this clinical perspective can even view itself as taking priority over fundamental human rights. For example, it provided part of the basis for a Supreme Court decision that affirmed the primacy of professional judgment over the rights of mentally retarded people (*Youngberg* v. *Romeo*, 1982). In most cases, however, the conflict between the rights of disabled people and professional judgment is not so blatant or even apparent. Nonetheless, it emerges in almost every journal article that reports research regarding residential settings. It is almost *pro forma* for the introduction to state that the purpose of the research is to inform the debate over the "best" environment for disabled people. The unstated implication is that the optimal environment for disabled people is somehow fundamentally different from the environments where everyone else lives, attends school, or works, and that *the answer* will be *found* through clinical research and implemented through professional practice.

Lack of Technical Expertise. The weakest argument for the continued segregation of people with severe disabilities is that they cannot be served in the community because they are *too* disabled, *too* medically involved, or have behaviors that are *too* difficult to deal with. Regardless of the research method used—matched pairs, survey, or site visit (Conroy, Efthimiou, & Lemanowicz, 1982; Hauber et al., 1984; Silver, Silverman, & Lubin, 1982; Taylor, Racino, Knoll, & Lutfiyya, Chapter 3 of this volume)—research findings consistently demonstrate that individuals with equivalent needs can be served as well or better in small community settings than in institutions. When this is reviewed in light of the finding that individuals with the most severe disabilities appear to benefit the most from living in smaller homelike settings (Conroy et al., 1982; Hemming, Lavender, & Pill, 1981; Keith & Ferdinand, 1984; Raynes, 1980), the continuation of large segregated settings is indefensible. Nonetheless, support for the perpetuation of institutions frequently presumes that the expertise necessary to serve the most severely disabled people is not and cannot be available in general community settings.

Conclusion: Strategies for Integration

The most significant barrier to community integration of people with severe disabilities is not technical. Every day in literally every community in America people with severe medical problems, multiple disabilities, and serious behavior problems live their lives in safety and comfort without being artificially segregated from the rest of society. Communities have demonstrated the ability to ameliorate the technical barriers. Fiscal disincentives to integration can be reordered. Existing institutions can be converted for alternative uses. Alternative work can be fashioned for current institutional employees. Functional community-based programming can and does work. Individualized community supports have been demonstrated. But no amount of technical, legislative, or regulatory tinkering will bring about integration.

On the surface, integration concerns where and how people live, but more fundamentally it reflects the relationship of people who happen to have a disability with the other members of their community. Integration does not exist as long as disabled people are viewed as intrinsically different from those who have no functional limitation or socially imposed label. As long as some people are rejected economically, socially, and politically, they will remain segregated no matter where they live. As we suggested in the introduction to this chapter, integration will not come for people with severe intellectual disabilities unless we reconcile ourselves to confronting the systemic stereotyping, prejudice, and discrimination (i.e., handicapism) that pursues people with disabilities.

Successful strategies for developing integrated community services demand the presence of certain nontechnical elements. In some instances there are beliefs or ideologies; in other cases, there are broad principles for guiding practice. All are oriented toward combating handicapism. In sum, these crucial elements provide a framework within which to reorder services for meaningful community integration.

1. *Common Human Needs.* There needs to be a clear and unambiguous affirmation by human service professionals that the needs of people with severe disabilities are the same as those of other people (i.e., nondisabled people). They may require some "special" supports, but fundamentally people with severe disabilities need

- A secure, stable home, not a facility or constant movement toward some mythical state called "independence"

- Enduring human relationships, not merely transitory paid ones
- Some real control over their environment, via at least partial participation in every aspect of daily life.

2. *Truly Individualized Services.* Services to disabled persons must become truly individualized. People must enjoy choices in their lives, a measure of self-determination. The priority must be meeting the unique needs and desires of a particular person within the context of his or her personal community. The fiction that individualized services mean "placing" someone in the most appropriate setting in some predefined continuum of "options" must be recognized for what it is—an administrative artifact. People with severe disabilities desire options and choices in living arrangements, employment, recreation, and the people with whom they interact—just like everyone else. This type of service system stands in stark contrast to the "take it or leave it" array of "options" available in most localities. In the final analysis, a society that asks, "What are your interests and needs?" is not so much extravagant as sensitive.

3. *Self-Determination.* There needs to be a realization that:

> A new voice is beginning to make itself heard in our midst, and demanding that we should listen. It is the voice of persons with mental handicaps. Until now, others have spoken for them, in the belief that they would lack the skill to speak for themselves. Our task now is to listen to them, to help them to participate as equals in the life of the community and to provide them with the opportunity to make meaningful choices. To assert their right to participate is one thing; making it a reality is another. But the obstacles to greater participation and self-expression do not lie entirely with persons with mental handicaps; they spring partly from the low expectation of others, even those with a lifetime's experience as family members or professionals. (International League of Societies for Persons with Mental Handicap, 1984, p. 1)

4. *Holistic Perspective.* We must begin to recognize that the lives of people with severe disabilities (like all our lives) cannot be broken up into discrete boxes. All of the elements in a person's life—home, work or school, recreation, relationships, and so on—form a whole fabric. Thus, if people with a disability have a home where they are treated as active adult members of the household but are devalued in the workplace, the quality of life in general is diminished. If schools are preparing their graduates with severe disabilities to live in individualized homes as adults, but then are graduating those students into residential systems that provide only 10-person group homes, in effect students and their families are bound to feel an extraordinary dissonance between the goal of individual choice and the reality of enforced congregate living. All aspects of people's lives are interrelated; integration requires coherence across these elements.

5. *Quality and Equity.* One of the cornerstones of our society is a belief that there are no qualifiers on the statement that all people "are created equal." The implication of this is that the quality of society, the quality of communities, the quality of social existence demand equity, since an arbitrary restriction of any individual or group potential is a restriction on everyone. This faith, which has been constitutionally canonized, has been consistently affirmed in the judicial system's finding that the mandate for equity at the very least requires that *everyone* have equal access to opportunity. Hence no one receives a quality education, lives in a quality neighborhood, or works in the best possible work environment if that "quality" is based on the exploitation or exclusion of some other group. In other words, the quality of life available to anyone is, in a very real sense, tied to the full inclusion of people with severe disabilities.

6. *"Generic" Communities.* One fundamental tenet of community-based services has long been that whenever possible people should use typical, "generic" community resources and avoid specialized "handicapped-only" or disability-specific clinics, recreation clubs, and so forth. The problem has been that, in many communities, generic service providers continue to refer disabled consumers to specialized agencies. This often happens because the adaptations or accommodations needed in order for the community resource to become accessible to the consumer with a disability are regarded as unique or exceptional, an add-on. Instead we must view special accommodations as routine, ordinary, and expected. We must design schools, homes, workplaces, health care systems, transportation, and other social environments in such a way that they take in everyone. Our communities and our services must be pluralistic, rather than exclusionary.

7. *Shared Problems.* The logical implication of the two previous points is a realization that the needs of people with disabilities are not theirs alone. To speak of an issue as a "disability problem" is to deny the fact that questions of equity and accessibility belong to everyone. Thus, part of the process of developing integrated community services involves educating the nondisabled public to see the needs of people with disabilities as public needs and problems, directly affecting the entire society.

8. *Fiscal Responsibility.* Nearly everyone values fiscal responsibility. Without responsible services, the public may well begin to view people with disabilities as "expensive burdens" consuming limited public resources in luxury service settings. In a society that is committed to integration, true fiscal responsibility has two corollaries:

- The closer that residential services parallel typical living situations and use generic resources, the less likely they are to be publicly perceived as extravagant and the more likely they are actually to be economical. On the other hand, services in specially constructed residential facilities have their costs escalated by expenditures for bond payments, maintenance, administration, and a proliferation of professional staff.

- A long-term perspective is needed on cost. While a short-term exceptionalistic response to an issue (e.g., a subsidized wheelchair-van taxi service) may be perceived as cheaper, such costs are never absorbed. On the other hand, capital investment in generic services, even if initially substantial (e.g., a fully accessible regular public transportation system) ultimately generates cost savings.

9. *Shared Experience.* Particular prejudices are not inevitable. Negative reactions to physical and behavioral differences are not "in people's nature," they are learned. One way of overcoming these barriers to the membership of disabled people in communities is to confront consciously the various social attitudes that reinforce them. This re-education of society means that "the disabled experience" must take center stage. Factual information regarding disabilities, as well as real-life and *honestly* fictionalized accounts of the experience of disabled persons and their families, must find an enduring place in our school curricula, for example. The media and the arts must be held to using the image of people with disabilities not as caricatures of alienation, impending doom, or plucky stick-to-it-iveness but as fully drawn, complex persons.

10. *Minority Status.* To return to our discussion at the beginning of this chapter, we need to foster the perception of disability as merely one of a wide range of possible human differences. This done, individuals with a disability can then be seen as members of one of the myriad minority groups that together equal the human community. From this perspective, denial of access to community living, whether through nursing home placement, institutionalization, or placement in other large congregate residences, can be viewed not as a treatment option but as discrimination. Similarly, the guarantee of a personal home, whether in a supported apartment, a small group home, a family home, independent living, or a housing cooperative, is not a treatment option but an expression of basic rights.

The term *community integration,* like *deinstitutionalization,* must become a historical artifact. We will no longer need such terms when integration exists, when people with disabilities have support in their natural communities, use generic services, and are full partners in the decision-making processes that affect their lives. After all, integration survives as an issue only so long as someone is segregated.

References

Asch, A. (1984, May). Personal reflection. *American Psychologist, 39*(5), 551–552.

Bercovici, S. M. (1983). *Barriers to normalization: The restrictive management of retarded people*. Baltimore: University Park Press.

Berry, J. (1975). *Daily experience in residential life: A study of children and their caregivers*. London: Routledge & Kegan Paul.

Biklen, D. (1985). *Achieving the complete school: Effective strategies for mainstreaming*. New York: Teachers College Press.

Biklen, D., & Knoll, J. (in press). The community imperative revisited. In J. A. Mulick & R. F. Antonak (Eds.), *Transitions in mental retardation* (Vol. 3). Norwood, NJ: Ablex.

Blatt, B., & Kaplan, F. (1966). *Christmas in purgatory*. Boston: Allyn and Bacon.

Blatt, B., Ozolins, A., & McNally, J. (1979). *The family papers: A return to purgatory*. New York: Longman.

Bogdan, R. (1986). Exhibiting mentally retarded people for amusement and profit, 1850–1940. *American Journal of Mental Deficiency, 91*, 120–126.

Bogdan, R., & Biklen, D. (1977, March/April). Handicapism. *Social Policy*, 14–19.

Bogdan, R., & Taylor, S. (1983). *Inside out*. Toronto: University of Toronto Press.

Braddock, D., Hemp, R., & Howes, R. (1985). *Public expenditures for mental retardation and developmental disabilities in the United States*. Chicago: The University of Illinois at Chicago.

Brightman, A. (Ed.). (1984). *Ordinary moments*. Syracuse, NY: Human Policy Press.

Bruininks, R. H., Kudla, M. J., Wieck, C. A., & Hauber, F. A. (1980). Management problems in community residential facilities. *Mental Retardation, 18*, 125–129.

Center on Human Policy. (1979). *The community imperative: A refutation of all arguments for institutionalizing anyone because of mental retardation*. Syracuse, NY: Author.

Cherniss, G. (1981). Organizational design and the social environment in group homes for mentally retarded persons. In H. C. Haywood & J. R. Newbrough (Eds.), *Living environments for developmentally retarded persons*. Baltimore: University Park Press.

City of Cleburne v. *Cleburne Living Center*, No. 84-468, Amicus Curiae brief of American Association on Mental Deficiency, et al., U.S. Supreme Court. (1984a).

City of Cleburne v. *Cleburne Living Center*, No. 84-468, Amicus Curiae brief of Association for Retarded Citizens/USA, et al., U.S. Supreme Court. (1984b).

Conroy, J. W., & Bradley, V. J. (1985). *The Pennhurst longitudinal study: Combined report of five years of research and analysis*. Philadelphia: Temple University Developmental Disabilities Center.

Conroy, J., Efthimiou, J., & Lemanowicz, J. (1982). A matched comparison of the developmental growth of institutionalized and deinstitutionalized mentally retarded clients. *American Journal of Mental Deficiency, 86*, 581–587.

Featherstone, H. (1982). *A difference in the family*. New York: Penguin Books.

Fiorelli, J. S. (1982). Community residential services during the 1980's: Challenges and future trends. *Journal of the Association for the Severely Handicapped*, 7(4), 14–18.

Foster, S. (1983). *They've got you coming and going: The process of institutionalization of mentally retarded people in 1981*. Unpublished doctoral dissertation. Syracuse, NY: Syracuse University.

Gallup Organization. (1976). Report for the President's Committee on Mental Retardation: Public attitudes regarding mental retardation. In R. Nathan (Ed.), *Mental retardation: A century of decision* (DHEW 76-21013, pp. 106–113). Washington, DC: U.S. Government Printing Office.

Gleidman, J., & Roth, W. (1980). *The unexpected minority*. New York: Harcourt, Brace, Jovanovich.

Goddard, H. H. (1912). *The Kallikak family*. New York: MacMillan.

Goldenberg, I. I. (1971). *Build me a mountain: Youth, poverty, and the creation of new settings*. Cambridge, MA: MIT Press.

Goodlad, J. (1984). *A place called school*. New York: McGraw-Hill.

Hahn, H. (1984). *Civil rights for disabled Americans: The foundation of a political agenda*. Paper prepared for the Wingspread Conference on Images of Disability, November 8–10, Racine, WI.

Hauber, F. A., Bruininks, R. H., Hill, B. K., Lakin, C., Scheerenberger, R., & White, C. C. (1984). National census of residential facilities: A 1982 profile of facilities and residents. *American Journal of Mental Deficiency, 89*, 236–245.

Hemming, H., Lavender, T., & Pill, R. (1981). Quality of life of mentally retarded adults transferred from large institutions to small units. *American Journal of Mental Deficiency, 86*, 157–169.

International League of Societies for Persons with Mental Handicap. (1984). *Participation in family and community life*. Brussels: Author.

Jones, P. A., Conroy, J. W., Feinstein, C. S., & Lemanowicz, J. A. (1984). A matched comparison study of cost-effectiveness: Institutionalized and deinstitutionalized people. *Journal of the Association for Persons with Severe Handicaps, 9*, 304–313.

Jones, R. (Ed.). (1983). *Reflections on growing up disabled*. Reston, VA: Council for Exceptional Children.

Keating, R. (1979, Sept. 17). The war against the mentally retarded. *New York Magazine*, pp. 87–94.

Keith, K. D., & Ferdinand, L. R. (1984). Changes in levels of mental retardation: A comparison of institutional and community populations. *Journal of the Association for Persons with Severe Handicaps, 9(1)*, 26–30.

Krastner, L. S., Reppucci, N. D., & Pezzoli, J. J. (1979). Assessing community attitudes toward mentally retarded persons. *American Journal of Mental Deficiency, 84*, 137–144.

Kupfner, F. (1982, Dec. 13). Institutions is not a dirty word. *Newsweek*, p. 170.

McCarthy, T. J. (1980). *Managing group homes: A training manual*. Nashville, TN: TMAC Behavior Development.

McCord, W. T. (1981). Community residences: The staffing. In J. Wortis (Ed.). *Mental retardation and developmental disabilities* (12th ed.) (pp. 111–128). New York: Brunner/Mazel.

National Commission on Excellence in Education. (1983). *A nation at risk*. Washington, DC: U.S. Government Printing Office.

New York Times. (1978, Nov. 26). Hindsight on helping the handicapped. P. D20.

Raynes, N. V. (1980). The less you've got the less you get: Functional grouping, a cause for concern. *Mental Retardation, 18,* 217–220.

Roth, R., & Smith, T. E. C. (1983). A statewide assessment of attitudes towards the handicapped and community living programs. *Education and Training of the Mentally Retarded, 18,* 164–168.

Roth, W. (Ed.). (1981). *The handicapped speak.* Jefferson, NC: McFarland.

Rothman, D. J., & Rothman, S. M. (1984). *The Willowbrook wars.* New York: Harper & Row.

Scull, A. (1981). The new trade in lunacy: The recommodification of the mental patient. *American Behavioral Scientist, 24,* 741–754.

Seltzer, M. M. (1984). Correlates of community opposition to community residences for mentally retarded persons. *American Journal of Mental Deficiency, 89,* 1–8.

Silver, E. J., Silverman, W. P., & Lubin, R. A. (1982). *Community living for severely and profoundly retarded persons.* Albany, NY: Office of Mental Retardation and Developmental Disabilities.

Sizer, T. R. (1984). *Horace's compromise.* Boston: Houghton Mifflin.

Starr, R. (1982, Jan., Vol. 264, No. 1580). Wheels of misfortune. *Harper's,* pp. 7–15.

Steinbeck, J. (1937). *Of mice and men.* New York: Bantam.

Taylor, S. J., Brown, K., McCord, W., Giambetti, A., Searl, S., Mlinarcik, S., Atkinson, T., & Lichter, S. (1981). *Title XIX and deinstitutionalization: The issue for the 80's.* Syracuse, NY: Center on Human Policy.

Terman, L. M. (1916). *The measurement of intelligence.* Boston: Houghton Mifflin.

Tomlinson, S. (1982). *A sociology of special education.* London: Routledge & Kegan Paul.

U.S. Senate. (1982). *Care of the retarded, 1981. Hearing before the Subcommittee on the Handicapped of the Committee on Labor and Human Resources, at Hartford, CT, on April 13 & 15, 1981.* Washington, DC: U.S. Government Printing Office.

Willer, B., & Intagliata, J. (1983). *Promises and realities for mentally retarded citizens.* Austin, TX: Pro-Ed.

Youngberg v. *Romeo,* 102 S. Ct. 2452 (1982).

Youngblood, G. S., & Bensberg, G. J. (1983). *Planning and operating group homes for the handicapped.* Lubbock, TX: Research and Training Center in Mental Retardation, Texas Tech University.

2

Continuum Traps

STEVEN J. TAYLOR

The LRE Principle

Since the late 1960s and early 1970s, the concept of the *least restrictive environment* (LRE) has been a guiding principle for the design of services for people with developmental disabilities. The LRE principle has been incorporated into federal and state policy and court decisions and has been widely accepted by professionals in the field.

Translated into practical terms, the LRE principle has been represented in terms of a *continuum* of services, ranging from the most to the least restrictive environment. Like the LRE principle on which it is based, the continuum is a popular way of thinking about residential, vocational, and educational services.

The LRE principle has its roots in both professional writings and law (Biklen, 1982). In the 1960s, special educators like Reynolds (1962) began to describe the idea of a continuum of educational placements as an alternative to segregated facilities for all children with disabilities. In 1962, Reynolds called for a continuum of placements, from the least restrictive setting to the most restrictive, for children with handicaps.

Later in the 1960s and early 1970s, when federal courts began to address the rights of children and adults with disabilities in schools and institutions, they incorporated the concept of a continuum from "least restrictive" to "most restrictive" into their rulings. From a legal standpoint, the idea of the "least restrictive alternative" is simple: The state must do things in a manner that least intrudes upon, or restricts, individual rights.

In the Mills (*Mills* v. *Board of Education,* 1972) and *PARC* (*Pennsylvania ARC* v. *Pennsylvania,* 1971) right-to-education cases in the early 1970s,

---

The author would like to thank Julie Racino, Doug Biklen, and Bob Bogdan for their assistance in the preparation of this chapter.

federal judges strongly endorsed the right of children with disabilities to placement in the least restrictive environment. Similarly, federal courts in the early institutional right-to-treatment cases ruled that institutionalized persons had a right to treatment or habilitation in the least restrictive environment. In the landmark *Wyatt* case (*Wyatt* v. *Stickney*) in 1972, Judge Frank Johnson ruled that residents should have a right to the least restrictive conditions necessary to achieve the purposes of habilitation.

In passing Public Law 94–142 and the Developmentally Disabled Assistance and Bill of Rights Act in 1975, Congress also lent its support to LRE. The Public Law 94–142 regulations require educational agencies to provide a continuum of alternate placements:

> Each public agency shall insure that a continuum of alternative placements is available to meet the needs of handicapped children for special education and related services. . . . The continuum must . . . include . . . instruction in regular classes, special classes, special school, home instruction, and instruction in hospitals and institutions.

The Developmentally Disabled Act, which according to the Supreme Court in *Pennhurst State School and Hospital* v. *Halderman* is an expression of national policy, mandates that services be provided to people with developmental disabilities in the setting "least restrictive of the person's personal liberty."

LRE quickly caught hold in the 1970s and continues to be a guiding principle for the design of services (Bruininks & Lakin, 1985; Turnbull, 1981).

The LRE principle is commonly conceptualized in terms of a continuum of services represented by a straight line. One end of the continuum represents the "most restrictive" or "most segregated" placements, although this end is also sometimes thought of in terms of the "most intensive services." The opposite end of the continuum represents the "least restrictive" or "most integrated" placements, or "least intensive" services. The assumption is that every person with a developmental disability can be placed somewhere along the continuum. As a general rule, people with severe disabilities will end up at the most restrictive end of the continuum, while those with mild disabilities will be at the least restrictive end. As people acquire additional skills, they are expected to move to less and less restrictive placements.

In the fields of residential services, vocational services, and special education, the continuum usually looks something like this (see Hitzing, 1980):

- *Residential continuum:* public institution → on-grounds "community residence" → nursing home and private institution → community intermediate care facility for the mentally retarded (ICF/MR) → group home (or community residence) → foster home → semi-independent living → independent living.

- *Vocational continuum:* day treatment → day training → sheltered workshop → work station in industry → job placement and follow-up → competitive employment.
- *Special education continuum:* residential school → special school → special class in regular school → regular class with resource room → regular class.

For the purposes of this chapter, we will limit our discussion to the residential continuum.

The Residential Continuum

When the LRE continuum first emerged as a concept, people with developmental disabilities had few options regarding where they could live. With few exceptions, they either lived in institutions or in the community, with little or no support in the latter. The past 20 years have witnessed dramatic changes in residential services for people with developmental disabilities. Today, there is a continuum of services. Let's look at what the continuum means for people with severe disabilities.

Public Institutions

The populations of public institutions have declined at a steady pace over the past two decades. In the late 1960s, the institutions housed approximately 200,000 people. As of this writing, that number has probably dropped to under 100,000 (Braddock, Hemp, & Howes, 1984; Epple, Jacobson, & Janicki, 1985; Lakin, Hill, & Bruininks, 1985). Public institutions continue to house a large number of people with severe disabilities; in fact, the percentage of people with severe disabilities living in institutions has increased over the years (Lakin et al., 1985).

Despite the steady decline in institutional populations nationally, it would be wrong to assume that the institutional battle has been won. To the contrary, most states continue to spend more money for institutions than for services in the community (Braddock et al., 1984). In addition to allocating large sums for institutional operating expenses, states spent millions of dollars on capital improvements to institutional facilities throughout the 1970s and 1980s. According to one estimate, states spent over $821 million for institutional construction and renovation in the period 1977 to 1980 alone (Taylor, McCord, & Searl, 1981).

As a policy, "deinstitutionalization" continues to generate considerable controversy nationally, as evidenced by the Senate hearings held on the Community and Family Living Amendments (U.S. Senate, 1984). In addition, professional articles and books defending institutions continue to be published (Crissey & Rosen, 1986). The most common rationale for institutions is that some people are too severely disabled to live in the community.

On-grounds "Community" Facilities

An unknown number of states have developed new small facilities on the grounds of public institutions. While this is not a new idea, what is new is that some states refer to these facilities as "community" residences. For example, New York classifies small facilities, which primarily were formerly staff housing, on the grounds of large state institutions that contain over 400 beds, as "community" settings.

Several states are involved in the construction of clusters of 8- to 12-bed group homes on institutional grounds. New York plans to construct new facilities of this type containing a total of over 1,000 beds over the next few years (Center on Human Policy, 1986). According to New York's Office of Mental Retardation and Developmental Disabilities, these new facilities, referred to as "small residential units," represent a "new niche in the continuum." New York identifies people with severe disabilities as the prime candidates to live in these new facilities.

Nursing Homes

In some states, deinstitutionalization has meant "transinstitutionalization," the transfer of people from large public institutions to somewhat smaller private institutions and nursing homes (Warren, 1981). Lakin, Bruininks, Doth, Hill, and Hauber (1982) estimate that, as of 1980, over 69,000 people with mental retardation were living in nursing homes. Some states like Wisconsin have a higher number of people with developmental disabilities living in nursing homes than in state developmental disability institutions.

Community Intermediate Care Facilities for the Mentally Retarded (ICF/MRs)

Under Medicaid amendments passed in 1971, states can receive 50% to approximately 78% federal reimbursement for services provided in an ICF/MR. While Medicaid has been used as a major funding source for public institutions, states began to look to the ICF/MR program to fund community settings in the mid to late 1970s (Taylor et al., 1981). In the period 1977 to

1984, 18.2% of ICF/MR funds were spent for "community services," as opposed to institutions (Braddock et al., 1984).

ICF/MRs range from small group homes to private mini-institutions to large public institutions. As of 1982, according to Lakin et al. (1985), 9,714 people were living in ICF/MRs for 15 or fewer people, while 130,970 were in ICF/MRs for 16 or more.

Some states have developed a large number of relatively small community ICF/MRs. In Michigan, the typical size of a community ICF/MR, referred to as an AIS/MR (alternative intermediate services for the mentally retarded), is 6 persons. Michigan's Macomb Oakland Regional Center, in particular, has placed many people with severe and profound retardation, multiple disabilities, and challenging behavior in 6-person community facilities (Taylor et al., 1981).

When people with severe disabilities are served in the community, they often end up in community ICF/MRs. In fact, it is not uncommon to hear it said that the severely handicapped *need* to be in an ICF/MR.

Group Homes

Until relatively recently, community living was associated almost exclusively with group homes, also referred to now as community residences and previously as halfway houses. The phrase *group home* is used to include a diverse range of facilities, including small community settings and large mini-institutions. According to Lakin et al. (1985), approximately 53,989 people with mental retardation were living in residential facilities (other than ICF/MRs) for 15 or fewer people, as of 1982. Except in states like Nebraska, which do not use ICF/MR funds for community settings, relatively few people with severe disabilities have been placed in regular group homes.

Foster Care

Foster or family care programs specifically for people with mental retardation stem back to the 1930s; however, it was not until the late 1960s and early 1970s that states began using foster care for a large number of people with mental retardation. According to Lakin et al. (1982), an estimated 8,700 people with mental retardation were living in specially licensed foster homes in 1980. Like other statistics, this number is misleading, because some states use generic foster care for children with developmental disabilities.

Until recently, foster or family care was defined in terms of providing room, board, and minimum supervision. More recent schemes provide for a payment for families to provide training and personal care to people placed in their homes. Some states maintain a dual system of "regular" and "specialized" family care homes.

The names used for foster care programs for people with developmental disabilities vary widely by state; community training homes, extended families, shared homes, host homes, personal care, family care, and specialized foster care are some of them.

In most states, foster or family care has been used primarily for children and adults with mild or moderate disabilities. However, some states, such as Michigan and Nebraska, are placing people with the most severe disabilities, especially children, in foster homes.

Semi-independent Living

This refers to a range of living arrangements in which people receive supervision and support on an "as-needed" basis (Halpern, Close, & Nelson, 1985). Examples include "transitional apartments" and "apartment clusters." Typically, people in semi-independent living programs are expected to move on to independent living as they gain community living skills. People with severe disabilities have almost never been served in these programs.

Independent Living

Independent living has been heralded as a goal for people with developmental disabilities. In a sense, independent living is what stands at the end of the continuum. For people with developmental disabilities, independent living means everything from living in decent houses and apartments in the community, often with the support of friends, to living in substandard conditions in urban slums. Many cities count ex-residents of institutions among their street people.

Independent living has not been an option proposed for people with severe disabilities.

Pitfalls in the LRE Principle

As a guiding principle for the design of services for people with developmental disabilities, the LRE principle has serious flaws. For people with severe disabilities, in particular, LRE is full of pitfalls.

Legitimation of Restrictive Environments

To conceptualize services in terms of the most to the least restrictive environment is to legitimate the most restrictive settings. As long as services are conceptualized in this manner, some people will end up in more restrictive settings; namely, institutions, segregated day programs, and special schools. In most cases, these will be the people with the most severe disabilities. In short, implicit in the LRE principle is the assumption that certain people should be placed in the most restrictive environments.

The lack of specificity of the LRE principle undoubtedly explains much of its appeal. People are free to define LRE differently. For some, LRE is defined in terms of integration, while for others it may include segregated settings. As long as the goal is viewed in terms of the least restrictive environment, some people will continue to support institutions and other segregated settings merely by defining them as the least restrictive environment for certain people. Thus, states with entrenched institutions can adopt the LRE principle as official policy.

In addition, in some states, debates have been waged over the meaning of the *least restrictive environment,* as opposed to the *less restrictive environment.* For example, in the Willowbrook case (*New York State ARC* v. *Rockefeller,* 1973) in the 1970s, New York State argued that transfers from Willowbrook to the Bronx Developmental Center represented movement to a less restrictive environment. More recently, New York justified the proposed construction of on-grounds "small residential units" in terms of moving people to less restrictive settings.

Segregation/Integration vs. Intensity of Services

The LRE principle confuses segregation and integration, on the one hand, with intensity of services, on the other. As represented by the continuum, the LRE principle equates segregation with the most intensive services and integration with the least intensive services. When viewed from this perspective, it follows that people with severe disabilities will require the most restrictive environments. However, segregation and integration, on the one hand, and intensity of services on the other, are separate dimensions. In fact, some of the most segregated settings have provided the least services.

Beginning in the late 1970s and early 1980s, a number of people started to argue that the traditional continuum of services was conceptually flawed (Bronston, 1980; Galloway, 1980; Haring & Hansen, 1981; Hitzing, 1980). As they explained, the continuum concept confused people's needs for normal housing with their needs for specialized services and supports. Bronston (1980) distinguished between a "housing continuum" and a "program continuum." As an alternative to any kind of continuum, Hitzing (1980) proposed the placement of people in "natural settings" with an array of services available to meet their needs (in-home staff or services, financial support, transportation, advocacy, vocational training, legal assistance, home health care, recreation, respite services, counseling, and so forth).

The 1980s have been characterized by the emergence of a range of approaches for supporting people with severe disabilities in integrated community, work, and school settings. For example, in the area of vocational services, the supported work model is based on the assumption that services can be provided in typical job sites. In terms of community living, the "state of the art" includes family supports to enable children with severe disabilities to live at home, the recruitment and support of adoptive and foster families for children who cannot remain at home, and the development of supportive living arrangements for adults with a range of disabilities (see Chapter 3 of this volume).

Despite the emergence of approaches for supporting people with severe disabilities in the community, most resources continue to be devoted to settings on the most restrictive end of the continuum. According to Braddock et al. (1984), states allocated over $4.2 billion to institutions while allocating slightly over $3 billion to community services in 1984 (note that the community figure includes all funds spent for nonpublic institutions, including nursing homes and private institutions). In most states, it is easier to obtain funding for segregated services than for services and supports in integrated settings.

The Readiness Model

The LRE principle is based on a "readiness model." Implicit in LRE is the assumption that people with developmental disabilities must earn the right to move to the least restrictive environment. In other words, people must "get ready" to live, work, or go to school in integrated settings. As Hitzing (1980, p. 84) noted in his critique of the continuum model,

> Another negative feature of most service continua is that they place a tremendous burden on clients for movement. . . . The notion was that a person moved into the residential system initially by being placed in a nursing home or a large group home. Once clients "shaped up," they "graduated" to a smaller group home. If they learned certain skills in the group home, they "graduated" to a more independent placement unit.

The irony is that the most restrictive placements do not prepare people for the least restrictive placements (Brown et al., 1977). In other words, institutions do not prepare people for community living; segregated vocational programs do not prepare people for competitive employment; segregated schooling does not prepare students for integrated schooling. The demands of segregated settings are different from those of integrated settings.

Disruptiveness of New Placements

The LRE principle suggests that people must be uprooted continuously. Even if people could move smoothly through progressively less restrictive environments, their lives would be in a constant state of flux. Life becomes a series of stops between each new, transitional placement. This destroys any sense of home and disrupts relationships with roommates, neighbors, and friends.

Many residential programs are based on a transitional approach that looks to the readiness model in deciding who will be placed where. As a consequence, people with severe disabilities are usually denied the opportunity to live in apartments and other individualized arrangements because they will never be able to move on to independent living.

Infringement of Rights

The LRE principle is a seductive concept: It sounds good to say that government should act in a manner that least intrudes on individual rights. Yet when applied to people with developmental disabilities, as a class, the LRE principle sanctions infringements on basic rights to freedom and community participation. The question implied by LRE is not *whether or not* people with developmental disabilities should be restricted, but to what extent.

As a legal principle, LRE has often served as a useful tool for forcing changes in institutions and schools. However, as a guiding principle for the design of services for people with developmental disabilities, the LRE principle is seriously flawed. To say that people should live in the least restrictive environment is like saying they should live in the least obnoxious or least aversive environment. Instead, we should be thinking in terms of creating nonrestrictive environments.

Services Defined in Terms of Facilities

As Gunnar Dybwad once stated in a personal conversation, "Every time we identify a need in this field, we build a building." This strikes at the heart of the matter. Stripped to its essentials, the LRE principle has to do with facilities designed specifically for people with developmental disabilities. The continuum refers to facilities, not to services. As a field, we have been successful in constructing facilities, first large ones and now smaller and more normalized ones. We have not been nearly as successful in meeting people's needs.

Conclusion

The principle of the least restrictive environment was extremely forward-looking for its time. It emerged in an era in which people with developmental disabilities and their families were offered segregation or nothing at all. The LRE principle helped to create options and alternatives when none existed.

Concepts and principles can help us get from one place to another, to move closer toward a vision of society based on enduring human values such as freedom, community, dignity, and autonomy. Yet they must be viewed in historical context. The concepts that guide us today—normalization, handicapism, mainstreaming, competent communities, functional life skills, deinstitutionalization, supported work, life-sharing—may mislead us tomorrow. Indeed, as stated earlier, integration only makes sense in the context of a segregated society (see Chapter 11 of this volume). End segregation and the concept of integration singles out people with developmental disabilities as different from the rest of us.

There comes a time when we must find new ideas, concepts, and principles to guide us. The LRE principle defined the challenge in terms of creating homelike settings, normalized facilities, and least restrictive environments. It is time to define the challenge in terms of enabling people with developmental disabilities to enjoy equal citizenship rights and achieve full participation in community life.

References

Biklen, D. (1982). The least restrictive environment: Its application to education. In G. Melton (Ed.), *Child and youth services* (pp. 121–44). New York: Haworth.

Braddock, D., Hemp, R., & Howes, R. (1984). *Public expenditures for mental retardation and developmental disabilities in the United States*. Chicago, IL: Institute for the Study of Developmental Disabilities.

Bronston, W. (1980). Matters of design. In T. Apolloni, J. Cappuccilli, & T. P. Cooke (Eds.), *Towards excellence: Achievements in residential services for persons with disabilities* (7–17). Baltimore: University Park Press.

Brown, L., Wilcox, B., Sontag, E., Vincent, B., Dodd, N., & Gruenewald, L. (1977). Towards the realization of the least restrictive educational environment for severely handicapped students. *Journal of the Association for the Severely Handicapped, 2*(4), 195–201.

Bruininks, R. H., & Lakin, K. C. (Eds.). (1985). *Living and learning in the least restrictive environment*. Baltimore: Paul H. Brookes.

Center on Human Policy. (1986). On the issue of "small residential units" on the grounds of New York State institutions. Syracuse, NY: Author.

Crissey, M. S., & Rosen, M. (Eds.). (1986). *Institutions for the mentally retarded*. Austin, TX: Pro-Ed.

Epple, W. A., Jacobson, J. W., & Janicki, M. P. (1985). Staffing ratios in public institutions for persons with mental retardation in the United States. *Mental Retardation, 23*, 115–124.

Galloway, C. (1980). The "continuum" and the need for caution. Unpublished manuscript. Prepared for the National Association of State Directors of Special Education, Washington, DC.

Halpern, A. S., Close, D. W., & Nelson, D. J. (1985). *On my own*. Baltimore, MD: Paul H. Brookes.
Haring, N. G., & Hansen, C. L. (1981). Perspectives in communitization. In C. L. Hansen (Ed.), *Severely handicapped persons in the community* (pp. 1–28). Seattle, WA: Program Development Assistance System.
Hitzing, W. (1980). ENCOR and beyond. In T. Apolloni, J. Cappuccilli, & T. P. Cooke (Eds.), *Towards excellence: Achievements in residential services for persons with disabilities* (71–93). Baltimore: University Park Press.
Lakin, K. C., Bruininks, R. H., Doth, D., Hill, B., & Hauber, F. (1982). *Sourcebook on long-term care of developmentally disabled people*. Minneapolis: University of Minnesota.
Lakin, K. C., Hill, B., & Bruininks, R. (1985). *An analysis of Medicaid's intermediate care facility for the mentally retarded (ICF-MR) program*. Minneapolis: Center for Residential and Community Services.
Mills v. *Board of Education*, 348 F. Supp. 866 (D.D.C. 1972).
New York State ARC v. *Rockefeller*, 357 F. Supp. 764, 759, 770 (E.D. N.Y. 1973).
Pennsylvania Association for Retarded Citizens v. *Commonwealth of Pennsylvania*, 334 F. Supp. 1257 (E.D. Pa. 1971).
Reynolds, M. (1962). A framework for considering some issues in special education. *Exceptional Children, 28*, 367–370.
Taylor, S. J., McCord, W., & Searl, S. J. (1981). Medicaid dollars and community homes: The community ICF/MR controversy. *The Journal of the Association for the Severely Handicapped, 6*(1), 59–64.
Turnbull, R. (Ed.). (1981). *Least restrictive alternatives: Principles and practices*. Washington, DC: American Association on Mental Deficiency.
U.S. Senate. (1984). Community and Family Living Amendments of 1983: Hearing before the Subcommittee on Health of the Committee on Finance. Washington, DC: Government Printing Office.
Warren, C. A. B. (Ed.). (1981). New forms of social control: The myth of deinstitutionalization. *American Behavioral Scientist, 24*(6), 721–846.
Wyatt v. *Stickney*, 344 F. Supp. 373, 379 (M.D. Ala. 1972).

3

Down Home

Community Integration for People with the Most Severe Disabilities

STEVEN J. TAYLOR
JULIE RACINO
JAMES KNOLL
ZANA LUTFIYYA

The state of the art in community integration is evolving at an incredibly rapid pace. The professional and research literature do not reflect this. Reading most of the latest books and journal articles on residential services, you get a rehash of the arguments in favor of institutions versus large group homes. When, however, you take a close look at the most experienced community service systems and agencies,[1] you find that the debates that have dominated the field over the past decade and a half are largely irrelevant to what is actually happening in the community. The state of the art today is moving beyond the notion of a continuum (institution→group home→independent living) and toward more individualized, integrated, and responsive services.

If you went to the widely heralded Macomb Oakland Regional Center in Michigan; Options in Community Living in Madison, Wisconsin; Region V Mental Retardation Services in Nebraska; Seven Counties Services in Louisville, Kentucky; or a number of other places around the country, you would

---

This chapter is based in large part on site visits made to Macomb Oakland Regional Center in Michigan; Region V Mental Retardation Services in Nebraska; Seven Counties Services in Kentucky; the State of Michigan; Options in Community Living in Wisconsin, Dane, LaCrosse, and Columbia counties in Wisconsin; and the Working Organization for Retarded Children in New York City. Unless otherwise indicated, quotations used in this chapter were taken from reports based on these site visits.

hear people talking about new ways to support people with severe disabilities in the community. People are talking about *homes*, not "homelike facilities" or "normalized environments," for all people with developmental disabilities. The approach is deceptively simple: Find a home for people—with their natural families, with a foster or adoptive family, or with others they happen to get along with—and build in the supports and services they need to live successfully in the community.

It is easier to define what is not a home than to define exactly what is. At least in our society, we assume that a home is a place where things are arranged according to your own personal preferences and not the needs of a group. A home is where you live with people with whom you have mutual attachments. A home is where you cannot be kicked out because you do not fit in.

Families for Children

Amy* is a girl and Jimmy* is a boy. Otherwise they have a lot in common. For one thing, both are 8 years old. They both have hydrocephaly and a multitude of associated problems, including blindness, seizures, and hypothermia. Both are tube-fed and are susceptible to choking, infection, bedsores, and sudden drops in body temperature. Fortunately for Amy and Jimmy, they happen to live in states where people are committed to serving children with severe disabilities in the community. Jimmy lives with 5 other children in a Medicaid-certified group home just outside Ypsilanti, Michigan. Amy lives with her foster parents, Mr. and Mrs. Parker,* in Lincoln, Nebraska.

Jimmy's house is new and modern and nicely furnished. A single-story house, it's fully accessible, with extra-wide hallways, and it's fireproof. By contrast, Amy's house is rather modest, a small two-story house in a middle-class neighborhood. The doorways seem just wide enough for Amy's wheelchair, and to leave the house she has to be wheeled onto a mechanical lift.

Jimmy's room, which he shares with another child, is clean. It has two beds, a suction machine, a vaporizer, an oxygen machine, a picture on the wall, curtains on the window, and two dressers. There are a half-dozen or so toys and stuffed animals in the room. Amy's room is bright, colorful, warm, and filled with pictures, mobiles, decorations, toys, and statues, in addition to a thermometer and a control device for a heated water mattress on the top of her bed. A red and yellow handmade cloth "AMY" sign hangs on the wall by her bed. A radio playing soft music is by her bed. Mrs. Parker thinks Amy enjoys this.

---

*Throughout this chapter, all names with asterisks are pseudonyms.

Mrs. Parker spends a lot of time with Amy. She talks to her, gently caresses her, changes her diapers, dresses her, and feeds her. She has to take Amy's temperature frequently, clear her throat of mucus, and change her position in bed. She also provides range-of-motion exercises. A physical therapist used to come to the house to do this, but Mrs. Parker does not think it is a good idea to have a lot of different hands touching the child. One can see Amy tenses up when she is touched.

The 10 or so staff members at Jimmy's house also have to spend a lot of time with him, feeding him, taking his temperature regularly, rotating him, and so on. Staff members can be observed touching and talking to Jimmy and the 5 other children in the home.

According to Jimmy's house manager, the staff enjoys working at the house. As she sees it, caring for these children in a community setting is not difficult: "These guys aren't hard at all." Similarly, Mrs. Parker doesn't think it's difficult to care for Amy. She speaks with pride when she recalls what doctors said to her when she took Amy in at 2 months of age: "They said she'd have to be in an institution. I said to myself, 'That's all I need to hear. We'll see about that.' I knew I could take care of Amy, and I have."

Mrs. Parker keeps a scrapbook of Amy's progress that she takes out for visitors. She speaks lovingly of Amy as she goes through the pictures, locks of hair, and other mementos. She also speaks freely of how much Amy has done for her life.

At Jimmy's house, the house manager tries to build in consistency in how staff members handle and treat the children. She reports that open communication and frequent staff meetings are a must.

One senses that Mrs. Parker may be a bit overprotective of Amy. She doesn't trust too many people to provide respite, although she has an older woman come in every once in a while just to keep an eye on Amy so she can go out.

The stories of Amy and Jimmy are incomplete without thinking about similar children in institutions. Compared to where they could be, both Amy and Jimmy are doing quite well. After visiting both of them, however, one cannot help but conclude that Amy is doing better.

Amy and Jimmy are as severely disabled as any child at any institution for the developmentally disabled in the country. One would have to go to intensive care or neonatal units at general hospitals to find more severely disabled children. Yet Amy and Jimmy are exactly the kind of children whom many people think have to live in institutions. If Amy and Jimmy can have their needs met in the community, any child in any institution can also. The question is not whether they should live in the community, but how and where.

Just a few years ago, group homes constituted the state of the art in community living for children with severe medical involvements. The Eastern Nebraska Community Office of Retardation (ENCOR) was probably the first service system to serve medically complex children in the community, through its "developmental maximation unit" (DMU), located in a wing of a general hospital. The DMU is now referred to as the Specialized Medical Unit and is a group home for 6 children in the community. Today, the state of the art is to support the rights of children with severe and multiple disabilities to a permanent home and enduring relationships with adults, whether in natural, adoptive, or foster families. As Nancy Rosenau of Michigan's Macomb Oakland Regional Center explained, "There isn't a kid in the world who can't do better in a family than a group home."

Permanency Planning

For a number of years now, advocates for abused and neglected children have argued in favor of their right to a permanent home, whether through adoption or reunification with the natural family (see Knitzer, Allen, & McGowan, 1978).

In 1980, Congress passed the Adoption Assistance and Child Welfare Act (Public Law 96-272), which requires state social services agencies periodically to review the status of children in foster care, with a view toward obtaining a permanent home for each, whether through family reunification, adoption, or permanent foster care. Since most mental retardation and developmental disability agencies do not receive funds under Public Law 96-272, they are presumably not bound to adhere to the requirements of the law.

It has taken a while for the concept of "permanency planning" to make its way into the field of developmental disabilities. In fact, most states and agencies have actually discouraged children with developmental disabilities from having a permanent and stable home. Family support services have only recently been offered to families; children placed out-of-home have often been bounced from institution to group home, from foster home to foster home; legal and financial barriers have stood in the way of adoption. In an evaluation of one state's specialized family care program for people with developmental disabilities, Taylor, Lutfiyya, Racino, Walker, and Knoll (1986) found that 7 out of 10 families interviewed had considered adopting children placed in their home, but had encountered various roadblocks to doing so.

Some states are beginning to take a serious look at permanency planning for children with developmental disabilities. The concept has taken hold at Macomb Oakland and now is catching on throughout the State of Michigan. As Ben Censoni of the Michigan Department of Mental Health described it, "Permanency planning is a fundamental change in the way we do business." It can best be described as a philosophy that endorses each child's right to a stable home and lasting relationships. The thrust is to find a permanent home for every child. As it should be, permanency planning starts with the natural family, the aim being to provide the services that families need to keep their children at home.

Even with the best support services, some families cannot care for their children at home. This is where the permanency planning approach makes all the difference in the world. In most communities, out-of-home placement signals an end to the family's responsibility for the child. Indeed, many service systems actually discourage family involvement with the child after placement. Permanency planning supports the family's ongoing relationship with the child and aims toward family reunification.

Macomb Oakland has discontinued what one person there referred to as the "smorgasbord" of placements (institution, group home, and foster care) commonly presented to families. For children, there is only one option: foster care. As one administrator stated, "We tell families when they can't care for their children, 'If you're looking for out-of-home placement, we can help you. What we have available is a foster family.' " Parents are approached with empathy and understanding:

> We try to break down parents' feeling threatened by foster care. We tell them, "A foster parent is different. You didn't *choose* to have a child with a disability, you didn't *choose* the type of child, you didn't have training prior to having the child, you didn't choose the time of life to have a child with a disability, and you didn't have an out clause. All of that is what makes a foster family different."

When a child is placed in foster care, this is viewed as a *temporary* placement and plans are made to reunite the family. Macomb Oakland, together with other agencies, develops a written memorandum of understanding with the family and the foster family. This specifies the reason for the placement, the conditions necessary for the child to return home, the parents' responsibilities for changing things to enable the child to return home, the parents' agreement to visit the child regularly, Macomb Oakland's and other agencies' responsibilities to provide services to families to enable them to take their children home, and the foster parents' agreement to encourage and cooperate with parental visits. In short, permanency planning aims at encouraging continued parental involvement during placement, with the goal of returning the child to the natural family. When this is not possible, other options, including adoption, are pursued.

Family Supports

A number of years ago, Ed Skarnulis, then in Nebraska and now Minnesota State Director of Mental Retardation and Developmental Disabilities, admonished agencies, "Support, don't supplant, the natural family." It is only in the past several years, however, that state and local agencies have begun to fund support services to families. Many communities have family support programs such as respite, home aide services, or home nursing. In some communities, agencies have developed specialized respite facilities or earmarked "beds" in group homes or even institutions for respite.

While increased funds for family support services are a positive sign, many family support programs are not designed to meet the diverse needs of families. Family support services are often operated like group homes or other residential facilities: develop the program and then find families to fit in. For example, in some places, family support is defined almost exclusively in terms of respite. This may provide relief to some parents, but many families neither want nor need out-of-home respite.

Several states and communities have developed innovative approaches to supporting families, based on the individual needs of families themselves. Three approaches stand out: family cash subsidies, the "smorgasbord" plan, and the family support program.

Family Cash Subsidies. The first approach is the cash subsidy. A number of states now have family subsidy programs. In Michigan, for example, the state pays direct cash subsidies to families of children (up to 18 years of age) with *severe* disabilities, who have an annual income of less than $60,000. The subsidy is designed to help parents pay for the extra expenses incurred in having a child with severe disabilities (for example, equipment, respite, home renovation, diapers, and sitters). The subsidy amounts to $225 per month, an annual subsidy of $2,700 for eligible families.

Passed by the Michigan legislature with strong support from parent and advocacy groups, the Family Subsidy Act appealed to people with diverse political persuasions ("liberal," "conservative," "right-to-life"). As an economic measure, supporters argued that passage of the legislation would result in cost savings to the state by preventing out-of-home placements and encouraging families to take their children home from institutions and nursing homes. As a philosophical rationale, they pointed out that the legislation supported traditional family values.

Some Michigan agencies were not supportive of the legislation. They took the position that families would be better off if the funds were provided to the agencies to operate family support programs. They also questioned whether families might use the funds for other things not related to their children with disabilities. Supporters countered that families themselves were in the best position to determine their needs. As one of the key legislators supporting the Family Subsidy Act put it, "We made the assumption that families are capable of making good decisions." It might also be argued that, even if families used the subsidy for general household expenses, this can make it easier to maintain their children at home. Over 2,000 families participate in the Family Subsidy Program throughout Michigan.

The "Smorgasbord" Plan. The second innovative approach to family support services might be termed a "smorgasbord" approach. This is used by Community Services for the Developmentally Disabled, a community mental health center in the Clinton-Easton-Ingham counties area of Michigan. Under this approach, families are provided with an allotment with which to purchase one or more types of respite from a "menu" of services. Community Services for the Developmentally Disabled provides families with $255 worth of respite per quarter (every three months), in addition to family subsidies from the state. With this allotment, families can select from the following services: (1) foster home respite care; (2) home-based respite care; (3) family friend respite care; and (4) drop-in day care.

Families may be able to exceed their quarterly allotment in exceptional cases, if they receive prior approval. Families can also use their own funds to purchase additional respite care services.

The Family Support Program. The third innovative approach to family support services is modeled on a voucher system, although this might also be called, "Tell us what you want, and we'll try to get it for you."

Wisconsin has one of the most innovative family support programs in the country. While many states have begun to establish respite and other programs for families, Wisconsin's Family Support Program stands out for its responsiveness to the needs of individual families. Unlike many other schemes, the program is flexible, individualized, and family centered.

Like other community services, Wisconsin's Family Support Program is administered by the counties, with approximately one-third of Wisconsin's counties participating. Counties may either provide services directly or contract with local agencies. The Family Support Program provides up to $3,000 in services, per child, for families of children with severe disabilities. The state is authorized to approve additional funds to families upon the request of the local administering agency. Under state legislation, 10 percent of the funds allocated to a county may be used to pay for staff and other administrative costs; the rest must be spent directly for family support services.

The Family Support Program can be used to pay for a broad range of services families may need. As Linda Brown, one of the parents participating in the program in Dane County, points out, families of children with severe disabilities can have a variety of extraordinary expenses:

> Along with the stress that arises from living much of the time on the edge of life, we families deal with things most families never have to consider:

occupational, physical, and speech therapy; special feeding techniques, utensils, and foods; special equipment like wheelchairs, bolsters, wedges, seats, splints, braces, and hearing aids; life-support equipment like oxygen, apnea monitors, ventilators, nebulizers, and compressors; various tubing, trachs, trach masks, and suctioning equipment. There are even special dressings for all of the tubes inserted and sterile water for all the special techniques. On top of these are countless medications, diapers, usually far past the normal toilet-training stage, and often special clothing.

The Family Support Program lists 15 specific categories of services a family can receive:

1. Architectural modifications to the home
2. Child care
3. Counseling and therapeutic resources
4. Dental and medical care not otherwise covered
5. Specialized diagnosis and evaluation
6. Specialized nutrition and clothing
7. Specialized equipment and supplies
8. Homemaker services
9. In-home nursing and attendant care
10. Home training and parent courses
11. Recreation and alternative activities
12. Respite care
13. Transportation
14. Specialized utility costs
15. Vehicle modification

In addition, the program can pay for the costs of other goods or services, as approved by the state.

As the first step in participating in the program, families receive a needs assessment and family plan. To be eligible, families must have a child with a severe disability according to state criteria that parallel the federal definition of developmental disabilities. While there is no income test for the program, families may be expected to share some of the costs of services. Under state legislation, a child is defined as a person under the age of 24. In practice, however, the program is directed at families of children in school. The state must approve services for families of children ages 21 through 23.

According to documents describing the Family Support Program (Wisconsin Department of Health and Social Services, 1985), the needs assessment looks at the family's existing formal and informal support networks, and the family plan attempts to build on these. For example, a state document indicates that a neighbor may be asked to provide transportation for a child. The plan specifies what services a family will receive through the program. These services may be paid for directly by the agency, or the family can be given a grant to pay for them (families must keep receipts).

In addition to providing support services, the Family Support Program is intended to help coordinate other services a family receives. According to the Wisconsin Department of Health and Social Services (1985),

> An important role for the family support coordinator or case manager is to act as a kind of service broker assisting the family through the bureaucratic maze of available programs and services. The worker can also act as an advocate in helping the family to make maximum use of community services, such as community recreation programs, medical and dental services, public transportation, and other generic service providers.

In Dane County, Wisconsin, family support services are provided by the Family Support and Resource Center, a private agency. Fifty percent of its members are consumers of support services. The center has a range of funding sources and administers the state's Family Support Program. Located in a typical-looking storefront, the Family Support and Resource Center has seven people employed as one and one-half family coordinators, two respite workers, a part-time director, a bookkeeper, and a secretary. The center provides information and referral and offers in-home and out-of-home respite in foster homes. As the director explained, "We're a central place. We offer parents a place to start, and serve as a clearinghouse." The center supports families through state Family Support Program funds, as described earlier, and state COP (Community Options Program for people at risk for institutionalization) funds. The center supports 50 families through the Family Support Program, with 15 to be added this year, and 20 natural and foster families through COP. Under the COP program, families can receive up to $550 worth of services.

According to the director, the center can pay for "anything that will help the family take care of the child." She described one rural family with a teenage son with spina bifida who requires an enema every other day. She characterized this as a "stress point" for the family. The program pays for a neighbor to provide the enemas at $5 to $6 per hour. She also mentioned a family who bought an alarm that alerted the parents when their teenage child with autism tried to run away.

The director compared Wisconsin's Family Support Program with Michigan's, which entails a cash subsidy paid directly to families. She commented that Wisconsin's approach has more "accountability" and ensures that funds are spent on expenses directly related to the child with the disability. She also stated that Wisconsin's approach puts families in touch with people who can help them: "Although some families don't want this, we can offer case coordination and an ally."

In designing family support services, it is important to think in terms of what families need to keep their children at home. The best family support services are flexible and individualized, build on informal sources of support and existing social networks, and place control in the hands of families themselves.

Adoption

Adoption is being viewed increasingly as the option of choice for children who do not have actively involved families. Seven Counties Services in Kentucky, Macomb Oakland and other places in Michigan, and several other agencies around the country are finding families to adopt children with developmental disabilities. Contrary to conventional wisdom, people in these places report that even children with the most severe disabilities are adoptable. According to Jeff Strully, formerly of Seven Counties Services, age is a more important factor than severity of disability in finding families to adopt children. In other words, the younger the child, the easier it is to find adoptive families, regardless of severity of the child's disability.

As part of their permanency planning approach, Macomb Oakland and other Michigan agencies are looking for adoptive families for children whose natural parents are no longer involved in their lives. Adoptive families are often recruited among foster families. As Macomb Oakland administrators describe it, they push hard for adoption for children who do not have involved families. Michigan agencies also explore "open adoption" for some children. This is a nonlegal arrangement whereby a family agrees to adoption, but the adoptive family agrees to cooperate with the natural parents' visits and continuing involvement.

In Michigan, as in several other states, adoptive families can qualify for a range of subsidies, including a foster care payment and either a medical care subsidy or the state's family support subsidy. These subsidies are designed to help adoptive parents pay for the extra expenses entailed in taking care of the child.

Foster Families

Children who cannot live with their natural families or with adoptive families should have the opportunity to live in foster homes. While it is a poor second choice to living with natural or adoptive families, foster care is a preferred alternative to group homes or any other residential placement for children with developmental disabilities.

For some children, foster placement will be a temporary arrangement. Macomb Oakland's permanency planning approach calls for temporary foster placement until the natural family can be reunited or an adoptive family can be found. (Macomb Oakland also looks to foster families for adoption.) For other children, foster placement is likely to be a long-term arrangement. Even when children cannot live with their natural families and cannot be found adoptive families, they should be able to live with a family that not only cares for them, but cares *about* them as well. Thus, as part of its permanency planning approach, Macomb Oakland pursues options known as *shared care* and *permanent foster care*. Shared care is an arrangement in which the natural and foster parents agree to share responsibility for raising the child; for example, the child might spend weekdays with the foster family and weekends with the natural family. Permanent foster care refers to a nonlegal agreement by foster families to serve as primary parents for children until adulthood.

Many states and agencies have developed a special foster care program for children with developmental disabilities. Depending on the state and locality, foster homes are called *host homes*, *community training homes*, *extended families*, *family care*, *personal care*, *shared homes*, *developmental homes*, *specialized foster care*, and *professional foster homes*. Until relatively recently, foster care has not been viewed as an alternative for children with the most severe disabilities. However, throughout Michigan, Nebraska, and Wisconsin and at Seven Counties Services in Kentucky, agencies are recruiting foster homes for children with the most challenging needs.

Seven Counties Services and Macomb Oakland represent contrasting styles in placing children with severe disabilities in foster homes. Seven Counties Services proceeds cautiously in finding foster homes. People there look for deeply committed, almost missionary families to take children with developmental disabilities into their homes. They reject aggressive recruitment of foster families and believe that the payment of families can corrupt their relationship with children. As a consequence, they move slowly in placing people in foster homes or other kinds of living arrangements, even if this means that people must remain in institutions.

By contrast, Macomb Oakland, driven by the mission to move people out of institutions, operates like a finely tuned machine when it comes to recruiting foster families. In line with the announced goal of Michigan's governor of returning all children with developmental disabilities from state institutions and nursing homes to the community, Macomb Oakland planned to have all children from its catchment area (with a population base of approximately 2 million) in the community by the end of 1986. For children who cannot live with their families or be found adoptive families, Macomb Oakland is committed to finding foster families. In fact, Macomb Oakland no longer places children in group homes.

"We can't find enough good foster families" is a common lament among agencies. A Macomb Oakland resource manual (Dewey, 1980) is entitled, *Recruitment of Foster Homes . . . Can Good Homes Really Be Found?* In characteristic fashion, the last sentence of the manual reads, "Yes! They can be found!"

According to Macomb Oakland staff, there's a foster parent somewhere for every child. As Nancy Rosenau explained, "There's somebody for everybody. Foster parents aren't interchangeable, though. Some aren't good with kids with behavior problems, but they're good with medically fragile kids. You have to match the kid with the family. The toughest kid will be taken in by someone who likes him." The best estimate is that Macomb Oakland has placed in foster homes 25 children with severe multiple disabilities and medical involvements.

So how does Macomb Oakland find these wonderful foster parents, these "saints"? First of all, Macomb Oakland thinks that you don't have to be a saint to be a foster parent. To be sure, foster parents should be caring and committed people and willing to treat the child "as their own." According to people at Macomb Oakland, though, the image of foster parent as saint has driven many otherwise good people away from being foster parents. In looking for foster parents, they try to downplay the romanticized version of foster parenting. As long as foster parents are decent people, they don't mind if they are attracted to foster parenting by the opportunity to supplement family income or to practice professional skills.

Second, you have to be prepared to stand behind foster parents. Good service systems offer a lot of support services to foster parents: respite, home aide services, consultation, in-home nursing and professional services, and financial assistance for purchasing equipment and supplies and making necessary modifications to a house. Perhaps the biggest support to foster parents is being there when they need some help. This is what good case managers do. At Macomb Oakland, case managers (who have an average caseload of 20 to 25) stay in close touch with foster parents. Part of the reason for this is monitoring foster homes, making sure people placed in foster care are doing well. It is also a matter of supporting foster parents. As one Macomb Oakland case manager commented, "I'll stop by during the evening or on weekends. They also know they can call me anytime day or night. You can't just drop in unannounced without reciprocating."

Third, according to Macomb Oakland, it helps if you pay foster parents a decent stipend. For some people, especially those who view themselves as professionals, this will mean the difference between becoming a foster parent or doing something else. Many states and service systems today offer foster parents both a room-and-board payment and a stipend to provide training and services within the home. Region V in Nebraska recruits both foster parents, who receive from $322.00 to $359.50 per month for room and board, and "extended families," who are paid an additional $125 to $500 per month for training and services. Macomb Oakland refers to foster homes as "community training homes"; they receive between $25 and $35 per day ($9,125 to

$12,775 per year) and higher in some instances. Macomb Oakland's community training homes serve from 1 to 3 people, although it also contracts with some families to operate "alternative family residences" for 4 people. These homes are provided with an additional budget for hiring staff to come into the home. While it is true that the opportunity to supplement family income can attract many good people to being foster parents for children with severe disabilities, it is equally true that some people neither need nor want to be paid a salary for doing what comes naturally, namely being a loving parent to a child. These people too have to be sought out.

Finally, you have to know where and how to look for foster parents. Places that have been successful in finding foster homes for children with severe disabilities seem to start with the assumption that there are decent people in the world and proceed to look for them. Places that have not been successful seem to assume that only people who are "just in it for the money" will become foster parents.

Service systems and agencies have used different strategies to recruit foster families, including ads, public service announcements, newspaper articles, radio and television appearances, community presentations, newsletters, flyers, posters, and referrals from other agencies and people. Some places have focused on presentations at religious groups and service clubs. Others have relied on the media.

Macomb Oakland makes foster parent recruitment an agency priority and employs three full-time specialists who recruit and screen foster families. Macomb Oakland's strategy is to achieve high visibility for foster care. It attempts to generate a large number of phone calls and inquiries in order to come up with a small number of good families. As Nancy Rosenau put it, "What we need to do is generate thousands of inquiries about foster care. You have to get large numbers. Then you need a staff of people to call and stay in touch with them, to nurture and shape them into being able to give what a kid needs." Macomb Oakland has found that referrals from other foster parents and agency staff, newspaper articles on foster care, and classified ads yield the most foster parents. Their recruitment efforts downplay the saintly image and stress the income available through foster care and the opportunity for home employment. Typical classified ads read, "Looking for a new career?" and "NURSES, Your skills are needed in a unique program." Macomb Oakland officials are only slightly embarrassed by the mercenary tone of their foster parent recruitment efforts. As they see it, their specialists can easily screen out people who are not caring and committed.

"Every child," says internationally recognized child development psychologist Urie Bronfenbrenner (personal conversation), "needs at least one adult irrationally committed to his welfare." Bronfenbrenner wasn't referring specifically to children with disabilities, but his words apply to these children just as well. What he was referring to can only happen in a home, in a family.

Supportive Living Arrangements

Charles* and Peggy,* a middle-aged couple, live in a trailer in Wahoo, Nebraska, as do some other people in that town. Charles lived first in an institution for people with mental retardation and then in a group home; Peggy also previously lived in a group home for mentally retarded people. According to staff, Charles and Peggy did not always get along with other people in their respective group homes. Peggy has some behavior problems. Fortunately for Charles and Peggy, they seemed to get along with each other, so they got married. Their marriage isn't perfect, but this hardly makes them unique. They receive marriage counseling regularly.

Their trailer is clean and nicely furnished. Charles planted a small garden out in front and simply cut down some weeds in the back. Charles and Peggy probably wouldn't be doing so well in most places around the country. They would probably be living in institutions or group homes. Left on their own, they would be living in substandard conditions and perhaps even wandering the streets. They are doing well in Wahoo, however, with support from Region V.

Their trailer is actually a "supervised apartment." Each day a Region V staff member comes in from 2:00 P.M. to 10:00 P.M. (One staff member covers weekends while another works on weekdays.) The staff member cooks for them, makes sure their trailer and small yard are clean, helps them with budgeting and personal hygiene, and works with them on developing skills. He also checks in every once in a while on a nearby trailer where three men with mental retardation live and have a staff member visit for 4 hours each day.

Charles and Peggy rent their trailer themselves, although Region V found it for them. It is not simply a "homelike setting." It's their home. They seem very proud of it. When asked whether people living in their own homes receiving support from Region V ever kick staff out, a Region V administrator answered, "Yes, that happens." When asked what happens then, she said, "Oh, the staff member will go away for an hour or two, and by the time they go back, the people are sorry about the whole thing and apologize." Charles and Peggy are indeed doing well in Wahoo. Their basic needs are being met. They also have something that too few people with mental retardation seem to have. They are living with dignity.

The Case for Individualized Living

Since the beginning of the national trend toward deinstitutionalization, group homes have sprung up across the country. In most places, for adults, community living is equated with living in a group home. The problem with group homes is that they are almost never homes. This is not to suggest that group homes are abusive or dehumanizing settings. To the contrary, many group homes are nice places, staffed by caring and committed people. Many are, indeed, "homelike" and "normalized." For people living in group homes, life is richer and more fulfilling than for those in institutions. However, group homes almost always lack the warmth and intimacy that makes a house a home.

In Wisconsin, Nebraska, Michigan, Vermont, Kentucky, New Hampshire, and other places across the country, agencies are beginning to develop individualized community living arrangements as alternatives to group homes for people with severe and moderate disabilities. In fact, some agencies with the most experience in operating group homes are among the first to explore individualized alternatives.

These alternatives are variously called *supportive apartments*, *individualized service options* (ISOs), and *options in community living* in Wisconsin; *supervised apartments* in Region V in Nebraska; and *supported independence* at Macomb Oakland. In contrast to the group home model, these alternatives are designed to fit the program to the individual, not vice versa. A county administrator in rural Columbia County, Wisconsin, commented, "I don't want to see any group homes. The way group homes operate is that you identify the needs of the people through the needs of the program." In contrast to "transitional" living programs, people are not expected to leave their homes and move on to independent living; they stay in their homes while staffing and supports are adjusted.

As a concept, these supportive living alternatives are simple and straightforward: Find a home—whether a house, apartment, duplex, trailer, condominium, or what have you—and provide the supports people need to live successfully in the community. People live in homes, not agency-owned or -operated facilities. Inherent in the concept is flexibility. As Gail Jacob, Director of Options in Community Living in Wisconsin, explained, "Our models are flexible. If it is not working, change it." Some people—for example, those with mild disabilities who function relatively independently—may need only part-time support or merely someone to drop by to make sure they are doing okay. Others, such as people with severe disabilities and challenging needs, may require full-time staff support. Nothing in the concept precludes small groups of people from living together. However, when people are placed together, this should be because they choose to live together or happen to get along.

Region V in Nebraska has adopted a goal of becoming a "facility-free" community service system. The region is committed to phasing out both sheltered vocational centers and residential facilities. In recent years, the region has placed a number of people like Charles and Peggy in supervised apartments, which they themselves own or rent. Region V has both "live-in" and "live-out" homes. The live-out homes provide staff support for periods ranging from 30 minutes to 8 hours per day.

Macomb Oakland just developed its supported independence program in 1985, which it describes this way:

> The support provided will be based on identified needs, and will cover many areas: rent or living expense subsidy, resource and information referral, transportation, homemaker services, counseling, home health care aide, social and recreational, medical support, and skill building. Staff will be made available on a "P.R.N." basis up to twenty-four hours daily, if needed. Utilization of previous supports will be encouraged, i.e., family, employer, advocates, friends.

According to one Macomb Oakland administrator, the supported independence program is designed "to leave the bureaucracy behind." Macomb Oakland prefers to have people rent or own their own homes, but is prepared to arrange for agencies to rent places on people's behalf. A description of the supported independence program prepared by Macomb Oakland explains why homes shouldn't be licensed:

> It is preferred that these sites be unlicensed, as licensing has several undesirable aspects. Limits would be automatically placed on the type of setting used. For example, single apartments in a building and mobile homes cannot be licensed. Fire marshal and room size requirements would further limit options, as would the distance-between-licensed-facilities rule. Licensed facilities must offer twenty-four-hour supervision, which would be grossly restrictive for some participants. Lastly, it is provocative to the community to be notified when a foster care license is being issued. It not only promotes community resistance, but it is degrading to the program residents and to be avoided whenever possible.

While many agencies in Wisconsin are exploring individualized community living arrangements, Options in Community Living (not to be confused with the state's Community Options Program or COP), a private, nonprofit agency based in Dane County, has led the way in developing and refining this approach. They recently developed an excellent resource manual that describes their approach in depth (Johnson, 1985). This is must reading for anyone interested in developing individualized community living arrangements.

Options in Community Living supports approximately 100 people living in apartments and houses in the community. Initially, they served people with mild mental disabilities. With special project funding, including the state Community Integration Program, they have begun to serve people coming out of institutions who have more challenging needs, including people with physical disabilities.

All Options clients rent their own homes. For a number of people (17), Options arranges for live-in staff to provide full-time support. Attendants provide personal care to some clients who have physical disabilities. Some Options clients hire their own staff, referred to as attendants. For these people, Options acts as a broker. They recruit and train attendants and teach clients to supervise their own attendants. Options staff maintain close contact with clients and attendants and provide regular support and training to both. In other cases Options uses foster care funding and licensing to arrange for paid "roommates" who provide companionship and support in clients' homes. Options provides oversight and monitoring to these situations as well.

Rural Columbia County in Wisconsin contracts with a small private agency to support people with mental and developmental disabilities living on their own. It hires support workers or "friendly visitors" recruited from the local neighborhood to provide support to people for up to 20 hours per week. Describing the support workers, the county director stated,

> They're ordinary people in the community, but extraordinary in many ways. We look for people with the following qualities. They have to be ordinary in the community. They have to be respected people, not people who have to earn respect. They have to be local folks. They know other people. The person has to be of the community. People have to be connected to the community. They get out and around and know things in the community.

The county director gave some examples of what the support workers do for people:

> They get the person to church if the person wants to go. They take the person grocery shopping. They get the person out for recreation in the community. They work on appropriate social and sexual responses, either individually or in groups. . . . You have to start out giving a lot of support to people. If you're setting up an apartment for the first time, you need someone to help you with where to put your knives, forks, and spoons.

The agency hires one supervisor and supports about 25 people in the community at any given time. The county pays the agency about $15 an hour for services, and this covers transportation, insurance, office expenses, and wages. The support workers, who are employed by the agency, earn around the minimum wage. In order to help prevent a cash flow problem for the agency, the county advances the agency its expenses for the first several months of the year.

Columbia County has also set aside funds to help people living on their own to deal with the expenses of setting up a home. As the county director explained,

> We set up a closet of materials for people. We went out and bought a lot of stuff on sale. They can use or rent things. We had a TV they could rent. We had dishes, brooms, dustpans, bicycles, colanders. When people start out, they have a lot of front-end expenses. You have to have some stuff available so they can live. You let them buy their own things over time. . . . We also had a pot of money to help people with things like security deposits. We'll put down a security deposit and then they pay us back over time.

Issues in Meeting Individualized Needs

These supportive living approaches springing up across the country are innovative and responsive to people's needs. The only rule about supporting people this way is that it has to be individualized. This stands in stark contrast to the usual way of doing things. You must start with the person and his or her needs, then find a home and design the program. Here are some questions to ask:

1. What kind of housing does the person need? Does the person need an accessible house or apartment? What kinds of renovations will have to be made?

2. Where does the person work? It makes sense to find places for people to live that are near or accessible to where they work.

3. Where do the person's friends and family live? You should try to support people's social networks and encourage relationships with family and friends.

4. Should the person live alone or with others? Some people will probably be better off living alone. As Lyn Rucker has written, "People with behavioral needs or severe or profound retardation may need to start with a one-to-one living environment; roommates can be added if it makes sense." However, one-to-one arrangements between staff and clients have to be approached cautiously. As one Wisconsin case manager explained, "We might be asking too much of one person in this kind of situation." Other people, probably the majority, will most likely want to live with others. When people live with others, this should be for the same reason that any people choose to live together—because they like each other and get along. Some people might even choose communal (small group) living arrangements.

5. Should the person live with a family? Like most service systems, Region

V, Macomb Oakland, and other agencies look to families to provide homes for many adults. Region V views its extended family homes as the "model of choice" for both adults and children with severe disabilities. The strength of this is that it enables people to live in typical homes and can foster strong human bonds that are usually missing for people in group facilities and sometimes those living independently. The drawback is that this can lead to a dependent parent–child relationship that inhibits independence. It also raises the question of what will happen to people when, later in life, families die. Perhaps the best advice is that anyone placing adults with families should have a specific reason for doing so. A Macomb Oakland administrator recalled one woman placed with a family who had grown up in an institution and longed to live with a typical family. Finally, it should be pointed out that "family care" can be a flexible and individualized approach. Region V views its extended family homes this way. These include not only traditional families who accept people into their own homes, but also roommates who are contracted with to provide training to a person in a shared apartment.

6. How will you support the staff? In other words, how will you make sure that staff members get a break when they need it, receive training and assistance, and have someone to talk with about how things are going?

7. How will the living arrangements be monitored? How will you know if people are doing okay in the community? Who is responsible for making sure that people do not become lost in the community?

8. How will you help people become involved in their communities? Community integration does not simply mean living in a typical home in the community. It also means that people should have the opportunity to interact with other people, to form close relationships, and to achieve full participation in community life. How will you make sure that people are not simply *in* the community, but are *part* of the community?

People with severe disabilities have a lot of needs. They have some special needs. They may need staff support, medical assistance, and special programming. But they also have *human* needs. In attempting to address their special needs, too often we have overlooked their human needs. All people, regardless of disability, need a warm and pleasant place to live, companionship and friendship, and respect and human dignity. Everybody needs a home.

Making Community Integration Work

What makes community integration work? That is, what distinguishes good agencies from bad ones? Why is it that some places do a good job of serving people with the most severe disabilities in the community, while others don't serve these people at all?

There are professional and technical answers to these questions. To be sure, the best, most integrated programs have the technical know-how they need to serve people in the community. If you are placing people in the community, you had better know how to fund the supports they need to live successfully. If you are serving people with medical involvements, you had better be sure that staff or families are trained in how to use medical equipment and adaptive devices; how to recognize medical warning signs; how to feed, handle, and position people; and so forth. Similarly, if you are serving people with challenging behaviors, you should know how to implement nonaversive behavioral programs. These are just a few examples.

Yet it would be misleading to portray community integration simply as a technical matter. It is not. While professional and technical expertise may be important, it takes more than this to make community integration work.

Commitment

When you take a close look at the best, most innovative service systems and agencies—those that serve people with the most severe disabilities in integrated community settings—you find a common strand that ties them together: a deep commitment and belief in what they are doing. Commitment is the key to community integration.

At Macomb Oakland, at Region V, at the Working Organization for Retarded Children in New York City, at Options in Community Living, and at Seven Counties Services in Kentucky, people are committed to a philosophy and a vision of what services should look like. The philosophy and vision may vary somewhat from place to place. As an agency, Macomb Oakland is driven by the goal of getting everyone out of institutions and into the community in the shortest possible time. This is what Jerry Provencal, Macomb Oakland director, refers to as a "sense of urgency." As he described Macomb Oakland, "What we have done best is to serve a large number of people in the community in a short period of time." Region V is committed to social integration, the fullest possible participation of people with developmental disabilities in community life. This is why Region V has adopted the goal of becoming a "facility-free" service system. At Seven Counties Services, people emphasize the importance of developing relationships with people with disabilities. From this vantage point, it is not enough to serve people in the community or even to integrate them into community life; people also have to make a personal commitment to people with disabilities and develop mutual relationships with them. The Working Organization for Retarded Children is a relatively small agency that serves people with severe, multiple disabilities in ICF/MR-certified apartments. Its mission is to offer the most normalized services possible, given state-imposed bureaucratic and regulatory obstacles. Options in Community Living is committed to integration, autonomy, and quality of life.

Broad-based commitment does not happen on its own. This is where leadership comes in. You don't have to have a charismatic leader to have good services (although this does not seem to hurt). However, you do have to have competent and committed administrators who can set a direction and support and reward staff members who follow that direction.

At Region V and Macomb Oakland, administrators talk about the need for all staff members to feel personal involvement and responsibility in what they do. As Lyn Rucker, Region V's executive director explained, "You have to respect the staff. They have to feel ownership of what they do. If you don't own it, you won't do it." Thus, all staff members are involved in goal setting and monitoring services. Similarly, Macomb Oakland administrators are committed to involving staff in agency decision making. They are the first to admit, though, that not everyone shares the same exact philosophy and principles. As a state agency, Macomb Oakland has a number of long-term civil service employees who may not subscribe to the direction set by the administration. According to administrators, it is not necessary for everyone in the service system to share the same vision. As they see it, it takes about 6 hard-working and highly committed people in key leadership positions to make a service system work.

Flexibility

The best service systems and agencies allow for flexibility, creativity, and innovation. Region V, ENCOR, Seven Counties Services, and many others fall into this category. As a state-operated agency, Macomb Oakland may be somewhat of an anomaly, as most state agencies do not seem to have anywhere near the degree of flexibility found there. The Michigan Department of Mental Health seems to support Macomb Oakland's direction and gives it more autonomy than agencies in most states. Macomb Oakland administrators, in turn, seem to reward and encourage staff creativity and initiative.

If we were to design a service system that would maximize flexibility without sacrificing accountability, we would probably do so along the lines of the Nebraska system. Nebraska's 6 community mental retardation services regions are independent of state government. The state establishes regulations and funnels—but does not control—funds to the regions. Each region is controlled by local counties, each of which has a representative on the multicounty governing board. As part of a philosophy of placing "control as close to the individual being served as possible," Nebraska's regions have moved to an "area management" system. Each region is subdivided into smaller management units corresponding to one or more counties. These areas have their own directors. While the regional office sets policy, establishes general procedures, implements monitoring and evaluation systems, and approves area budgets, the areas seem to have a great deal of flexibility in designing services to meet individual needs and fit with local circumstances.

This area management system seems to have a lot to do with what makes Region V an innovative and responsive community service system. The area agencies are "human-scale" organizations, especially in rural communities. They are relatively small and manageable; one of Region V's areas serves 28 people. This ensures that decisions about people are made by staff who know them personally. Area agency staff also seem to have a strong sense of identity and hence feel "ownership" over what they do. This contributes to the high level of commitment found at Region V. Finally, when one visits Region V area agencies, one senses close ties between the area agencies and the local communities. Area agency staff live in and know their local communities.

While many states are moving toward regional systems, most place responsibility for the operation of community services with state agencies or local counties. This is not likely to change in the near future, if at all. Macomb Oakland's experience is instructive. According to Jerry Provencal, the State of Michigan was not committed to community services when Macomb Oakland was getting off the ground: "We had to persuade them to let us try new things. We talked them into giving us autonomy." Macomb Oakland created its own momentum. It won the flexibility it needs to try new ideas and models.

Accountability

One of the things that distinguishes successful programs (those that are integrating people with severe disabilities into the community) from unsuccessful ones is a willingness to be subjected to independent review and consumer evaluation. Self-evaluation also is important. Places like Options in Community Living, Region V, and Seven Counties Services seem to welcome external review. This has a lot to do with the quality of their services and their openness to innovation and change.

All services should be subject to independent evaluation. The history of institutions teaches us what can happen when places are out of sight and out of mind. When you serve people in dispersed settings throughout the community, it is just as important to keep a close eye on how people are doing. As bad as it might be, you can always go to an institution to see what things are like. Once you move people into the community, the danger is that no one will know how they are faring.

Practically every state has established certification procedures for services. Federal laws and regulations often require these. Institutions and community settings alike undergo life-safety inspections, fiscal audits, compliance surveys, professional reviews, utilization reviews, and a host of other licensing and certification requirements. These formal surveys and reviews yield certain kinds of information. They might tell you if a facility meets fire codes, if the record keeping and paperwork are in order, and maybe if people are involved in some kind of programming. But they never tell you about the quality of life and degree of integration. For this, you have to go to the people whose lives are affected by the services.

Consumer Monitoring. Some agencies seem to resent external monitoring of their services. Many objections are raised in order to exclude outsiders: "We have to respect clients' confidentiality." "It's too disruptive." "We're already licensed and certified." "We can't let people visit, because these are people's homes." By contrast, Macomb Oakland welcomes external monitoring.

Since 1980, parents have been monitoring Macomb Oakland group homes, under the auspices of an external advisory committee. A core committee of 6 to 8 parents coordinates the monitoring; as many as 25 additional parents may be involved in visiting the group homes. The core committee meets monthly, prepares monitoring reports, and makes recommendations for changes in group homes.

Consumer advisory committees are another way of building in external review and consumer involvement. Many agencies have established external advisory boards. What makes some places stand out is that they actually solicit advice and take it seriously when given.

External Review Committees. These committees, which include consumers and parents, review all programs that might involve a restriction on people's rights. Region V maintains an external program ethics committee. According to committee members, Region V has never gone against the committee's recommendations. Committee members' biggest complaint about Region V is that the administration and staff sometimes bring cases to the committee that do not involve restrictions on people's rights. In other words, Region V errs on the side of being too cautious, a commendable trait for an agency.

Self-Evaluation. Region V undertakes a thorough and lengthy annual "systems review." This is in addition to its having been accredited by the Accreditation Council for Services to the Mentally Retarded and Other Developmentally Disabled since 1978. In fact, in 1974, one of its area agencies, Saunders County Office of Mental Retardation, was the first community service system in the country to be accredited. Yet Region V does not feel the accreditation system goes far enough in guaranteeing a high quality of services and a high degree of integration. As they explain it, they feel that accreditation standards focus too heavily on paper compliance and ignore many aspects that they feel are important. So Region V developed its own review procedures which focus not just on record keeping but on people and programs. As part of this annual review, Region V surveys parents and consumers on what they like and dislike about its services.

Commitment, flexibility, and accountability—these things, and not just technical expertise, are what make community integration work. In fact, if you have these characteristics, you can often figure out how to solve the most challenging technical problems. As Jerry Provencal put it, "The answers are easy; the work is hard."

Making Lives Better while Developing Good Services

It is a healthy sign for the community integration movement, and a sign of its maturity, that people equally committed to helping people with developmental disabilities to achieve their rightful place in the community disagree on some things. Today, there are new controversies and debates. In looking at good programs and talking with people across the country, we have found that it is easy to get agreement on basic principles and values. We have also found that there are some issues on which there are legitimate disagreements.

Is the mission today one of developing only the highest quality, most integrated services, complete with full participation in community life for people with developmental disabilities? *Or,* is the mission one of ending the suffering of people in institutions and preventing other people from having to live through the institutional experiences?

We have argued that *everyone,* including people with the most severe disabilities, needs a *home,* not a "homelike" setting, or a natural environment, or a group facility, but a true home. For children, this means living with a family; for adults, this means living alone or with a very small number of other people in a house, apartment, or other place where typical people live. Is this a vision of what services should look like—something we should work toward—or is it a yardstick for practical day-to-day decision making? If you believe that everyone needs a home, can you justify developing group homes if this means that you can get people out of institutions more quickly? This is the controversy.

Some people believe that you only develop the highest quality and most integrated services, no matter what. For example, you should only place children with families and adults in small supportive arrangements in typical community homes. As a corollary to this belief, if you cannot develop the best services, do not develop any services at all. If, for example, funding mechanisms prevent the development of individualized placements or if caring and committed families cannot be found for all children, then people will have to remain in institutions or go unserved in the community.

Many other people just as passionately believe that the mission is to return everyone in institutions to the community in the shortest possible time. Jerry Provencal, Macomb Oakland's director, warns against what he calls the "purist trap," the belief that only ideal services should be created. As he and others at Macomb Oakland argue, they will not let their inability to develop the most normalized or integrated services stand in the way of developing a large number of community placements. They readily admit that they operate too many group homes and sheltered workshops, but they do not apologize for these. They developed them to get people out of institutions. Today, Macomb Oakland is moving toward more integrated and individualized services; it no longer places children in group homes, let alone in institutions, and is developing a supported independence program for adults. If, however, it had to develop all of its group homes and sheltered workshops again, it would readily do so.

As with any philosophical issue, there is no right answer in this controversy. If we were pressed to give our own answer, we would be inclined to say that both sides are right. Having looked at some of the best group facilities and home- and family-based services in the country, it would be a philosophical compromise to suggest that group homes should be developed, especially in the case of children. Just as surely, though, having looked at many institutions, it too would be a philosophical compromise to suggest that some people should continue to live there because we cannot develop the best services quickly enough. How can you explain to people living in institutions and their families that staying there is better than living in a small group home in the community?

It's up to you to decide where you stand on this controversy. If, on the one hand, you believe that only the most integrated and individualized services should be developed, then the burden is on you to figure out what to do with all of the people in institutions or those left unserved in the community. You can't just write these people off. This is what Jerry Provencal means when he refers to a "sense of urgency."

No service system has developed a large number of integrated and individualized community living arrangements in a short period of time, but this does not mean that it cannot be done. No one has really tried. In fact, it is only in the past several years that people have started trying to find homes in the community for people with severe disabilities. As places in Wisconsin,

Michigan, Nebraska, Kentucky, and elsewhere place more and more people with severe disabilities in homes in the community, we are slowly accumulating the experience needed to do this on a broader scale.

If, on the other hand, you are committed to getting people out of institutions and into "better" places in the community, even if this means operating group homes, then, it seems, the burden is on you to show that you can move toward "good" services in the future. A couple of things seem important. First of all, do not lock yourself into group homes. Do not buy facilities. Many states and agencies act as though they are in the real estate business. The more resources that are tied up in facilities, the harder it will be to move people out. This is one of the lessons of institutions. Second, develop some alternatives to group facilities, if only on a small scale. Find and support some families for children; develop some nonfacility-based services for adults. In doing this, serve people with the most severe disabilities. In the long run, this will give you a base of practical experience and demonstrate that everyone can live in a home. Good models always drive out bad ones.

There are also some better or worse, more or less integrated, ways to operate group homes. Here are some suggestions.

1. *Develop Smaller Facilities.* If you have to develop group homes, make them smaller rather than larger. As we have argued, small size alone does not guarantee a high quality of life or high degree of integration. However, smaller settings are almost always more "homelike" and less "restrictive" than larger ones.

2. *Place People with a Range of Disabilities Together.* In other words, try "heterogeneous," rather than "homogeneous" groups. When selecting people to live at group facilities, don't group them according to categories (e.g., severe or profound mental retardation, autism, medical involvements, challenging behaviors, or multiple disabilities).

3. *Integrate People into the Community.* Just because people happen to live in a group facility, this does not mean that they have to be cut off from community life. When we refer to integrating people into the community, we are talking about one, two, or perhaps three people going shopping, eating in restaurants, attending community activities, and interacting with people as individuals rather than as members of a group.

4. *Teach People "Functional" Life Skills.* People with severe disabilities need opportunities to learn practical skills, in order to participate as fully as possible in home and community life. This does not mean that people have to be "programmed" 24 hours a day, with all of their activities recorded and charted. It does mean that opportunities for people to learn life skills should not be lost. In any community setting, somebody has to cook, clean, grocery

shop, and perform dozens of other daily tasks. People with severe disabilities should participate in these activities, if only partially (see Baumgart et al., 1982).

5. *Avoid Institutional Trappings*. This could be stated in a more positive way; namely, make the setting as "normalized" as possible. The problem with saying this is that much of the true meaning of *normalization* has been lost. Indeed, Wolfensberger (1983) has abandoned the term for what he calls *social role valorization*: placing people with disabilities in valued social roles. The point is to avoid re-creating institutions in the community. Some practices associated with institutions are creeping into community facilities: separate bathrooms for staff; kitchens and other rooms being off-limits to "residents"; mealtimes revolving around staff routines; separate meals for staff and "residents"; and others.

6. *Help People Develop Relationships with Community Members*. Encourage visits and contacts with family members and friends. Help people become involved with local community associations and organizations. Seek out volunteers and community members to become involved in people's lives.

Finally, if you are operating or developing group homes, there seems to be some truth in the saying that compromises are more acceptable when one acknowledges them as such. When you admit that you are making a compromise, you reduce your personal stake in what you have done and develop a sense of what you must do in the future.

Conclusion

Recently we were at a meeting when a discussion broke out about whether we, as a field or movement, really *know* how to achieve community integration. On the one side stood people who argued that the know-how exists today to integrate people with the most severe disabilities into the community. On the other side were those who took the position that there are no simple solutions to helping people with disabilities lead the good life in the community.

Do we know how to achieve community integration? We know that in many parts of the country an increasing number of people with the most severe disabilities are living and thriving in the community. We know how to design funding mechanisms, recruit foster families, and implement quality safeguards. We know how to teach people with severe and profound retardation, we can design alternative communication systems for people who cannot speak, we know how to suction and position people with medical involvements, and we have learned how to develop nonaversive behavior programs for people with challenging behaviors.

There are things we do not know. We do not know how to get complex service systems always to do what we think they should. We do not know how to take ideas developed in fertile environments and apply them to ones not so open to innovation and change. We do not know what makes for the right chemistry in matching families or staff with people with severe disabilities. We do not understand exactly how communities work. We do not know which compromises are called for in which situations.

We do know, however, that good people across the country are doing good things for people with the most severe disabilities. They are committed to community integration and are providing answers to some of the things we do not know. They are making community integration work, not perfectly perhaps, but making it work nonetheless. This much we know.

References

Baumgart, D., Brown, L., Pumpian, I., Nisbet, J., Ford, A., Sweet, M., Messina, R., & Schroeder, J. (1982). Principle of partial participation and individualized adaptation in education programs for severely handicapped students. *Journal of the Association for Persons with Severe Handicaps*, 7(2), 17–27.

Dewey, J. (1980). *Recruitment of foster homes: An instructional manual of foster home recruitment techniques*. Mt. Clemens, MI: Macomb Oakland Regional Center.

Johnson, T. (1985). *Belonging to the community*. Madison, WI: Options in Community Living.

Knitzer, J., Allen, M. L., & McGowan, B. (1978). *Children without homes: An examination of public responsibility to children in out-of-home care*. Washington, DC: Children's Defense Fund.

Taylor, S. J., Lutfiyya, Z., Racino, J., Walker, P., & Knoll, J. (1986). *An evaluation of Connecticut's Community Training Home Program*. Syracuse, NY: Center on Human Policy, Syracuse University.

Wisconsin Department of Health and Social Services. (1985). *Family support program: Guidelines and procedures*. Madison, WI: Author.

Wolfensberger, W. (1983). Social role valorization: A proposed new term for the principle of normalization. *Mental Retardation, 21*, 234–239.

Part II

LEADERSHIP

4

Culturing Commitment

GERALD PROVENCAL

> There was never any more inception than there is now,
> nor any more youth or age than there is now,
> and will never be any more perfection than there is now,
> nor any more heaven or hell than there is now.
>
> —Walt Whitman, "Song of Myself"

Recently a friend asked me if I thought it were possible for staff who work in the field of developmental disabilities to sustain their commitment over time. This question is getting a lot of attention lately, as the fear of burn-out seems to be on every mind. In fact it has gotten to a point where many see burning-out as an inevitable condition that must eventually afflict us all; the only question is when.

Frankly, I do not subscribe to the pessimism. I cannot but feel that this phenomenon, like many others in human services, has received more credit for being an obstacle than it deserves. Accepting burn-out as a kind of legitimate condition gives an air of respectability to quitting on the job. It adds another excuse to our medley of excuses for not producing. People do get tired. People do experience frustration. People do fail to pace themselves properly. But these problems are part of every vocational pursuit from barking at carnivals to discounting jewelry. It seems that it is mostly in human services, however, that a natural byproduct of employment has become a badge of courage. Surely there are ways to dilute the effects of natural fatigue without elevating the experience to a "wounded in battle" status, accompanied by a purple heart and a paid trip to the sidelines.

The way I would describe staff "commitment" is that it is a kind of motivation by habit. Its origin differs from person to person but usually has roots anchored to a personal experience that movingly called attention to the great injustice perpetrated on people with disabilities—an experience that refuses to be forgotten. Commitment takes form in the attitude and, more importantly, in the behavior of people in our field. The behavior is predictably energetic, productive, and unwavering in purpose. The drive is to close all the gaps that prevent consumers from being treated as full citizens.

My observation of those who have sustained their commitment is that they are people who have gained a level of satisfaction in their work that has become virtually self-propelling. Their satisfaction tends to drive them toward achievement that leads to new satisfaction, that pushes for another achievement, and so on. Regardless of what initially sets the cadence in motion, whether guilt, goodness, or vanity, it evolves into a highly personal need to produce.

It is not that such individuals are beyond being influenced; however, once they reach the stage of being personally driven they seem to get locked into their own power source. Once there, they seem to become indifferent to the creature comforts, the fringe benefit arguments that preoccupy so many who complain of burning-out.

The compulsion to produce does not appear to begin spontaneously; in fact, it even seems to have a developmental sequence. Any number of things can generate the process, but what is perhaps more important than what sparks interest is the climate it finds to grow in. Fortunately there are a great many things we can do to affect that climate, to help our initial interest to become caught up in a rhythm that builds toward a personal drive to create rich and full lives for those we serve. This chapter is devoted to exploring the attitudes and strategies that help to maintain this momentum. My own notions about ways human services administrators, in particular, can contribute to an environment that nurtures a developing sense of personal commitment are offered here. Some are the products of my personal experience; some have been gleaned from watching others from a distance.

The Leader Holds the Bag

It is the leader's job to lead. This requires that she or he accept the stewardship for seeing to it that a productively charged atmosphere exists in the organization. Whether it is the director or someone else who is the cheerleader, the person in charge has no more fundamental duty than to see to it that the agency energy level is high enough to move the organization forward to meet its objectives. The agency personality that takes shape during this process is one the director has no choice but to take responsibility for, whether the organization emerges as robust and ambitious or whiney and aimless. Staff, whether burned out or spirited, trace their performance lineage to their leaders.

So, for starters, if you run the show you also hold the bag. You can't blame the capitol, the budget, the unions, or your predecessor for your agency's mindset or pulse rate. Accepting the responsibility for setting a rejuvenated tone, rather than explaining its absence, is primordial.

The Need for Objective Clarity

In order for people to feel a commitment to an organization, they have to accept its doctrine. More immediately they have to agree with the most obvious single objective the agency pursues. When an agency is without such an objective or has one that is vague or inconsequential, instead of the organization having the feel of purpose, it will seem adrift. Direction will be random and expeditious.

Human services work is demanding, sometimes homely work, and the altruism that leads so many here is seldom enough to coax high energy over a long campaign. Among other things necessary to motivating this kind of investment is the presence of a clear objective that staff feel is worthy of their heart, an objective that is ambitious but not so distant as to be impossible to reach, an objective that all members of the agency can feel they have some part in attaining.

At the agency where I have spent most of my professional life, the Macomb Oakland Regional Center in Michigan (MORC), there are many objectives, but one stands above the rest. We chase it like the great white whale: "To provide a home down the street for every person with a developmental disability from our corner of the world who is living in an institution or who is at risk of living in one." Oh yes, ultimately we want self-actualization and lives that are filled with colorful adventure for the people from Macomb and Oakland, but what we seek first, and with an obsession, is housing—housing that is indistinguishable from mine, yours, and the mayor's.

Having locked in on the brass ring, the rest becomes obvious, not easy. Layer after layer reveals the obvious. The process of determining how long it will take to access enough homes; of deciding who will leave and when; of creating funding structures, support configurations, real work opportunities, and more, all become manageable functions when they exist in a context that recognizes gaining a residential foothold in the larger community as the most fundamental step toward citizenship.

Recognizing these functions as mechanical pieces of an apparatus that has an unmistakable purpose also keeps any single function from taking on more significance than the objective. The MORC objective is distinctive. It is one that the staff identify with; it recognizes the critical nature of the full range of consumer needs but places housing above the rest in sequence.

The leader's function, once the objective has been crisply defined, is to make certain that all staff members see themselves as part of the chase and are invigorated by the exercise.

The Romance of Ingenuity

The agency tenor should assume obvious respect for creativity and innovation, just as staff dependability and longevity are respected. In an attempt to establish this tenor, it is important to groom excitement and elevate displays of ingenuity to a place of importance by applauding new approaches to old problems and encouraging even outrageous ideas, just to keep the organization's creative juices flowing.

It is necessary that neither the agency as a whole nor its individual members become satisfied with a modest balance of success for any sustained period. Push, pull, stroke, coax. Dare staff to be more like Andy Warhol (even the Marx brothers) than society's image of the modest civil servant. Tom Robbins (1980, p. 19) has perceptively written, "Humanity has advanced where it has advanced, not because it has been sober, responsible, and cautious, but because it has been playful, rebellious, and immature."

When you feel yourself becoming more and more pleased with thoughtful, quiet, problem-solving approaches, it is probably time to unbutton the collar. Give in to staff eccentricities, even if they undermine the notion of a dignified agency demeanor. Let people wear Bermuda shorts, have their offices in an abandoned garage, devote days to planting spring flowers, have "administrative leave" to tour programs in other states, and plaster maps and zany signs all over walls and ceilings. We should be building a sense of creative freedom along with a sense of purpose. Give staff the opportunity and the atmosphere, and the agency will advance.

The director must make the objectives clear, then incite improvisation. If no one has walked on the conference table in over a month it's probably time to see "A Day at the Races."

A Sharp Sense of the Present and the Past

The work being done in the field today is revolutionary. We are in the midst of changing Western society's collective mind; radically altering the way it treats one stratum of its people. We are trading caricature communities that have existed on the margin of society for integrated housing and guaranteed education. We are trading puzzles for paychecks, food carts for carry-out Chinese, dayrooms for family rooms. Whether you are a romantic or not, the change and its significance cannot be denied. It is what it is: social revolution.

Now this is all very powerful stuff, not only for the consumer but also for the staff who are helping to make it happen. Yet many staff lack the sense of history needed to recognize the spectacular differences they are a part of making. In fact, many people who are working right in the midst of the whirlwind of progress have no real sense of the proportion of change that has occurred in recent times, and consequently the significance of their own roles is lost. For example, there is often a lack of understanding of the enormous difference living in the larger community can have on someone who has lived for 20 years in the state school.

The organization's leader has to make certain that staff gain a sharp sense of contemporary history so both the gravity of the consumers' situation and their dependence on human service activists are brought into dramatic perspective. When we come to appreciate the absolute reliance citizens with disabilities have upon the labor of human service workers, and when we accept a role in dismantling the social structure traps that have ensnared those citizens as a matter of tradition, our altruism can truly begin to mature. Further, we can look forward to our job satisfaction no longer being tethered to creature comforts but being linked to a gratification that propels itself.

The phenomenon that develops for many in this field is similar to other matters of the heart. Early on it is easy to be captivated by the novelty, the rightness, the excitement of it all. But for the relationship to gain in strength until its presence is unquestioned takes giving and trust. It takes risk, too, and the recognition that a balance must be struck that carries the gifts and the handicaps of each party with equal respect.

The leader's job is not to make sense of the love metaphor; rather, it is to help the people he or she works with to find romance in this field. Part of it comes from communicating what things were like before the recent changes and what they can be like someday.

Identification with Social Activism

Staying on the social revolution theme, it is important for staff to recognize the parallels that exist between all groups that have been oppressed because they differed from the norm of the dominant group. It is important because both the illness of elitist discrimination and the antidote apply cleanly to the plight of people with developmental disabilities. Virtually every group in this country that has been discriminated against for whatever reason has followed the same road on their march toward full citizenship. In condensed form, this process involves dramatizing the disparity between their lifestyles and those of the privileged class and simultaneously working for a raising of public consciousness and statutory change that will give them access to their version of the American dream.

The major difference between the developmentally disabled segment of the population and other oppressed groups, of course, is that the former is far less likely than the latter to produce spokespersons and activists in significant numbers from their ranks. As a result they depend heavily, to near exclusion, on professionals and outside advocates. It follows then that we should pay close attention to the strategies that have been employed by the Gray Panthers and Southern Christian Leadership Council, and not just the administrative dicta written for ponderous bureaucracies. We should read more Saul Alinsky than John T. Molloy.

It has been my experience that not only does the consumer stand to gain more when we emulate social activists, but staff seem to inhale pure oxygen. Unlike the tepid satisfaction that comes from following volumes of procedural manuals, which have removed any possibility for creative thought on the job, the deepest kind of gratification—the kind that is most likely to become a personality fixture—is gained by staff who represent the consumer as other activists represent themselves.

Never Underestimate the Power of Rah-Rah

A few years ago a friend of mine said that her work had changed, it wasn't "fun any more." What had been a labor of love had become only labor. The drudgery she used to associate with the business world now clung like barnacles to her own job. She blamed the increasing size of her agency, the change in administration attitude, and the quality of new staff.

Most of my friends and I have felt this kind of exasperation and more than once considered moving from human services to balloon sales because of it. The "no-fun" phenomenon seems to hit us hard in this field, and I am convinced that one of the reasons is because there is a tendency for people in our work to feel special and deserving of special treatment. After all, aunts and uncles have told us for years that our work takes great patience, requires a special kind of person. The systems we work for, however, treat us with less awe.

The truth of the matter is that, unless we deliberately do something to gain control of the rhythm of work, time is on the side of the system, not the special people. The idealism that brought us to this field originally, even the pride of our relatives, wears thin in time. And all the while the bureaucracy grows more entangling.

Nothing I know of counters more consistently the slide of work becoming just work than paying respect to someone's fresh, even fabricated enthusiasm. The fact is that, until a more naturally invigorating spirit kicks in, we can manufacture events and situations that will change the "no-fun" atmosphere. Going out of the way to compliment someone on a letter, speech, or just an idea can be perceived as unnecessary for professionals, but of course it is not. These simple gestures can be the start of turning the mood momentum around and back in the direction of enjoyment. Telling someone that working with them is a real pleasure or showing excitement over a consumer's progress either can remain a solitary burst of pleasantry or, if we work at it, can be the start of putting vigor back into the work experience.

Softball games, agency T-shirts, spontaneous celebrations, parties because it is Friday, becoming invested in one another's success, being hurt by one another's failures, and making a serious effort to promote fraternity and affection are not necessarily superficial components of work satisfaction. More and more I find them one heartbeat from it all. The objectives we have for our agencies give us a sense of mission, but the interpersonal relationships we develop and the climate they are given to grow within give us a bond.

Agencies with identical salary structures and bureaucratic inhibitors can differ sharply in work performance and reputation. One group may allow themselves the joy of being knocked out with the opening of a new group home or with a new work placement, while the other may trudge along dispassionately, another day at the office.

Rah-rah approaches might be seen as sophomoric, as glossing over the essence of a professional's discontent. But rah-rah can effectively help to interrupt the cadence of job depression because it playfully diverts self-indulgence; it can break the blues grip and allow other, more productive influences into work life.

The tenor of an agency should be upbeat, positive, and confident, but it doesn't happen spontaneously or stay in place because we are good, deserving people. We have to work at it. I know for certain that it is a dead-end set-up to act as if we are entitled to contentment and success on the job, expecting each to come floating through the air duct. We need to have as much respect for the principles of learning in our own lives as we do in the lives of our consumers. Enthusiasm, idealism, and optimism should be shaped and reinforced. Cynicism and pessimism should be slated for extinction.

At all costs we must not pass on our own depression or pessimism to someone else. It is larcenous to steal the idealism that moves our colleagues. It is unforgivable to squelch their happiness for the job with our cynicism. As the leader you must help people find the delight, the spirit that led you to this work. Your job, your responsibility is to infect others with a sense of mission, not to convince them that they will lose their interest as they gain wisdom. Having others become as thrilled as you are when you feel your best is your ticket to immortality.

The high-energy personal-involvement style advocated here might not seem to fit the traditionally dignified professional image some would choose for themselves or their agencies; however, this tempo is well suited, in a complementary way, to the nature of contemporary problems that are so often sterile, impersonal, and trance-inducing.

Never underestimate the power of rah-rah.

Beware of Leadership Gone Awry

In the desire to be the best possible director of an organization it is tempting to take oneself too seriously. While this is really just another shade of generic vanity, which touches everyone, we need to be especially watchful of it here because the director's style and expectations so greatly affect the building of staff commitment. Two illustrations of leadership gone awry follow.

Self-Appointed Superman/Superwoman

One of the seductions a director faces is that of feeling that, in order to have the respect of staff, he or she has to be the acknowledged expert in every phase of the organization. The epitome of this is illustrated by the director who hoards information, influential contacts, and decisions and, worse, hoards the credit for success. Such directors demand that staff behold them as *the* authority, as *the* seat of all wisdom, whether concerning daily routine or future policy. Even speculation as to distant trends and "vision" are presumed to be the exclusive property of this person in charge. Staff members can debate pertinent topics, offering opinions here and there, but the director's thoughts are delivered as if they are bolts of truth sent by a god.

Such directors operate as if effective leadership were a matter of control. They develop procedures and circulate memoranda that spell out responsibilities in the narrowest of terms so that no staff come to rival their broad-based expertise. They allow only the slightest individual initiative to be taken, preferring instead to step into any phase of the operation when the occasion suits them and usurp decision making from employees who have the routine duty of making such decisions. It is reminiscent of the approach taken by those teachers who are driven above all else by the desire to exact compliance from students, as if spirit must be broken before learning can take place.

Great teachers do not teach by denying opportunities for learning. Great leaders do not lead by denying opportunities for gaining recognition. Great leaders and teachers do not extract the most from people with control but with freedom. They do not coax the most from people with selfishness but with generosity. I had a boss who always made a point of introducing his staff personally to visiting dignitaries. The introductions were intimate, flattering, never rushed or perfunctory, and they focused on some quality that each of us was proud of—energy, dedication, or a special skill. These brief moments of being singled out for recognition and having our importance to the organization highlighted (even exaggerated) swelled our heads as well as our hearts, but the pride that ensued was the invigorating type. We were important contributors to an agency that was coming to stand for something.

Rather than hoard credit, directors need publicly and freely to give praise to staff for their unique specialties; to admit openly that the budget officer knows more about accounting principles than anyone in the field, and that the training director is able to get more out of a class in one hour than the director could in a week.

Rather than striving to build a superman/superwoman directorship, create a super organization. If the latter is the choice, then staff need to be unbridled and given the room to run.

The Reign of Terror

This is another style of management to avoid sharply. It is characterized by a one-dimensional punishment approach. Here the administrator takes on the appearance of a latter-day Ivan the Terrible. In this scenario a premium is placed on having the correct response to any conceivable question the boss might ask, as great pain is usually experienced in the form of a fall from grace, and the descent is steep and fast and public. Questions might be data oriented or simply intended to tap opinion. They may be anticipated and put in writing or come from some cloud and delivered by telephone on a Saturday night.

This administrator relies heavily on surprise and fright, assuming unpredictability will keep staff so off balance they will prepare themselves for anything. The problem is that staff in these organizations come to feel less prepared than anxious, defensive, and resentful. They increasingly become less likely to take chances or try new methods because the risk of error is too great. In extreme cases they take on a nervous glaze like National Geographic antelope who pray that the lion will dart right instead of left.

The administrators themselves are often popular with the news media, elected officials, and citizens, many of whom admire get-tough approaches for civil servants. Ironically, while this administrator and those in the inner circle move about the agency at will, they communicate to staff in the most formal manner. It almost snows memoranda, carefully written, initialed, and copied. New policies, procedures, and directives are issued in volume and prepared in such exacting terms that they simultaneously cover the administrator and make supervisors vulnerable.

There are many conclusions that can be drawn about this style of leadership, but ultimately it comes to this: You cannot scare people into loving their work, and commitment to any labor requires love above all else. Being good to people seems to work better than being frightening. Fear breeds fear; what we give tends to be recycled in one way or another.

Closing the Distance; Putting an End to Anonymity

I am not sure when it began to change; when social work became less social; when human services became less human. My first awareness that things were different came sometime during the early 1970s, when I noticed that more and more of us were converting head bands to camera straps and paying $10 for razor cuts. The slide was a gradual one, away from altruism for its own sake, away from identifying with social reformers who made personal sacrifices and who assumed gigantic responsibilities on their own.

This slide unequivocally changed the character of human services work because it altered the breadth of the individual professional's involvement in the life of the consumer. Habits and practices that had proven successful within the world of free enterprise began to appear in human service operations. Management by objectives, PERT charts, cost-effectiveness analyses, and the like crept into conversations of social workers, psychologists, and other colleagues. More and more these concepts exerted strong influence in the network of agencies devoted to improving social conditions in America.

In some respects we learned some good things from Wall Street and Madison Avenue. For example, we began to make serious evaluations of our goals and outcomes, which gave direction to effort that had sometimes meandered. Modeling the business community also drew our attention to pay scales, fringe benefits, and the provision of working climates that would attract and hold staff.

One of the dubious benefits of this association, however, was the depersonalization of the professional's role. The new expectation became for staff to make discrete contributions to an agency, which in turn fit into a "system" of services. The "system" became the accountable party. It became the problem, the solution, and the hope, and in order for it to function at maximum efficiency professionals became more and more specialized and their responsibilities more and more diffuse. In fact, the times today seem to find the field of developmental disabilities in a situation where few staff have the impression that they are ethically accountable for more than one facet of a consumer's life.

There is a growing practice of projecting ownership for a consumer's condition onto a group—an interdisciplinary team, central office, board of commissioners, or a legislature—rather than on a single identifiable individual. Trades are being made: activist for technician, generalist for specialist, intimacy for anonymity, wheel for cog, guilt for innocence. When they are made, the trades improve the mechanical functions of our "systems" but they surgically remove the soul from our work. They largely separate us from the romance of human services by reducing contributions to piecework production. Tasks are narrow and circumscribed, intended to take us beyond the bounds of error commission, beyond the circles of individual judgment. The trouble is that they can also take us beyond the thrill of personal triumph which so often comes from knowing that each of us—with our judgment, and at our risk—acted without blueprint and made a major difference in someone's life.

A large part of the reason for people feeling like they are burning out is that the essence of their own participation, the full impact of their energy and imagination, is seen as insignificant when compared to the omniscient "system" that arches over everything like some socialistic Emerald City of Oz.

The work in human services is hard; even the technical work is hard. Fatigue is real. But burn-out doesn't come from working too hard, it comes from being cut off from the joy of knowing your work is of consequence, undeniable consequence.

It is fortuitous that one of the things that institutionalized people with developmental disabilities need to set them free is a perfect complement to what has been missing in the professional's diet. With the overdependence on the "system," professionals are in a situation similar to citizens in general who are set apart from the handicapped community. There is often only a distant or esoteric appreciation for the gravity of the consumer's plight. The conditions that make up this plight are so far outside the world of experience of noninstitutionalized people, whether professional or not, that little urgency for change is sensed. This state of oblivion is reminiscent of a cryptic remark written by Alexander Solzhenitsyn (1963, p. 19) in *One Day in the Life of Ivan Denisovitch.* In an attempt to explain the indifference of Russian guards in the dead of winter, comfortable in their wool overcoats at a Siberian Gulag, the hero asks, "How can a man who is warm understand a man who is cold?"

In a recent interview with a middle-aged homemaker, a member of Amnesty International, a reporter asked why she had become so committed to the cause of freeing political prisoners from around the world. She replied, "Once you read about them, learn about them, they become a part of you."

The irrefutable fact is that we have to put a check on the anonymity that has spread throughout so much of our work. Each person who lives in an institution, nursing home, or other residence that robs and dehumanizes people is someone's son, someone's daughter. They have names, faces, family, and memories of vacations spent out of the institution. Likewise, professionals with a role in reparation are not inanimate objects whose professionalism is judged by the empathy they can temper. Liberating people from life in exile is an emotional business. It is a personal business. Freedom is the most emotional and personal of all businesses. We should not shun this truth because it no longer fits the evolving contemporary image of the cool, dispassionate professional. We should accept the nature of this work for what it is and use the sentiment it naturally stimulates to propel us onward.

To regain the sense of personal appreciation that is necessary for changing ingrained social practices, we might immerse ourselves in the consumer's world. Periodically we might spend a day on the ward of the institution someone calls home. We might eat where they eat, sleep where they sleep, shower where they shower, fill our lungs with the odors that fill their nostrils. Look into the eyes of people who live there and ask what they think about their lives, about their futures.

In fact, we should make it a requirement once and for all that each worker who gives service and every member of a board that presides over developmental disabilities agencies must spend some time in direct contact with consumers—on the consumer's turf. Case managers who have clients living in a nursing home, for example, should be required periodically to spend Sunday on a ward. No member of a county oversight board that, for example, ostensibly is in the business of assuring appropriate services to county citizens who have a developmental disability should be spared the experience of eating a meal on the ward of an institution. Nor should they miss the opportunity their fellow citizens have every day of sitting on hard furniture and trying to find a corner of the room, or their mind, to which they can retreat for peace.

This "reality rub-in" should not just be directed toward board members or practitioners. Clerical staff, accountants, and members of the housekeeping crew gain from spending time in the client's world. The most important benefit will be to the consumers, because their situation will come alive. They will occupy a permanent place in the memories of people who need reminders.

The names and photographs of every person waiting in an institution, waiting for community placement, should be vivid to the staff responsible for the placement. The person from your county and mine, sitting on the floor of some state school dayroom, should not be a faceless blur. The conference room or some other escape-proof place could well be decorated with those faces and those stories.

There are countless warm, moving, outrageous experiences that unfold around our clients every day. We should share them. When we trade experiences that bring laughter and anger, we also bring the consumer into focus and bring what needs to be done to the unmistakable foreground. My observation has been that when it is the agency norm to talk about the people who are affected directly by us, share anecdotes that give them dimension, both employees and those depending on them gain purpose.

The leader can make a powerful difference in both the staff's search for job satisfaction and the consumer's search for life satisfaction, by promoting an agency norm that keeps the client alive and in full view of the organization, ahead of "system" abstractions. The leader in a human services agency has to find ways of making the client so real that "once you read about them, learn about them, they become a part of you."

Testing the Mettle

Recently I sat on an interview team that was screening applicants for the vacant directorship of an area agency. I was struck by the remarks of one applicant in particular because her expectations for the job were understandable as desires yet presumptuously off the mark as conditions. The applicant was qualified and made a favorable impression on the panel. Verbal skills and presentation were fine. She was a young woman, energetic, quick, intelligent. She was enthused, acted interested, and was connected. She interviewed positively. What struck me about the applicant, however, was her saying she would only consider the position if she would be given the "freedom to do some really interesting things." She asked the panel members for assurance that the funding be stable, the support from the department guaranteed. These were not outlandish things to ask for, but they were great conditions for her to require prior to considering acceptance of a position. The applicant was politely told that she could expect no such environment. In fact, rather than being guaranteed creative freedom and funding, she would do better to anticipate each budget year being a fistfight. She could expect some initial flexibility in order to permit her to show her capabilities, but everything thereafter would have to be earned.

It seems to me that a mistake that many people make today is in assuming that the work atmosphere they are "entitled" to is a wonderful one. It is almost as though they feel that since they have chosen to offer themselves to human services they should at least be given the consideration of a well-stocked agency larder. When it turns out to be quite different, they act as if they have been taken for granted, betrayed. When such conditions are sustained, the feelings of underappreciation build toward bitterness, cynicism, disinterest, and the dread condition of burn-out.

It is best to prepare staff for their work being more like the raid on Entebbe than an afternoon at Epcot Center. If we want to groom staff to work for the liberation of people with disabilities, staff who can perform in a hailstorm and not be rattled, then we prepare them for hailstorms, we don't promise bright dawns.

It is best to sell your staff on your need of them and the consumer's dependence on them. This is a rescue mission they are being asked to join. The odds are great and the terrain treacherous. From you they can expect strength of conviction and support where you are capable of delivering, and they will extract gratitude from people they will not always see. The real pride, however, will come from knowing that one stratum of the population will move in from the margin because of them, and historians will write differently about our society because of them.

In this business of social reform, so many oxen will be gored that not only can committed professionals expect lack of support from the central office and the legislature, they can anticipate the questioning of everything from their budget and purpose to their sanity. Local officials will say, "You want to move too fast." Legislators will say, "Your dollar demands are unrealistic." Consumer interest groups will make accusations of greed.

If you truly call for the system to right itself, it will resist with all its gelatinous immensity. The bureaucracy will first ignore, then begrudgingly consider, study, evaluate, review, send out for reaction, sit on, then discard your suggestions and calls for change. But just as water relentlessly seeks its own level, the staff must be prepared to keep searching tenaciously for the opening, for the sympathetic ear in the system that will help promote the changes pursued.

For our clients to advance to citizenship, each of us has to keep true to our principles and take stands that will be unpopular from time to time. We cannot cower from positions that require character and integrity because our boards are indifferent or our boss is a jerk. Anyone can perform when they "have the freedom to do some interesting things." We are obligated to produce interesting things, even when the world has seemingly tipped on its axis, when lightning strikes the flour mill and all reason has gone fishing.

In a recent speech on the "gentle teaching" of people with behavior problems, John McGee (1986) recalled, "When the behavior is worst we have to be the best teachers." We teach one another what commitment is, what it is not, and how to sustain it when the times are most trying and most frightening. Administrators are not the only ones who teach by example, but the leader wears the mantle that requires as a condition of ownership that stamina and balance be most profound when conditions are most grim.

Our profession is not for timid souls, not for people who can only function when they hold all the cards. It takes courage, risk, and the ability to endure contrast anxiety, to labor conscientiously at any level in this field. When I am most effective I have this package. When I am least effective I have been temporarily separated from it. The difference is within me and what I bring to the encounter. The job owes no obligation. It is not my debtor.

Letting Yourself Be Moved

The one thing that can bring all the points of this discussion together and breathe meaning into our work is personal experience with the consumer population; experience that weighs heavily and cannot escape our conscience. In speaking to most of my friends about the variable that sparked their interest in developmental disabilities, I discovered that most all of them related a moving event with an individual or a family which touched them. The event might have actually launched them into the field or come sometime well after their careers were under way. But in either case, some intimate, personal involvement with a consumer was responsible for giving them a sense of mission that made all the difference.

Nancy Rosenau is one of those people I regard as highly committed, and I asked her once how it all began. A compelling story unfolded. She had gone to interview for a social work job, and a little 3-foot man of 21 years, a man she was told had no measurable intelligence, took hold of her finger and led her on a tour of the wards and dayroom that he and 34 of his friends knew as home. He could not speak. She was little more than a girl out of college, yet a charge of something pulsed between the two and it filled her life with a purpose that had not been there. Mark lives in a group home now, but his tour continues to pull. When everything else is a confused knot she can always go back to that moving experience that brought definition to opaque ideals, that experience that made so many others possible.

John McGee talks about the hollow-eyed stares, the gaunt emptiness peering out from the faces of people whose prime years have been spent caught in the maze of clinical treatments that all stop short of love. Those eyes, he says, haunt him and move him and keep his work in motion.

Gunnar Dybwad describes a scene where a nurse slipped unnoticed into the hospital room of an infant who, because of severe mental retardation and the dis-wisdom of physician and parents, was being starved to death. When he tells how the nurse dipped her fingers in cool water and then traced them across the parched lips of the baby, you know that chilling experiences do not come just once in a lifetime but at any time, any age, and as often as we put ourselves in a position to feel them, to see them.

I have had many wrenching experiences since I wandered into this work, but probably none more gripping than one that occurred in New England a few years ago. I was working for the plaintiffs in a lawsuit intended to close a large public institution. I was in the midst of touring that facility and had just walked into a crowded ward. As we entered the doorway a radio was playing a new popular song that I happened to like. It was Stevie Winwood's "While You See a Chance (Take It)" (Winwood, 1980). My entrance into the room was framed by the song and 35 people sitting in wheelchairs. All 35 were facing in the same direction—diagonal to the perimeter of the room, away from the door. Their heads were lolling to one side or the other, but each was directed toward the same wall. (I was later told that when we would decide to go to a particular building the staff were alerted by walkie-talkie so that they could get residents off mats and into their wheelchairs.) In this building the residents had all been hurriedly lifted onto their chairs and rolled toward one wall so that the floor could be quickly mopped behind them.

The scene was stunning in its irony. Everyone was parked, drive-in-movie style, in front of a wall that held only a radio speaker. It looked like a staging from an Ingmar Bergman film. There were 36 people in this room who were listening to the radio. Thirty-five were encumbered by their bodies, and by straps in chairs, by tile walls in a self-contained building on the vast acreage of an institution marooned in the rural northeast.

I, the 36th, was there by invitation. I could come and go as I pleased, with full freedom to roam. I could choose to stay for 10 minutes or for weeks. When I decided to leave I would be driven through breathtaking country, treated to lunch, thanked profusely for my time, and put on a plane for home. For my brief stay on the wards I would be paid more money than my grandfather made in a month. Thirty-six of us were listening to the same song, a song that had previously enthused me with the kind of excitement in fantasy that often comes from escape entertainment. This time, however, the experience was totally different. The new context changed everything. There was no escape.

I had been listening to the title line repeatedly and had been taking it personally, selfishly. Perhaps I should try for a new career move, a romantic adventure, or some high achievement. Whatever the "chance," I felt that for me "taking it" meant new, unlimited excitement. It meant reaching to accumulate even more middle-class accoutrements than the considerable stash I already had. Caribbean vacations, designer clothes, fast cars, flirtations, strength, wealth, success, and similar indicators of perfection were provoked for me by those lyrics. Previously the song had made me feel like the world was in a yawn while I was in a sprint.

Now here I was looking at 35 people who were more isolated than Napoleon on Elba Island. Without some dramatic happening, they had literally not the slightest possibility of ever "seeing a chance," let alone taking one. Here I was thinking about ways to add even more whipped cream to my idyllic life and they would soon be eating another meal of gray pap served by fast hands. The disparity scorched a hot line around the guilt I had heretofore managed fairly successfully to keep at bay. The pain was intense. Ernest Hemingway once said about F. Scott Fitzgerald, "It was clear enough that Scott had to be hurt like hell before he could write seriously. It was his obligation to use the damned hurt in his writing, not cheat with it" (Baker, 1969, p. 262).

This business is a mother-lode of hurt. But there is also a terrible beauty within our grasp, if we choose to use the pain and not run from it. Most of us are within just minutes of being moved by the drama in our work, if we put ourselves in position to be moved. It is our obligation to do so.

Four Proverbs

In order to help us keep our sense of commitment in good health, or to awaken old vitality, I offer four proverbs:

• *Be careful not to isolate yourself.* Reach out to friends and supporters who you know will give you hope when hope is needed. Remember that you are not in this campaign alone, nor do you have to be discouraged in solitary confinement. There are people who have faced barriers similar to the ones confronting you, and they can comfort you with their counsel. When a friend of mine gets the feeling, "Don't send me back in there, coach," he calls his mother. She tells him that he is good and that he makes her proud, and then she gently reminds him to do something that will make him better.

• *Reacquaint yourself with the heroes and the reading that led you to this field.* The lives of women and men who had the conviction to revolt against, to reform some part of their society, can serve to ignite the spirit again and again. Too often, however, the most fundamental lesson of heroics—that one individual can change the course of history—is either disbelieved or scoffed away because our problems are thought "too complex," our foes "too formidable." Of course this is just another way of excusing timidity. Better that we identify with Albert Schweitzer or even Captain Marvel than become known as someone who always has an explanation for why "it can't work here."

• *Stand for something.* Be sure that people come to recognize what your commitment is, what your obsession is. While you have to be true to your own style, go public with your commitment. Be clear about your objectives for the agency, but, more fundamentally, make the strength of your personal convictions unquestionably understood.

The reason I do this for myself is that I want the world to know what my obsession is because I want it adopted by everyone else—not "accepted" or "agreed with" as a "reasonable condition." I want it to become the popular crusade: Always want them out, out of institutions, out of nursing homes, out of variations on these themes. It must become an anthem of sorts, a deep roll-over-everything lyrical dirge in folk-opera voice: Our people do not belong in institutions of any size, shape, color, or creed.

• *Take care of yourself but avoid self-pity.* Of course there will be low periods, times when you feel like you have depleted all energy resources, when your tolerance is on empty, but these are temporary times if you choose them to be. Go home. Take a few days off. Fish for perch. Drink daiquiris with a straw. But veer sharply away from diagnosing yourself as having some kind of fatal white-collar syndrome.

There is really nothing un-American about getting tired and wanting to rest. There is something dishonest, however, about making fatigue experienced in human services seem exotic and righteous, to be taken more seriously than the weariness felt by people who work in other ways.

If any group of professionals should know about the debilitating effects of labeling, we should. There is no burn-out.

Shazaam!

References

Baker, C. (1969). *Ernest Hemingway: A Life Story.* New York: Charles Scribner.

McGee, J. (1986). "Gentle Teaching." Speech delivered on June 26 at Macomb Oakland Regional Center, Mt. Clemens, Michigan.

Robbins, T. (1980). *Still Life with Woodpecker.* New York: Bantam Books.

Solzhenitsyn, A. (1963). *One Day in the Life of Ivan Denisovitch.* New York: Signet.

Thalberg, I. (Producer). (1937). "A Day at the Races" (Motion Picture). Los Angeles: Metro-Goldwyn-Mayer.

Winwood, S. (1980). *While You See a Chance.* Fantasy Songs, Ltd.

5

Embracing Ignorance, Error, and Fallibility

Competencies for Leadership of Effective Services

JOHN O'BRIEN

The greatest barriers to community living are not inside people with severe handicaps or in the nature of community life but in the way necessary resources are organized. As long as those who design and govern human services wait for people with handicaps and ordinary citizens to get ready to live together, they will contribute to unnecessary isolation. As soon as they exercise leadership in creating opportunities and designing personalized assistance, everyone will begin to learn how to be a community that is competent to support all its members. The ability to learn from experiences of ignorance, error, and fallibility builds capable leaders.

This chapter is based on what I have learned from people who are developing effective human services and draws on methods for managing complex social systems that are emerging in other fields. My criteria for effectiveness are: creativity in redefining service patterns that exclude people from community life; significant effort to achieve consistency with the principle of normalization (as defined by Wolfensberger & Glenn, 1975; Wolfensberger & Thomas, 1983); and adaptiveness in managing the problems that arise in stabilizing and disseminating innovation. I discuss examples from small agencies that are not part of exemplary state systems because I want to explore the possibilities for responsible action under less-than-favorable circumstances, and because I think that those who lead good big systems have as much to learn from committed people who are exploring on a small scale as small operators have to learn from them. I have learned from many collaborative efforts with Connie Lyle to help leaders in my country—

Canada—and the United Kingdom to plan and to evaluate innovative services.[1]

In this chapter, ignorance, error, and fallibility are introduced as "the three teachers"; the contributions of leadership in complex systems are outlined; three examples of learning by embracing ignorance, error, and fallibility are presented; some reasons why these three teachers may be difficult to acknowledge as facts of life are discussed; and some implications for the design and governance of services and service systems are identified.

The Three Teachers

Leaders who embrace ignorance, error, and fallibility in the design and governance of community services develop important competencies. *Ignorance* results from incomplete knowledge of the possibilities of people for whom available technology is incompletely and variably effective. Embracing ignorance teaches careful attention to the opportunities a particular community offers and to each person's unique and changing interests, gifts, and requirements for accommodation and assistance. *Error* arises from managing complex activities with the ambiguities of a task that is bigger than any one organization's capacities. Embracing error teaches skillful resource management. *Fallibility* is a defining characteristic of human communities, especially in relationship to dependent, devalued people. Embracing fallibility defines the limits of service and teaches the importance and the possibilities of ordinary associations and relationships.

These three teachers are necessary but unpopular. Some advocates and decision makers have oversold themselves on blueprints for service reform which promise to deliver large-scale answers with certainty, as long as managers are given enough power and money. In the long run, such promises are disappointing because service designs and management tools based on them are a poor fit with complex, rapidly changing realities. Leaders with the courage to face the three unpopular teachers will discover ways to change devaluing social patterns, ways that are closed to managers who believe they can avoid them.

In commending ignorance, error, and fallibility as teachers, I do not want to discourage people who fight the injustice of segregation on the basis of

---

[1]This chapter owes a great deal to Jack Pealer, Sandy Landis, and John Winnenberg in southern Ohio; Bertha Young and Jack Yates in southeastern Massachusetts; and Kathy Bartholomew-Lorimer, Barbara Banazanski, and Jeff Strully in Louisville, Kentucky. Work with members of York University's Faculty of Environmental Studies—especially David Morley, Peter Dill, and Wayne Tebb—gave me access to current work on the design and leadership of complex systems in turbulent social environments. (For an overview, see Ackoff, Broholm, & Snow, 1984; Emery, 1981; and Williams, 1982.)

disability. Promoters of institutionalization (Skodak-Crissey & Rosen, 1986) argue that because community services experience uncertainties, mistakes, and imperfections, institutions deserve tolerance, a place among the range of necessary alternatives, and even greater investments of money. They are wrong. Some problems *are* ethically more worthy of engagement than others. The difficulties encountered in building communities that support people with severe handicaps are far more central to human development than the problems of repairing institutions that exclude ordinary relationships by design. Institutional defenders say that community service advocates cover their errors with the blanket claim that *any* community program is better. We must be sure they are mistaken. Wherever it is found, ignorance of common humanity is culpable; errors generated in procedural tinkering with segregated structures are, at their roots, foolish; and the eruption of fallibility into abuse is wrong.

I am interested in what we who are committed to "the community imperative" (Center on Human Policy, 1979) can learn of its meaning when we are thoughtful and decisive about what we don't know; what goes wrong as we act on our commitments; and where the limits to our abilities are.

The Contributions of Leadership

Leadership makes four closely related contributions in the design and governance of effective organizations (Bennis & Nanus, 1985).

1. *Vision:* forming and consistently focusing attention on a responsible vision of a desirable future and a definite statement of the values that will guide decisions toward the vision; staying clear about what is valued as circumstances change and offer new opportunities and threats.
2. *Social Architecture:* creating an organizational form and structure that offers a meaningful way for those committed to the vision to work; finding systematic ways to invite and support investment in the values that underlie the vision.
3. *Position:* negotiating a relationship with the environment that gathers the resources necessary to work.
4. *Learning:* investing in learning more about the meaning of the vision and better ways to work toward it by a process of reflection, criticism, and redesign.

The reality of ignorance, error, and fallibility test and strengthen human service leaders' abilities to make each contribution. The first example illustrates their place in each aspect of renewing an innovative agency.

The Three Teachers and Renewing Commitment

Residential, Inc. is a small agency serving people with moderate and severe handicaps in the southern part of Perry County, in rural southeastern Ohio. For the past three years its leaders have worked to renew and deepen its vision, restructure its social architecture, reposition its relationship to its community and the larger service system, and learn better ways of working. This extensive effort began when staff recognized their collective ignorance of the interests and desires of the people they serve. It has been motivated by a clear quality standard that makes error easy to define. And it has been tested by repeatedly facing the hard lessons of fallibility.

In 1983, Residential, Inc. initiated a self-evaluation. During its first 6 years, the management team worked hard to fulfill their mission: "to provide dignified living settings for small groups of people with mental retardation." They had paid careful attention to the principle of normalization as they opened 4 group homes—2 carefully designed for people with severe handicaps. They had attracted an innovation grant to set up an independent apartment living program that allowed people with mild handicaps to graduate from group home living. They could be proud of their good reputation for providing an innovative, well-managed alternative to institutionalization.

The self-evaluation method was simple: Managers and staff took time to listen carefully to what the people who lived with them said about the quality of their lives and questioned themselves closely about the implications of what they heard. Sandy Landis, a leader in this process, sums up the result: "It was bad news. The better we learned to listen to the people we serve, the more clearly we heard them say, *'It's not working for us. We don't like where we are living and we don't like the group of people we are living with.'* It smashed us. We had a clear mission and were working very hard, we liked the people we served and they liked us, but what we were doing didn't really fit their needs." Acting responsibly on this bad news has renewed Residential, Inc.

New Vision

Constructive action began as Residential, Inc.'s leaders embraced some sobering realities and made clear commitments to the people who rely on them for assistance. Sandy Landis summarized the following observations: Institutionalization has destroyed family ties for most people who rely on the agency. Many now have no one else to count on, celebrate with, or come to their funerals, so we have to be a family for people and help them build relationships outside the agency. Most people will need a good deal of assistance for years to come, so we make a lifelong commitment to people. People aren't where they want to be, so we will focus resources on people one by one rather than on the operation of group settings. Short-term thinking about next year's behavioral objectives won't create what people deserve, so we will become future thinkers and help each person develop a personal long-range plan and the means to follow it. These are grave responsibilities, so we must remain self-critical and widen the agency's leadership base by building our own skills and by making stronger individual and agency ties to the community. We have so much to learn about fulfilling these responsibilities to those we serve now that it would be a mistake to grow larger. Other people who deserve a community residence will have to look to another provider.

To better understand these commitments, the whole staff spent time defining their quality standard: "What do we believe would be good enough for the people we serve?" After talking at length about what makes their own lives good, staff decided that everyone is an expert on quality of life and that the same standard applies to everyone, regardless of disability. Residential, Inc. determined to focus its energies on learning to assist people in five areas in order to make a difference in their quality of life.

1. *Home:* providing the choice of people to live with and a secure place of one's own to live
2. *Relationships:* providing people to count on, people to share with, people to do things with
3. *Opportunities:* developing the chance to educate one's self, learn, and grow
4. *Money:* providing access to assets, possessions, and equity
5. *Status and a positive reputation* in the small, close-knit city people live in

Staff are confident that they can make clear judgments about the consistency between the quality standard and agency policy and practice. One staff member observes: "It's easy to see what fits and what doesn't. We won't get trapped again in the search for the good group home. What's hard is facing how far we still have to go and figuring out how to take the next step forward."

Renewed commitment and a clear standard of quality are the foundation of a new organizationl vision, which is summarized in the current mission statements, which is "to stand with, support, and represent the interests of the people with whom we affiliate as they gain and maintain respected citizenship in Perry County." For most people this mission means moving into one's own home with the assets and supports to live there comfortably and securely.

A New Social Architecture

Pursuit of this mission has created a new social architecture. John Winnenberg, Executive Director since the agency's beginning, describes the change like this:

"We were set up to run good group homes. Our structure was a traditional pyramid with me on top. Three college-educated people supervised the work of direct-service staff. Our management team had professional knowledge and put a lot of energy into going away to training and bringing back new ideas to try. We developed policies and individual plans and monitored others with less education, status, and pay in implementing them. Unless there was a serious problem, I had little direct contact with the people we served and only occasional contact with direct-service workers. The management team was well intentioned, respectful, and concerned about staff and residents, but the problems that developed as we tried to work on our new focus showed us that our organization was shaped all wrong for what we wanted to do.

"We turned the pyramid on its side. We talked with the people we serve and asked them which staff person they felt close to, and we talked to staff and asked them which person they wanted to represent. Most staff took responsibility for being a person's service planner, and everyone ended up with a service planner they chose. The service planner's job is to get to know the person and his interests better as time goes by; to help the person expand his closeness circle by reconnecting with family members and by connecting with unpaid community members; to spend time with the person, and others who are close, in asking and thinking about the future; to write annual and quarterly individual plans; to back the person up in difficult times; and to provide some of the day-to-day assistance the person needs. We decreased the number of supervisors and increased the pay that direct-service staff could earn for accepting new responsibilities.

"My job changed drastically as I became the back-up and support person for the service planners. It's up to me to find the resources and make decisions so the relationships work between service planners, the people they serve, and the rest of the staff a person needs. I spend my time teaching direct-service staff; encouraging people to dream specific, vivid dreams about their future; thinking about how the community I grew up in can help individual dreams come true; and talking to the board and to the state and county agencies that fund and monitor us about how they can help specific people attain their objectives. Day-to-day responsibility for the business end of the agency became the job of the assistant executive director.

"Some staff have found the increased responsibility and especially our commitment to self-criticism more than they wanted to deal with. But morale is good and turnover is low in comparison to other agencies (60% of the staff who were involved in the reorganization 3 years ago are still at work).

"As staff have learned more we have moved more responsibility and more opportunities for earning to them. The assistant executive director has just moved on to found another agency, and instead of replacing him we are dividing up his tasks and moving them out to other staff. And soon I will be sharing back-up and support responsibilities with two of our most effective service planners."

Renegotiating the Agency's Position

Gathering the resources to accomplish its mission calls for the agency to renegotiate its position in the local community, in relationship to people's families, and in the mental retardation service system. This is now the biggest challenge to Residential, Inc.'s leadership.

To operate good group homes, an agency needs community tolerance for site selection and rejoices at occasional, neighborly acts, volunteer involvement, and political support for expanded budgets. To assist people who want to participate in community life and become homeowners, Residential, Inc. needs much more from the local community. Staff and board members have to make—and show people the way to make—many connections with local people, activities, and associations. The agency shifts from an occasional, well-financed consumer in the local real estate market to one of the architects of new financial arrangements for assisting people without much money to own homes. It moves from being receiver of contributions to being a thoughtful contributor to local efforts aimed at overcoming discouraging economic conditions.

Families have been encouraged to trust, support, and cooperate with service staff and look to the state to provide. Some families have become discouraged and lost touch with their relatives. A number of service planners are locating missing family members, reacquainting people who have long been out of touch, and working with family members who want to assist their relatives to attain their goals.

The most problematic relationship is with the larger service system. Residential, Inc. depends almost completely on a state agency (the Ohio Department of Mental Retardation and Developmental Disabilities) for the authority to operate and for the funds to acquire property and provide services. State law requires eligible people to give up most of their assets and income in return for services. People who are almost ready to graduate to a situation that offers much less service can retain their income for a time in preparation for the move. Relationships between a person and the residential service she relies on are formalized by regulations and monitored by an external case manager. A person who needs as much staff time as the people Residential, Inc. serves who moves into her own apartment has to have that apartment licensed as a facility. Many people are under the guardianship of a statewide agency. State funds were granted to Residential, Inc. to buy houses based on an assumption of 40 years of use for mental retardation services; now some system administrators are concerned about underutilization as people move out and "beds become vacant."

The social architecture of the system is now as poorly suited to Residential, Inc.'s mission and commitment as the agency's internal structure used to be. Statewide trends—greater central authority, tighter managerial and programmatic controls to insure fiscal responsibility and protect the right to treatment, and a substantial increase in the number of "community beds" funded with Medicaid—make it unlikely that the whole system will shift in Residential, Inc.'s direction in the short run. The best option is to build on the agency's good reputation for innovation in order to get it into a position where it will be allowed to be a demonstration of new service options.

Agency leaders would prefer to devote all of their resources to supporting the new mission and are now discussing a plan to convert existing investments with the state department. Until the larger system shifts, Residential, Inc.'s strategy for dealing with the misalignment between system structures and its mission is a balance of three sometimes conflicting streams of activity: maintenance and reform of the old; preparing for the new; and learning by doing new things.

New Learning

Residential, Inc.'s leaders have not waited to gather enough power, permission, and money to implement change for everyone. Instead they have been learning by acting within existing authority and funds to find and take many smaller opportunities to enhance the quality standard for particular people. Everyone lives with fewer people and has a future plan that specifies what it will take for her to live well in her own place. Everyone is much better known personally to at least one staff person, a number of people have reconnected with their families, and others have developed new relationships with people in the community. Almost everyone has more assets than they did 3 years ago. Nine people have moved into places they hold in their own names, and 3 more await approval to move.

The three biggest remaining barriers to home ownership for several people are (1) the likelihood that their homes would be forfeited because of their need for paid assistance; (2) their need for more intensive assistance than the system is set up to provide outside of group homes or intermediate care facilities; and (3) most important, the agency's lack of flexibility to align existing resources with a person's plan.

Staff have new competencies and more responsible, interesting, and flexible jobs. They have collaborated in designing an effective individual service planning process, conducted two sophisticated program self-evaluations, designed and implemented individual development plans for themselves, discovered much more about their community, learned how to find room to move while complying with complicated regulations, and developed many skills for dealing with a wide variety of people. Most of them have also come to know people with handicaps better, and many agree with a service planner who said, "It sounds kind of funny to say it, but my relationship with the person I work with has taught me a lot about life. I feel a little bit wiser because I've known him."

Another service planner identifies the formula for individual and organizational learning. "We make a lot of mistakes around here because we are trying to do new things. Finding new ways to do things is valued around here. People in charge will think with you and help you out if you want them to, but they don't second guess you about the details. As long as we stand with the person we're serving and work toward the quality standard, we won't get hassled or punished if things don't turn out as planned."

Some of the lessons of the last 2 years have been very hard. Three people have been waiting for a long time to move into their own places because necessary state approvals have been slow in coming and the agency is close to the limit of the financial risk it can underwrite. Two people are now living in institutions because Residential, Inc. ran out of flexibility and staff time to provide the intensive, day-by-day assistance required by a person with a degenerating neurological disease and a person with an acute mental disorder. Once people have been transferred by the service system to the institutions that the system managers say have the resources to provide for them, they lose eligibility and Residential, Inc. loses formal standing in decision making about their futures. Both of these people enjoy unreimbursed, regular, continuing contact with people from the agency, but these situations teach sobering lessons about the fallibilities threatening even the best-intended commitments.

These hard lessons are as much a part of the agency's life as its many accomplishments. As staff members said during a recent agency planning meeting, "Hard work and clear goals sometimes aren't enough. We've asked some people to wait for what they deserve longer than they have been able to bear. No matter how hard we worked, no matter how many extra unpaid hours, two people have been lost to us." Said another, "It is very hard to face how much control is out of our hands. George and Albert want to move, and we are ready to help them move, but the state is in control and they move so very slowly." While the causes of these concerns can't be managed away, leaders who seriously consider their fallibility as they engage in action will be stronger. Their actions will be rooted in a deepening appreciation of the situation of the people they assist. Less energy will be wasted in denial and a search for perfect solutions, and more energy will be focused on mutual support and learning.

The key to constructive action in Residential, Inc.'s situation was identified during an agency planning meeting by a man who has spent many of his 67 years in institutions. He has lived with the agency through changes that have assisted him to live successfully in his own apartment and find a valued place in many agency and community activities. He listened to a summary of the discussion of the threats, opportunities, and options facing the agency and then made his contribution. "Put courage up on that list. This is all too hard to even start to do without courage. And we need each other, too. We can't do it without each other."

Revising Assumptions

Organizations shape what their occupants notice as important; what they talk about; how they interpret situations, what they define as opportunities, errors, or problems; how they deal with the problems they see; and their menu of solutions. Bringing unstated organizational assumptions up for discussion is an important part of good planning (Finney & Mitroff, 1986), and testing the validity of limiting assumptions by purposefully trying alternatives based on different assumptions is an important way to develop new competency. An organization's leadership is tested when reconsidering a key limiting assumption that would define much of its unquestioned routine as producing errors.

Beta Hostels assists 27 people with moderate and severe handicaps to live in 13 apartments in Attleboro, Massachusetts. A strong commitment to the principle of normalization, rigorous and regular external evaluations of agency performance, major investment in staff development and renewal, and strong initiative in planning and changing agency structures took Beta from operating group homes to supporting people in their own apartments. In 1983, Beta staff and friends could reflect on a decade of real progress.

Their reflections provided time to share a common but peripheral concern. Despite the very high value Beta places on personal social integration, most of the people Beta supports have very few close relationships and virtually no close relationships with nondisabled, unpaid people who are not family members. Extended discussion of this fact surfaced four unexamined, limiting assumptions:

1. If Beta breaks down the barriers to community presence so that one, two, or three people at the most live in ordinary apartments and use public transit, local doctors and dentists, and local recreation opportunities, then people will make friends with ordinary people naturally.
2. Beta's main role in relationship building is to support the person with a handicap, and if necessary to help her or him to change.
3. There are mysterious skills in helping people with handicaps form relationships, and none of the Beta staff have them or know how to get them.
4. Beta as an agency and most of its staff are justified in holding low expectations and disdain for most ordinary people in the community. The agency has better values, more skill, and deeper commitment than ordinary people could. Staff have nothing to gain personally from greater involvement in community affairs.

The entire area of personal relationships had not been the subject of disciplined discussion or action. The first assumption was usually justified by reference to a very few people Beta supports who did make friends on their own. A closer look showed that each of them holds a regular job—something that the larger system is unlikely to support for everyone, no matter how much they and Beta might want it—and each has a gift for meeting people which many others, including some staff, have not developed. The second, third, and fourth assumptions were usually covered by the first. The fourth assumption was unspoken and had to be constructed by asking, "What assumption does our behavior express about the community?"

Surfacing these assumptions by no means invalidated Beta's previous achievements, but it confronted staff with an important area of ignorance created and hidden by organizational routine. It defined a new class of routine errors of omission: Everyone knew relationships were important, but other things came first in everyone's daily schedule. Embracing and learning from this collective ignorance began a continuing cycle of development for Beta.

The agency decided that, instead of standing beside people with handicaps and waiting for relationships to happen, it should build stronger ties to the local community and invest in systematic ways to invite and support community members to form and sustain relationships. As staff thought about how best to do this, they came to terms with their own limitations. Their personal disconnection from ordinary people and community events made them uninformed about where there were opportunities for relationships to develop and awkward about approaching strangers to ask for personal involvement. Their own roles as professional service workers and daily assistants were not incompatible with having a close personal relationship with those they served, but relationships with staff cannot be the same as those that are freely given. Acceptance of these limitations led to a clear new direction: Beta will support stronger involvement in the local community, by the people it serves and by its staff.

The first action to implement this new direction was the creation of the volunteer program, a distinct part of the agency with the mission of inviting people into relationships and supporting their involvement with one another. Beta found funding outside the mental retardation services system to hire a very capable volunteer coordinator. She has limited human service experience and strong local connections, as she grew up and raised a family in Attleboro and is involved in more than 20 local groups and associations. She has learned to use her knowledge of community members and her growing knowledge of the people Beta serves to invite people into relationships based on mutual interests and to support them as the relationships grow and meet difficult times.

The volunteer program has made an important contribution to the people Beta supports. At present, there are 53 volunteers. Twelve people have more than one relationship, and one man, who needs extra personal support because of steadily worsening symptoms of Alzheimer's Disease, has five relationships because of the volunteer program. Twenty relationships have lasted since the program started in 1983, and 41 are over one year old. According to the people involved, these relationships have various good effects. People have new and different activities, visits, and meals in one another's home; someone to call on the phone with problems or good news or just to talk; another person to share holidays and special occasions with; advice and help with personal problems; and someone to count on when things are difficult. In addition, some of the people with handicaps have specifically benefited from a sense of belonging in someone's family, from finding job leads, and from having someone to advocate for their interests with the service system and Beta itself.

Beta staff have had a number of opportunities to clarify their beliefs about the meaning and value of friendships. In dealing with a number of problems that the volunteer program has created, staff have come to see relationships as ends in themselves, not as means for getting something done. So volunteers do not assume staff functions, staff do not attempt to change people's behavior by restricting contacts or arranging rewards in the context of relationships, and Beta has a policy of not hiring anyone who is involved in the volunteer program.

In a new emphasis, the coordinator recruits community association leaders to sponsor people to join their association. A person with an interest in the environment joins other volunteers in the local environmental action group's recycling operation. A man with a gift for cooking gives his Saturdays to a local church's effort to feed hungry people. A man with a desire to help young people is an assistant scoutmaster for a large, active troop.

Relationships take many forms, and each is valued in itself. People are as fallible in voluntary relationships as they are in paid ones. There have been missed connections, misunderstandings, arguments, and disappointments on both sides. But the community grows as people struggle with their limitations together instead of giving them away to professionals for repair.

The volunteer program is not all Beta can do to build bridges between the people who rely on it and their community. It has been a powerful way for the organization to test and disprove limiting assumptions through action.

Designing a New Response

The quality of vision, the design of social architecture, the strategy for organizational position, and the extent of learning are shaped by the character of response to ignorance, error, and fallibility (Korten, 1984). Maladaptive responses share the conviction that acquiring needed knowledge is no problem if only there is sufficient money and professional talent. Positive responses recognize that much relevant knowledge must be created and emphasize learning through action and reflection.

Self-deceiving organizations avoid noticing ignorance, error, and fallibility. Professional accounts of client deficiencies provide a scientific diagnosis of need and a prescription for appropriate treatment. Modern management techniques insure that things are done efficiently. The organization proclaims to all, "We already know how; we can do it!" If there are apparent failures, the solution lies in focusing resources on clients who are most likely to benefit and in aggressively seeking more money, more authority, more professional staff, and further scientific research. People with severe handicaps and the bearers of bad news are ignored, punished, and eliminated.

Self-defeating organizations wallow in error and fallibility but assign responsibility for constructive action somewhere else. Enlightened custodialism, according to such groups, is the only realistic expectation for people who are severely handicapped. Advocates who insist on a higher standard only make an impossible job harder. It makes no sense to plan, because those who control resources have no interest in providing the massive amounts of funds necessary to offer the enriched environment that represents the highest reasonable aspiration. When prodded to say anything, the organization mumbles, "We know what realistically can be done, but they won't let us do it. So why bother?" People with severe handicaps are contained, tolerated, and blamed in order to justify unacceptable treatment. Dissenters are ejected.

A learning organization defines itself as responsible for using whatever resources and opportunities are available to decrease ignorance, learn from error, and safeguard people who are especially vulnerable to fallibility. Beyond recognition that people with severe handicaps are very likely to need extra assistance all their lives, prediction and prescription are chancy. Knowledge about how to provide effective assistance is increasing at a rapid rate (Horner, Meyer, & Fredericks, 1986), so a learning organization reaches out in order to learn more effective ways of working. People with severe handicaps change in important and unpredictable ways in new settings with better supports, so a learning organization gets to know a person in ordinary community settings and invests in developing new supports as people change. The learning organization's message is, "We don't know all we need to, but we are responsible for finding out. How can you help?" There is a strong commitment to standing by people when things are most difficult and an unwillingness to cover up ignorance or error by blaming people for the consequences of their handicaps. Leaders work to build an organizational climate that accepts news of errors and mistaken assumptions and supports corrective changes in mission, social architecture, and position.

An organization whose beginnings exemplify the formation of a learning organization is Options for Individuals, founded in 1984 in Louisville,

Kentucky, to provide a day service to 23 people with severe handicaps and very few successful service experiences.

The founders set the agency's direction by making clear commitments based on their understanding of people's situations. Though most people live with their families, they are isolated and need personal connections in their neighborhood and in the larger community. The most effective way to make these connections is to provide people opportunities and support for occupying typical adult roles within their homes and in ordinary work, leisure, and other community settings. This is challenging because of people's lack of life experience, the extent of their handicaps, and negative attitudes that reinforce low, age-inappropriate expectations. People and their families have mostly had negative experiences with human services. They have been ignored, excluded, and rejected because they were unable to meet service providers' expectations. It is therefore understandable that people and their families would be slow to trust a new agency. It is important, therefore, for Options to deserve trust from people and their families, to stand by its commitments to people, and not to add another rejection to their lives.

Commitments were clear from the beginning, but the program's design was not. The founders were familiar with a number of recently developed model programs for severely handicapped adults, but they were unwilling to select one approach for all 23 people. They realized how little they or even people's families knew about each person's unique interests and possibilities. Treated as a group, only their most obvious individual differences were apparent: Some people can walk, others can't; some people can use their hands, others can't; some people have a few words, others do not. Past assessments only offered a variety of professional labels for these personal challenges, most prefixed with "severe" or "profound."

Taking their ignorance of people's identities seriously created anxiety. Both of the founders are experienced professionals who value their management and program skills. Opening an agency without having all the program details under careful control was most unlike them. But they realized that people will rely on Options for a long time, and it seemed wrong to specify the details of a program for people they hardly knew.

It seemed right to devote the initial months of program operation to discovering more about people's interests and preferences. So they created an action learning process that began with the assignment of newly recruited direct-service workers to a small group of people. The staff schedule was organized to allow each staff person several long periods of individual or one-to-two time each week. The task was to introduce the person to a variety of home and community experiences, get to know the person as well as possible, and identify at least one real interest the person has that could become the basis for developing an ongoing community work experience. Staff met regularly with agency leaders (daily at first) to share what they were learning, identify things that were working and things that were unsuccessful, and support one another. Leaders also spent time with people and their families and provided hands-on, person-specific training and assistance as staff needed it.

The rest of people's program week was spent in activities with a group of five or six. As many of these activities as possible were in community settings. For example, Options arranged downtown health club memberships for almost everyone. This provides exercise, a chance to be around a variety of people, and a good setting to work on physical and occupational therapy goals.

This blend of new employee orientation, staff training, individual program planning, and program design gave the people who rely on the program an unusually large influence over the program. A staff member comments, "I came here with no previous experience. I didn't learn about severe handicaps, I met Eva and Theresa and they taught me about themselves. The more new things we do together, the more I learn about them. I still don't know if I know much about mental retardation. But I sure have learned to do a lot of exciting things with the people I've gotten to know."

When a staff member felt she had identified a strong personal interest someone had, the program director and the staff member found community settings where the person could pursue his interests. This was the most relevant possible staff development for direct-service workers and the program director. They learned how to approach people and ask them to make room for a person with a handicap for a few hours a week. They learned how to design assistance based on the characteristics of the person with a handicap and the concerns of the people in the setting. They struggled with basic questions that remain central to Options' search for effectiveness: How much assistance is enough? What is reasonable to expect from ordinary people and settings? How do we decide if a community experience is good enough? How do we decide if a person who learns very slowly is learning enough? When is it time for us to leave?

This willingness to embrace ignorance and learn from errors as they emerge has had good results. Here are two examples from a description of Options written by the program director after about a year of work (Bartholomew, 1985):

> Greg is a man in his mid-twenties. His one great love is music, especially gospel music. Greg is very shy, and, although he stutters when he talks, we have found that he can sing along with gospel tunes. We contacted a local gospel radio station and now Greg goes to the station several times a week to do odd jobs, hang out, and listen to music. He is accompanied by one of our staff who is supporting a growing relationship between Greg and the employees of WDGS. We envision Greg associating with a gospel choir, traveling, and maybe

singing. The people at the radio station care about Greg, and we plan to reduce our presence there soon.

Eva, a woman 33 years old, began volunteering her time dishwashing at a local diner. Eva is accompanied by one of our staff because of her fear of new situations and her tendency to have tantrums when she is unhappy. Although Eva works at Frieda's diner clearing tables and washing dishes, we have focused primarily on Eva's feeling comfortable and on nurturing an understanding relationship between Eva and Frieda. Frieda's diner is a small "down-home" place. It's a place where women come in each afternoon to drink coffee, smoke cigarettes, and talk about their lives. Eva spends most of her time as a part of this informal association of women. Over the past 9 months, they have become very comfortable with Eva and Eva with them. Eva doesn't talk, but Jennifer (our staff member) has helped Frieda and the other women develop a better understanding of Eva and her ways.

We haven't changed Eva. She still has tantrums and in fact has had a couple at Frieda's. But Frieda hasn't asked her to leave. Instead, she has tried to understand her more. Last week, our staff member mentioned that we were starting to wonder if staff presence was necessary, and Frieda suggested that Eva start coming by herself. She said that she thought that Eva trusted her now. In time we know she will go every afternoon by herself. But this will not be because we have made her "independent." Eva is not independent. She stays at Frieda's without a paid service worker *because she can depend on the other people there*. (pp. 2–3)

The overall success of this foundation phase for Options can also be measured by the problems it creates. As unique people emerge from beneath layers of labels, and as staff become more skillful at developing community opportunities, the commitment to individualization becomes increasingly meaningful and the portion of program time that people spend in groups becomes less and less relevant. How much can Options differentiate its resources to support people with different interests in a variety of places at different times? As people begin to fit into places like WDGS and Frieda's Diner, how will the agency decide when a person begins to work, deserves wages, and loses eligibility for the Options program (not because of the amount of earnings, but because he would no longer "need day habilitation" if he were capable of "prevocational activity"). The local supported work initiative lacks the resources to serve people who learn as slowly as the people at Options have so far. Should Options try to open a supported work program of its own? How can Options be more effective for people whose physical disabilities require continuous attendant care? How can Options support people in becoming members of community associations like churches and civic clubs? How can Options work with families to help them recognize and support the changes in their relatives? How can Options survive as it evolves into a shape that fits people's interests better and better and thereby fits state and federal funders' ideas of what constitutes "active treatment" less and less well? Leaders' ability to manage all of these question marks will decide whether a positive future follows a promising beginning.

Some Implications for Practice

Each of the efforts described here is small, fragile, and incomplete. What can they contribute to advocates and decision makers whose concern is with justice for tens of thousands of people? They can't contribute big answers or even replicable models that can be mass produced to add up to big answers. They can contribute to foresight by surfacing and working on issues that are hard to see or evaluate properly from a broader, more distant vantage. They can be an early warning of negative effects of well-designed policies. They can teach a good deal about what it takes to realize the promise of the community imperative at the local level. They can be a good example of the confidence needed to face and learn from ignorance, error, and fallibility.

Leading Issues and Early Warnings

In all 3 cases leaders are occupied in redirecting the resources they can control into personalized supports that allow people to discover and amplify their interests. The shift from serving people in a group home or day program to supporting people in their own homes and community setttings of their choice turns the social architecture of programs inside out. At least 4 leading issues surface as people work to make this basic shift.

Personal Relationships. These include relationships with extended family members and unpaid, nonhandicapped people, which fulfill the desires of people's hearts and strengthen people's sense of their own interests. It seems difficult to make room for these relationships in professionally dominated environments, and there is no task analysis for their production. As relationships become important, the personal local connections of agency leaders and staff become central. Rich connections to local associations and personal networks offer the only way to expanded opportunity for people disconnected by generations of prejudiced avoidance.

Poverty. Many bureaucratic policies create or exacerbate poverty. Most harmful are those that bundle all necessary supports together into total packages and determine eligibility for all disadvantaged people according to long-term needs for some assistance. People are made poorer when eligibility for needed services requires spending down or confiscation of assets in return for service. The status and benefits of home ownership are within the reach of many severely handicapped people, even within existing levels of entitlements, if individually necessary services can be added on. The status and benefits of at least part-time work are within the reach of many people, if reasonable support and incentives are available in the long term. People can easily outgrow their need for service settings if they do not have to give up necessary supports.

Rights. Many well-formed measures to protect the rights of people who are vulnerable to abuse have negative effects when they are administered bureaucratically on a large scale. The guarantee of "active treatment" becomes a straitjacket when it comes to mean spending all day inside a service building under professional supervision working on deficit-focused behavioral goals. Concern for confidentiality becomes perverse when staff are cited for introducing a person to a neighbor without documenting a release of information. Insuring safe premises becomes a millstone when people must wait for months to move into the apartment they have leased while it is licensed as a mental retardation facility. Independent case management powers and guardianship cause confusion when people who spend relatively little time with a person have the power to move a person who has come upon hard times away from an agency with a strong commitment to supporting him or her into a "more appropriate level of care."

The long history and wide practice of neglect and abuse of people with handicaps makes this a dilemma. Every example I can give of negative effects can be countered with many examples of bad or silly practice. The only way through the dilemma is sober discussion and deliberate experimentation with answers to this question: "What local conditions—including governance, community involvement, safeguards, and record of performance—would allow us to exempt a program from routine, detailed scrutiny by a central authority? What measures would assure the central authority that things are not deteriorating?"

System Design. All 3 local innovators discussed in this chapter pose problems in the system they depend upon for resources. They stretch every loophole in their drive for flexibility. They interpret people's needs in idiosyncratic ways. They are critical of themselves and of other providers, and they often are in conflict with other local providers. They frequently break rules. They increase variety and risk. They do their paperwork well, but there is the constant suspicion that more is going on than shows up in their documentation. They pose system leaders these basic questions: "How do I know which of these troublesome, incomplete, risky projects to protect?" "How can I best use the relatively little flexibility I have to build new capacities and explore new issues at the local level?" "How can I influence other local programs to adopt promising directions and practices from people with whom they may be in conflict?"

These innovators provide system managers with an early warning. Reducing the size of living arrangements and declaring supported work of the policy goal are important current topics of policy debate. Programs that have made the shift to supporting people in settings of their choice can warn us that this will not be enough. Until the contract between a person who requires assistance and those who provide it is renegotiated to increase the person's power, negative patterns will not change. Most of the issues on tomorrow's policy agenda can be identified by listening carefully to small innovators like the 3 introduced here.

Some Lessons on What It Takes

These 3 innovators share a common feature of social architecture: They treat direct service like high-commitment work instead of trying to manage it like turn-of-the-century factory labor. The old-fashioned factory approach divides work into the smallest possible parts, constructs exhaustive job descriptions and policies to cover every contingency, and creates external controls to insure that workers do as they are told. Planning and judgment are separate kinds of work; that is, professional teams decide, while service workers do. As long as the job can be done by a reliable technology that can be broken into small coordinated parts, this approach has a chance of working.

High-commitment work is necessary in situations where threats and opportunities to an organization's mission occur unpredictably and tasks can't be successfully predefined in their details. Providing direct service focused on supporting community participation for severely handicapped people is high-commitment work. Staff frequently work without supervision; the stakes are high in human terms if staff exercise poor judgment; performance standards are high and complex when regulations are taken into account; the work calls for high levels of person-to-person involvement and skill at cooperating with others under what are often stressful conditions; and it takes judgment to apply most available technologies in changing individual circumstances. The distances among planning, doing, and controlling are short.

Eliciting and supporting high-commitment work requires different management structures. Innovative agency leaders put in time shaping and sharing a vision of a desirable future for people and their communities. Direct-service workers are responsible for helping the people they serve create and move toward a personal vision. The management task is to insure alignment between agency values, individual visions, and available resources. Direct-service workers participate in evaluation and planning. There is a strong commitment to staff development for everyone, and people are rewarded for learning new skills, doing expanded jobs, and teaching others.

Distinctions between professionally trained people and direct-service workers are minimized. Organizational structures are flat, with few levels of hierarchy. There is a trend toward narrowing the pay differential between direct-service workers, professionals, and managers by increasing the responsibilities direct-service workers assume. Women and people with limited formal education hold positions of status and responsibility. Personal knowledge and direct contact are valued, so managers and support staff spend considerable time with handicapped people. Leaders' families are involved in lots of meals, celebrations, and informal activities with handicapped people. Doing all this is such a big task it is no wonder these managers believe the basic building blocks of an effective system shouldn't involve more than 50 or 60 people, counting staff and the people they serve.

Why It Is Difficult to Acknowledge the Three Teachers

H. L. Mencken said, "There's always an easy solution to every human problem—neat, plausible, and wrong."

Human service leaders have difficulty learning from ignorance, error, and fallibility for at least 3 reasons:

1. Much recent progress in gaining political support for mental retardation services has come from confident assertion of solutions to outrageous institutional conditions.
2. The implementation of these solutions has come at a time of enthusiasm for reforming public administration with a set of management tools that are ill-matched to complex, ambiguous situations.
3. There is a widely held ethic of control that communicates the expectation that competent managers should be in unequivocal control of organizations that get problems solved efficiently.

Overconfidence as a Source of Power

Justified, politically well-directed optimism about the possibilities for the prevention and amelioration of mental retardation (President's Panel on Mental Retardation, 1962; Tizard, 1964) and outrage at the abuses inherent in institutional life (Blatt & Kaplan, 1966) combined during a period of increased spending on human services to thaw the frozen beliefs and policies that rationalized and perpetuated custodialism. The active cooperation of professional and administrative change agents with vigorous social and legal advocates greatly accelerated funding and created new policy and structures that embodied a recognition of the human and legal rights of people with disabilities (Kindred, Cohen, Penrod, & Shaffer, 1976; Rothman & Rothman, 1984).

This pattern of outrage at injustice followed by confident, expert assertion that remedies can be implemented if orders are given and money provided has been quite successful in influencing judges and somewhat successful in influencing legislators and executive decision makers. Practitioners of this strategy are understandably concerned that admissions of ignorance, error, and fallibility will dilute confidence and undermine support. But avoiding the massive error of institutionalization only creates the opportunity to face new questions and new errors. If new alternatives are to make a real difference, their leaders must invent community services out of something other than institutional patterns. This means learning new ways. Few inventions of any sort come out completely right the first time. Anything as complex and conflict ridden as the creation of a new relationship between devalued people and their communities can only evolve from many steps forward. Some forward steps will open promising new paths, others will turn out to be dead ends.

Admitting the limits of what we know and can do, while celebrating the many advances people with handicaps are making, builds a stronger foundation for change than overconfident promises that underestimate decision makers' ability to learn. Recognizing limits is not an excuse to avoid acting to develop competence, but a way to define the competencies we need.

Mismatched Tools for Administrative Reform

During the time that mental retardation services have grown, interest has spread in improving public management. Those interested in better management have adopted management by objectives, long-range planning, the rational design and reorganization of systems to achieve coordination and efficiency, and the creation of data bases to support quantitative analyses, among other things. Most of these reforms have had disappointing effects because they are poorly suited to the management of complex situations where there are conflicting interests and no technology sufficient to produce desired outcomes reliably (see Downs & Larkey, 1986, for an overall assessment of these reforms).

These techniques have been accepted by service leaders and many advocates as the right way to do things. On their advice, legal reforms and judicial remedies often call for comprehensive plans, detailed controls of agency behavior, and extensive interagency coordination mechanisms. They demand elaborate project designs which may require the on-time implementation of hundreds of precisely defined objectives which are only achievable if the proposed coordination mechanisms work flawlessly. They also involve frequent calls for more numbers as proof of need, proof of accomplishment, and justification of merit.

Whatever good they may do, these management techniques are very costly in their potential for misdirecting attention. Each of them creates hundreds of new errors as managers try to fit their operations into someone else's idea of the way things should be done. When system monitors discover problems, they often notice coincidentally that things are not being managed as they assume they should be. Because isolated decision makers hear little of the people who actually develop and deliver service besides their persistent inability to get the forms and the numbers right, they lose confidence in the service workers' ability. This leads to stronger central authority, elaboration of rules and controls, and the provision of technical assistance. These costs are justified if repairing errors in management technique proves to be the key to effective performance. If the link between technique and performance is weak, however, decision makers will feel like the frustrated viewer who has just discovered that a 60-channel cable TV hook-up still offers nothing he wants to watch. The temptation to pay more to add a few more channels is great, but the solution isn't in the way the wires are connected in the box. The solution lies in creating alternative pursuits.

The Ethic of Control

The struggle to learn the lessons taught by ignorance, error, and fallibility extends beyond public management into basic notions of how things get done. The world that most people see has been shaped by the notion that all things are controllable if the right person is in charge, if problems are broken up into manageable bits, and if sufficient authority and money are available. The measure of human effectiveness and worth is the capacity to use better and better information to achieve better and better results efficiently (Michael, 1983).

Viewed from the perspective of people with severe handicaps, the world is a less orderly, often uncontrollable place. Its limits are more obvious, its errors more easily felt. Big plans more often go awry, and promises are more easily forgotten. Perhaps this is because a severely handicapped person does poorly on conventional measures of the worth of human capital. In terms of the ethic of control, such a person's deficiencies are valuable because they create service work, but her or his unique assets are irrelevant because they create problems rather than solving them. For all of that, many people with severe handicaps deal with the fallibilities of their uncontrollable world with grace and courage when offered the support of personal relationships and a bit of practical help. Their example and their experience can be a gift to us if we let it be (Vanier, 1979).

Like the other counterperspectives on the world—those of women and racially oppressed people, for example—the experiences of people with severe handicaps challenge the basic notion that everything is controllable, and this challenge is often met with redoubled effort to increase control. We promise to prevent, we promise to cure, we promise to rehabilitate, we promise to make independence as if it were a Chevrolet. Our promises have been fruitful, up to a point. If we are to move beyond that point, we need the courage and the grace to learn the lessons of our collective ignorance and fallibility. There is much to learn in close attention to our errors and failings as we work to share and improve the lives of people with handicaps.

References

Ackoff, R., Broholm, P., & Snow, R. (1984). *Revitalizing western economies: A new agenda for business & government*. San Francisco: Jossey Bass.

Bartholomew, K. (1985, November). Options for individuals. *Institutions Etc.*, pp. 2–3.

Bennis, W. G., & Nanus, B. (1985). *Leaders: The strategies for taking charge*. New York: Harper & Row.

Blatt, B., & Kaplan, F. (1966). *Christmas in purgatory*. Boston: Allyn & Bacon.

Center on Human Policy. (1979). *The community imperative: A refutation of all arguments in support of institutionalizing anybody because of mental retardation*. Syracuse, NY: Author.

Downs, G., & Larkey, P. (1986). *The search for government efficiency: From hubris to helplessness*. Philadelphia: Temple University Press.

Emery, F. (1981). *Systems thinking* (rev. ed.; vols. 1 & 2). London: Penguin.

Finney, M., & Mitroff, I. (1986). Strategic plan failures: The organization as its own worst enemy. In H. Sims & D. Gioia (Eds.), *The thinking organization: Dynamics of organizational social cognition* (317–335). San Francisco: Jossey Bass.

Horner, R., Meyer, L., & Fredericks, H. (Eds.). (1986). *Education of learners with severe handicaps: Exemplary service strategies*. Baltimore: Brookes.

Kindred, M., Cohen, J., Penrod, D., & Shaffer, T. (1976). *The mentally retarded citizen & the law*. New York: Free Press.

Korten, D. (1984). Rural development programming: The learning process approach. In D. Korten & R. Klauss (Eds.), *People centered development: Contributions toward theory and planning frameworks* (pp. 176–188). West Hartford, CT: Kumarian Press.

Michael, D. (1983, January). Competence & compassion in an age of uncertainty. *World Future Society Bulletin*, pp. 1–6.

President's Panel on Mental Retardation. (1962). *A proposed program for national action to combat mental retardation*. Washington, DC: U. S. Government Printing Office.

Rothman, D., & Rothman, S. (1984). *The Willowbrook wars: A decade of struggle for social justice*. New York: Harper & Row.

Skodak-Crissey, M., & Rosen, M. (Eds.). (1986). *Institutions for the mentally retarded: A changing role in changing times*. Austin, TX: Pro-Ed.

Tizard, J. (1964). *Community services for the mentally handicapped*. London: Oxford University Press.

Vanier, J. (1979). *Community and growth: Our pilgrimage together*. Toronto: Griffin House.

Williams, T. (1982). *Learning to manage our futures: The participative redesign of societies in turbulent transition*. New York: John Wiley.

Wolfensberger, W., & Glenn, L. (1975). *PASS 3: Field manual*. Toronto: National Institute on Mental Retardation.

Wolfensberger, W., & Thomas, S. (1983). *PASSING: Normalization criteria & ratings*. Toronto: National Institute on Mental Retardation.

6

A Difference You Can See

One Example of Services to Persons with Severe Mental Retardation in the Community

LYN RUCKER

The purpose of this chapter is to describe how one rural Nebraska community-based program for persons with severe or profound mental retardation was established, why it was designed the way it was, and what we have learned from that experience. The following topics will be reviewed.

- General background information to familiarize the reader with the structure of services offered in Nebraska and specifically in Region V
- A description of one program that was specifically designed to provide services to persons with severe or profound mental retardation and behavioral or medical needs
- What we learned about what does or does not work
- Recommendations and conclusions

Background

Before the 1960s, families of persons with retardation had very limited choices in Nebraska. Most families could either send their family member to a state-supported institution or, if they could afford it, they could pay for care in a private or church-operated institution. For those families who rejected the institution, there were virtually no services or supports available. There was limited access to public or private schools, and there were few vocational, residential, or respite care services in the state.

In the 1960s, parents in Nebraska began to work to change the conditions that existed for their mentally retarded children and themselves. As a result of a request by the Association for Retarded Citizens, the governor appointed a citizens' committee of parents, professionals, and legislators to examine conditions at the state institution. A television documentary on the institution, "Out of the Darkness," shocked the general public and stimulated the governor to call this "the darkest period in Nebraska's history book."

After realizing that the institution could never be adequately reformed, the citizens' committee outlined a blueprint for future services to be developed in communities throughout Nebraska and drafted the foundation of what has become known as the "Nebraska system" (Paolini, 1980).

Foundation Principles

The most important legacy handed down by parents and other early designers of the Nebraska system was the foundation principles that acted always as their guideposts. These principles were not designed for a retardation system. They have existed since pioneer days and are reflective of a conservative Midwest that embraces traditional American values. The retardation system in Nebraska has simply adopted what the "normal" culture already valued. Those principles, in part, follow.

A Common-Sense Approach. Parents were not aware of systems or programs upon which to model changes at that time, and they had no research results from which to learn. Consequently, parents approached the development and planning of services using their own common sense and their understanding of the needs of their sons, daughters, sisters, and brothers with retardation. This led to such questions as, If this person were normal, where would he or she get this service? Why do we have to provide this service when it is already available in the community for the general public? Have you asked the individual or family what they want? Are we meeting the individual's needs or the system's? Addressing these types of questions helps managers develop simple approaches.

Build on the Strengths of the Family. Home and family are concepts deeply embedded in the tradition and heritage of human lives. Families are the natural environment in which people grow and learn. The relationships within a family gradually change as the children grow up. Unfortunately, the special demands of a child with a severe disability sometimes stretch the resources of a family to its limit. Society, the family, and the child are best served if public resources are allocated in a way that supports the family rather than requiring that the member with a disability leave the home to obtain services. Thus the service system in Nebraska places the highest priority on maintaining a child with a disability in his or her natural home (see Powell, Humphrey, & Rucker, 1983).

Focus on the Value and Strengths of the Individual. The rugged independence of individuals is a value deeply embedded in the Midwest. Consequently, the Nebraska retardation system was designed so that the focus would be on what the *individual* needs, not on what the system has traditionally provided to a group of people with retardation; and on *individual strengths,* what the individuals *can do,* not on a list or assessment that points out what they cannot do. Each person in the system must have an individualized service plan with specific goals and objectives. This plan acts as the road map for delivering services. Ultimately it also provides an evaluation tool for measuring the success of the services (see Powell et al., 1983).

Work toward the Least Amount of Governmental Intrusion. Parents wanted help for their offspring, but did not want to have them taken over by government or private providers. Consequently, services were designed to afford the least amount of governmental intrusion and thus maximize the individual's use of the normal community environment. In the final analysis a service system based on grass roots' decision making is responsible to the people in need of assistance. Further, to ensure stable, productive, and effective services, all levels of government should be accountably linked together (see Powell et al., 1983).

Taking Care of Our Own. Midwest values hold "welfare" systems or support in contempt, or certainly did at the time the Nebraska service system was developed. Consequently, there is a desire to keep people at home, keep government out of our lives if we can, get our sons and daughters off "welfare," and help the mental retardation regions to be as self-supporting as possible through the use of nontax-supported revenues. Now people with retardation are speaking up and demanding client-owned industries, paid vacation and sick leave, benefits, and so forth. No one likes to be dependent on someone else; this is another nail in the coffin of work activities centers.

Work Ethic. A common belief in the Midwest, as in many places, is that everyone is expected to contribute to the welfare of the family, community, and country, according to their own ability. That often translates into the value of working and making a wage. Many of us once misinterpreted this value to mean only sheltered workshops. In Nebraska, that has meant the development of highly industrial workshops that have subcontracts, primary manufacturing, and interstate and international contract sales and marketing. Unfortunately, this has given "face validity" to the whole concept of segregated worksites for persons with retardation. However, we created them; it is now our job truly to embrace the work ethic and get people real jobs.

The Wagon Train Approach. Perhaps one of the most critical principles that the parents adopted so many years ago was that, unless we join together, we will not ensure *permanence* of the services we wish to see develop, and we will not see a *statewide approach* to service development. Parents were not satisfied if their children received services. They weren't even satisfied if there was a program in their town. They knew that, if there were going to be services for their children after they were gone (permanence), they would have to continue to push on until there was a coherent statewide system. The wagon train can make it through if we all stay together, but one wagon will not survive for long.

The Regional Service System

There are 6 mental retardation regions in Nebraska, each controlled by local units of county government. There is one elected county official from each of the counties who sits as a member of the governing board for the particular region. The state Office of Mental Retardation serves as a conduit for funding and sets and monitors the compliance with rules and regulations for the services delivered by the 6 regions.

The largest geographic regions have 22 counties; the smallest, 5. The regional system is accountable to local government, many regulatory bodies, and (because of the procedures that have been adopted) most of all to the individuals who are served. A heavy emphasis has been placed on the involvement of consumers and consumer representatives, as well as professionals from related fields in an advisory capacity.

All of the regions have an area or local system of management that divides the region into smaller units. Control is therefore as close to the individual being served as is possible.

Region V Mental Retardation Services is comprised of 16 counties and provides or procures work training, residential alternatives, and therapeutic support to over 650 persons with mental retardation in community settings (see Figure 6.1*). Within this 16-county region, there are seven comprehensive "area or local programs" located in seven different counties within the region. (Figure 6.1 designates local "catchment" areas.) Some of the area program directors are responsible for coordinating services for one county, while others plan for up to four counties each. All of the Region V programs are located in rural areas except the one situated in Lincoln. Without exception, every program serves the behavioral and medical needs of persons with severe or profound mental retardation.

---

*Figure 6.1 provides a map of Region V and its seven catchment areas: Region V Industries, David City; Saunders County Office of Mental Retardation (SCOMR); Lancaster Office of Mental Retardation (LOMR); Region V, Nebraska City; South East Nebraska Developmental Services (SENDS); Region V Cooperative Industries, Saline; and Region V, Fairbury.

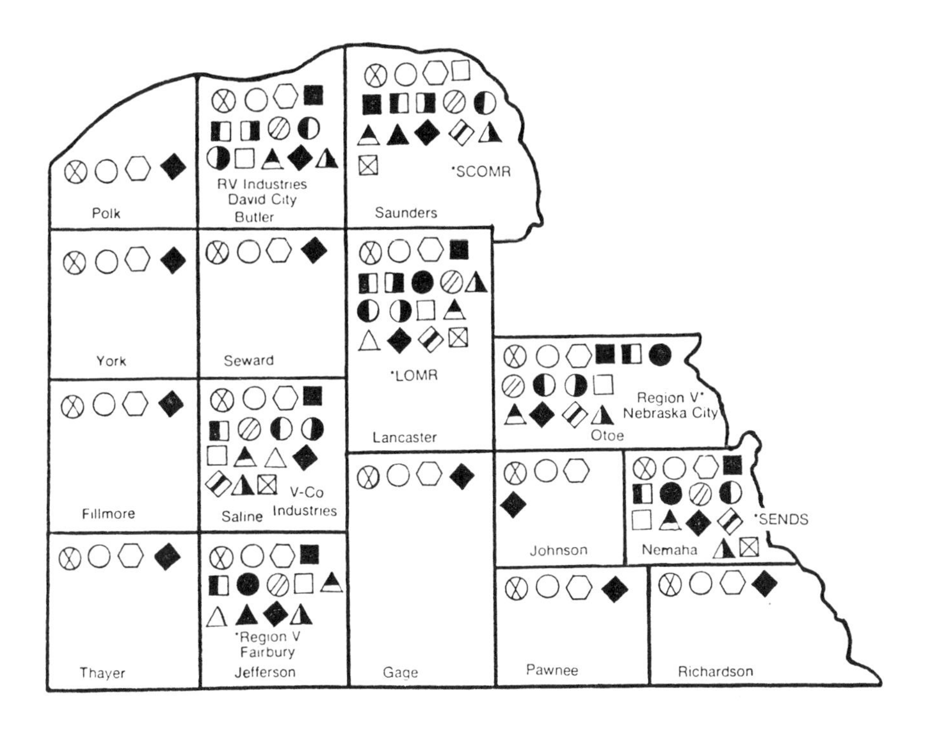

- ◆ Preliminary Planning/Community Services
- ⊗ Social Services
- ■ Workshops
- Work Crews
- Work Stations
- ⊠ Job Support
- Community Volunteer Work
- □ Job Placement
- ● Group homes (5-6 persons)
- ⊘ Mini-group homes (3-4 persons)
- Supervision in client's home
- Semi-independent
- ○ Foster/Respite Care, Adult Family Homes
- ⬡ Extended Family Homes
- Transportation
- △ Speech Therapy
- ▲ Physical/Occupational Therapy
- Behavioral Specialists

FIGURE 6.1. Map of Region V Mental Retardation Services.

The Fairbury Program: Integration in a Rural Community

Why Fairbury Was Established

As a result of revenue made available by the State of Nebraska to place persons out of the institution and into community-based mental retardation regions, Region V submitted a proposal to create a new area program that would serve persons with severe or profound mental retardation. In 1980, when this proposal was submitted, with few exceptions the individuals remaining at the institution from Region V counties were persons who fell within this range of retardation.

While 6 other programs existed within the region at that time, all of which served many persons with this same level of retardation, concern over saturating any one community, the desire to expand the capacity of the agency, and the wish to serve other geographic parts of the region dictated the decision to establish a new program site.

How Fairbury Was Chosen

During the 3 years preceding the establishment of the Fairbury program, Region V had established 3 new rural programs. That experience, coupled with the specific needs of the persons moving into the program, led us to the conclusion (which continues for new program sites today) that any city chosen as a potential site must possess the following characteristics:

• There must be a community or junior college in or near the city for 2 reasons:

1. We need a labor pool from which to recruit and hire staff.
2. We want the individuals who come to this or any of our programs to learn related skills, such as those taught through adult basic education, in the same environment as do other adults their age. We do not want to perpetuate segregation in the community by exclusively providing nonwork-related skills-training in our centers. Consequently, some of the persons served in our programs attend classes through the community college, rather than receiving all of their training through Region V.

• There must be a reasonable comprehensive core of medical staff available in the community, through either a physicians' clinic or a hospital. Many of the individuals being considered for the Fairbury program had complicating emotional and medical needs. The idea of transporting individuals who needed routine medical or psychological care to Lincoln, at least an hour away, was unacceptable.

• Available real estate for housing must lend itself to adequately meeting the needs of the proposed core of services and must have the ability to absorb reasonable growth.

• The Chamber of Commerce, mayor, and other community leaders must be willing to assist in securing sites for both the worksite and the houses we would need.

• The city needs to be in a county that is centrally located near previously identified persons with mental retardation. While the initial group of persons served was from the institution, we had lists of individuals residing in communities who had applied for services, or who were in the school systems and would need services within the next 2 to 5 years. Obviously, consideration had to be given to meeting the needs of those individuals as well.

With those stipulations in mind, we identified two cities as meeting all of the criteria established by the region. One had a population of 8,000; the other, 4,800.

It is not unusual for towns to "court" prospective businesses or industries, as they are the economic life of a community. A new industry brings new jobs and some new employees. They, in turn, buy or rent houses, purchase clothing and food, pay taxes, support churches, and more. It occurred to us that our approach to the establishment of new area programs had, in the past, not been in line with our philosophy or our view of the type of business we really are. Consequently, we changed our approach. Instead of asking for permission or expending large amounts of energy and time in order that we might "convince" communities of what a good "service" we provide (charity model) to a "special" population (pity model), we would

- Pick communities that met our established characteristics just listed
- Approach them like any large industry (our smallest area program has a budget of $500,000) and see what *they could offer us*
- Let them convince our board that they had the best all-around community for our new worksite.

With that "bidding" approach in mind, regional staff and local Association for Retarded Citizens (ARC) representatives approached the mayor and Chamber of Commerce in each of the cities. We provided information regarding the size of our budget, the number of persons we would employ, the number of facilities we would need, the type of industrial products that we produce, and a description of the employees with mental retardation we would train.

In addition, we indicated what level of support we would expect from the city with respect to the identification of potential work and housing site locations and asked for information on any zoning restrictions that might be a problem. Then we asked that they open doors for us with the medical, industrial, and religious communities, so that initial conversations could begin.

After all of the information was gathered, representatives from each city came to a meeting of the Region V Governing Board to bid on the receipt of the new program. In addition to slide shows and packets of information about each city, the two mayors presented over 30 letters each, offering support for the program and requesting that their city be chosen as the new worksite. Those letters were signed by every doctor, dentist, and therapist in their respective cities. In addition, letters were submitted from lawyers; ministers; parents of handicapped persons; judges; colleges; ARCs; Rotary, Jaycee, Kiwanis, Optimists, and Lions clubs; the Department of Labor; fire departments and rescue squads; local welfare offices; public schools; newspapers; industrial development corporations; banks; and so on.

With that information in hand, the governing board chose the city of Fairbury, with a population of 4,800. The presentations given by each city were comparable in almost every respect; however, the Fairbury area had more individuals waiting to come into services from both the institution and the community. Current and potential individual need proved to be the deciding factor in favor of the Fairbury location.

One of the exciting things we learned when we established this program was that if prospective community locations are given sufficient information, they will not only welcome a program, they will compete for it. The preliminary work in Fairbury helped the community understand its actual role in our program and set the stage for integrated activities later on.

Characteristics of the Employees

We had learned a good lesson about *how* to have new communities accept not only the program but the employees as well. The community expected new *workers* and a new *industry*. While they knew these workers would be severely and profoundly retarded, the image they were given was that of the mentally retarded person as a contributing member of the business community, not as a drain on the social or economic community.

Initially, 12 persons were chosen from the Region V population at the institution to be moved into the new program. In addition to these 12, 3 individuals from the community surrounding Fairbury were also served the first year.

Currently, the program serves 27 individuals, 13 men and 14 women. The average age of the individuals served is 36, and the average time spent in an institution is 27 years. After being in the program for 1 year or more, most of these people have made drastic improvements in their abilities, particularly in the self-help and behavioral areas.

The real story rests in the changes seen every day in both the individuals served and the agency itself.

Staff

After determining who was going to be served and where they were going to receive the service, we had to decide who the staff would be and what models we would put into place.

When hiring staff, we looked for characteristics that are valuable in staff working with any group of persons with mental retardation, specifically

- *Experience:* The staff hired for work training and home living had an average of over 3 years experience in the field of mental retardation. In addition, we felt that staff must demonstrate skills in the areas of behavior management, environmental control such as multiple scheduling, stimulus control, data collection, and multiple/individualized programming. Some staff needed to have skills in the area of sign language.
- *Attitude and Philosophy:* One of the most important characteristics we looked for in potential administrative staff was their attitude about the individuals whom they would be serving and about working with the public. We did not want someone who believed that it was enough to get people out of the institution. We wanted individuals who would not be satisfied until all of the individuals in the program were socially and vocationally integrated into the community. Individuals who had good public relations skills and enjoyed that aspect of the job were desirable.
- *Creativity:* A third characteristic we looked for was a willingness to develop new approaches. We wanted staff to search constantly for ways in which the people served could tap into community resources, and thereby grow and develop beyond the limiting expectations imposed by past history.

A management principle that is well known to many good administrators is that you are only as good as the people you hire. That same principle holds true as management works with staff in Fairbury and throughout Region V. All levels of staff are viewed as partners in the development, monitoring, and implementation of the system. It is central to the management's philosophy that staff must feel ownership of the system, both in the current decisions that are made and in the design of the future.

One of the most obvious ways this happens is in the "earned autonomy" of the local area programs. The basic philosophy of the Region V central administration is that the region must go to great lengths to recruit, hire, train, and reinforce staff. Once they are hired and trained, then the assumption is that they are the very best staff that exists in the field. Consequently, they are given the power and authority to manage and operate their programs in line with regional policies and procedures.

In addition, staff are reinforced and encouraged to "pilot" new ideas, take conceptual risks in proposing service changes, and actively criticize existing services when they do not fit with the system's philosophy.

The belief in participatory management has resulted in all levels of staff being involved in planning, budget development, monitoring and quality control, and personnel policy development and implementation.

This belief in the wisdom and integrity of the staff encourages new ideas to bubble to the top and keeps the system in a constant state of self-renewal.

From the start, we really expected breakthroughs from the Fairbury program.

Service Models

In setting up a framework for delivery of services, the initial inclination was to continue doing what we had been doing elsewhere; namely, create worksites and small living environments. To a great extent that is exactly what happened. Of the 27 individuals currently placed in this program, only 6 are involved in some off-site work environment. A description of the service models used follows.

Worksite. The worksite is located in the semi-industrial section of the city. Contract work from local companies, as well as products that have been designed and marketed by Region V, are used to teach job-related skills. Some of the products manufactured by Region V workers include waterbeds, mattress pads, folding chairs, snow fences, and small wooden products such as shipping pallets and lathing. In addition, a number of people are also employed in food service, recycling, packaging, and shipping. Many of the contracts serve as a natural form of advertisement that lets the general public know that the persons involved in this industry are working on real jobs and have a real income. However, competitive job placement or supported employment in integrated settings is the goal for every individual in the program.

Dramatic improvement in the acquisition of skills such as following directions, use of tools, and improved production rates has been seen since the contract work began. The worksite model is certainly not ideal; however, it does result in additional, sometimes more subtle benefits for the employees and the agency.

In line with the belief that individuals should not be isolated in work activities centers, some of the training activities take place away from the worksite. For example, the program has community contracts for lawn care, carpet cleaning, and a newspaper route. One individual is placed at Head Start.

One of the goals of this program is gradually to phase each individual out of the worksite and into a competitive placement, supported employment, or a work station in industry. This goal is shared by all of the worksites in the region. Where can an individual best learn work skills and habits than in a real job? That is the process by which we have all learned our professional skills. Ultimately, the industries and small businesses that already exist in the community should become our worksites.

Homes. If your child were having difficulty learning in a school classroom of 30 individuals, would you want him or her moved into a classroom of 60?

Obviously not. The same holds true for persons with mental retardation of any level or any behavioral or medical need. We have learned that group homes of 5 or 6 persons are too large. Two or 3 individuals living together with a staff person make for a much richer learning environment. It's easier to teach, to control the environment, to integrate with your neighbors, to travel in a car (not a van), to go downtown, and to learn in that environment. The attention individuals require is more readily available if it has to be shared with only 1 or 2 other individuals.

Persons with severe behavioral needs, in addition to severe or profound mental retardation, may need to start with a one-to-one living environment. As individuals adjust to controlling themselves and their environments, 1 or 2 roommates may be gradually added, if economically necessary and socially appropriate. Eighteen individuals in the Fairbury worksite came from an institution and now live in the small homes we are about to describe. The total number of individuals living in small homes is 21. Three individuals live with their natural families, and 1 individual lives in an adult family home.

- *Small Homes:* Of the individuals living in group environments, 14 live in a home with two other roommates. All of the houses are staffed for 1 full-time equivalent (FTE) staff weekdays and 1 FTE staff weekends. In addition, in order for most individuals to move into the community, the institutional staff stipulated that Region V would have to provide overnight awake supervision. That stipulation was made for any individual who had had a seizure during the past 5 years, for individuals who had to be "specialed" (taken to the toilet or had to be checked frequently), for some people who were nonverbal, and for anyone who got up during the middle of the night. *In every case,* overnight awake staff were phased out of the small group homes after a 30-day period. The phase-out was not done arbitrarily; rather, data were recorded and training initiated to eliminate the behaviors identified as necessitating the overnight awake staff.
- *Supervised Apartments:* Six individuals live in apartments with 1 other roommate whom they have picked. These apartments have a staff person who lives with the roommates and provides ongoing training and supervision. In addition, one individual lives in her own apartment and has a supervisor who "lives out" but visits with her and provides the training and support that are necessary or requested.
- *Adult Family Home:* One individual lives in an adult family home, which is similar to foster care for children. This alternative is provided with a family in a private home, licensed by the Department of Social Services (Welfare). Region V recruits, trains, and monitors the provider.

Quality of Life

No matter what the size or cost of the service "model of choice," the most important concern should be the quality of life experienced by each person with mental retardation. When we evaluate our agencies or train our staff, one of the exercises we all participate in is listing those things that make our lives meaningful or good (money, friends, family, lovers, independence, control, and so on). We talk in terms of what normal individuals of our age (as we grow older the sample age goes up) do to have fun and what it means to be a good neighbor, have money, and shop where we please. What we are really trying to get to are those components that give our lives quality. From those lists we talk about how many of these experiences persons with mental retardation participate in on a regular basis.

Some of the things we have done to improve the quality of life for individuals in the Fairbury and other programs follow:

- Individuals are involved with the community college in their Adult Basic Education Classes; this is seen as a real status builder. The fact that some individuals are interested in going over to the "college" demonstrates the increase in self-esteem and confidence many of the employees have gained during a short 3-year period. One of the region's goals is to turn most or all of the training over to technical, junior, or community colleges, as worksites are phased out.
- Some of the employees, when first moving to Fairbury, had never gone shopping or attended a church service. In many cases, behavioral outbursts precluded training during normal "open" hours for merchants or church services. The businesses and ministerial alliance responded openly and positively. We did the task analysis and program design, and they opened their businesses during off hours and held special church services until everyone was integrated into the normal business and church environments. That process took 3 years, but it is now complete, and no "special" or segregated training takes place in these areas. The only exception may be new individuals who enter the program and who may need this unusually intensive training.
- Leisure activities have also provided many firsts: the first opportunity to take regular vacations, catch fish, go to dances or concerts, participate in softball games, and see rodeos. The list goes on and on. The obvious issues with leisure time activities center around frequency, variety, integrated activities, and *small* numbers of persons with mental retardation traveling together.
- As a result of the internal evaluation done on each agency in Region V, a heavy emphasis has been placed on persons with mental retardation being given the opportunity to initiate and/or participate in community service activities. Instead of always expecting the community to give to us, we are expecting our staff and employees to give back to the community. For example, some communities have held CROP Walks to raise money for an international relief program and 2 local gardening projects. In response to the

request from the ministerial association, the Employee (Client) Advisory Board at Fairbury decided to participate in the fundraising event, as did some local employees. Others have chosen to adopt a senator (political action) or adopt a neighbor (elderly contact and call program). Others prefer not to be so formal and do a lot of contact with persons of their choice on their own.

Recommendations for Developing Services

After describing one experience with the establishment of a program that serves primarily persons with severe or profound mental retardation, I would like to share the following additional general recommendations for the development of integrated community-based services.

Demand leaders who insist that all people be served in the community. There are many reasons why a system works or doesn't work for *all* of the people for whom it has been conceived. If I were to identify the primary reason why every region within Nebraska provides services to persons with severe or profound mental, behavioral, and medical needs, it would be the attitude or philosophy of the decision makers. Lou Brown, from Madison, Wisconsin—one of this nation's prime movers for social integration of people with severe disabilities—has perhaps stated this philosophy best: "All individuals, regardless of the severity of their handicapping condition, will ultimately live in complex, heterogeneous integrated community settings." If decision makers truly believe that *everyone* will be served and integrated in the community, half of the struggle is over. In systems where that attitude is not embraced, I have seen every conceivable artificial barrier thrown up as a block to providing appropriate, integrated services for everyone.

The more handicapped the individuals, the smaller their living environment should be. Along with a philosophy that drives providers to develop services for all persons regardless of the severity of their handicapping conditions must come service models that provide the smallest living environment to those with the greatest handicap. We have found this to be true not only of persons with severe or profound mental retardation but also for those individuals who, in addition to their mental retardation, have severe medical or behavioral needs. This is not a minor observation. It is, I believe, one of the most critical factors in the successful integration of persons with severe needs.

Become facility free. One of the most distressing mistakes of the human services field, in my opinion, is the focus on owning and building "buildings." Once a system locks itself into owning group homes and workshops, then the focus shifts from meeting people's needs in the most natural environment to "keeping our beds full and our shops productive." It is an easy trap to fall into because buildings give us something to "show."

What we found in Region V is that individual needs change so quickly that even long-term leases are undesirable. For example, we made the traditional mistake of the 8-person group home. We compounded our mistake by entering into long-term (5- to 10-year) leases. It became very clear very rapidly that the persons with whom we worked did not want to live in large group homes and did not learn as quickly and were not accepted as readily by their neighbors when they did so. Unfortunately, we had them, so we had to keep them filled. What an outrage!

Rather than building a "facility empire," we should be focusing on building independence from the system by working to have persons with mental retardation own, rent, or lease their own apartments, condominiums, homes, or townhouses. Then, rather than trying to convince everyone that the system provides "homelike" environments, we will be talking about the supports and services we offer persons *in their homes!* Region V has gone from leasing every home living site that was supported by the region (including the natural home) to carrying the lease on only 40 of the 123 sites we support. We will continue to phase out leasing.

It is no different for the work-training sites. In harmony with a sound philosophy must come the consistent effort to restrict and/or eliminate the future development of segregated workshop settings. The workshops of today are rapidly becoming a dead-end placement for most persons with mental retardation, regardless of their functioning level. It is critical to integrate persons so that they can learn real work skills in a real work environment. How can that be done if our focus is on the maintenance of a building and the surrounding grounds? We must focus on getting everyone into an integrated, natural work environment. With ownership of buildings, we have put an enormous obstacle in the way of handicapped persons as they attempt to get free of *us*.

Serve a cross-section of developmental needs; develop staff expertise and build budgets slowly. This is probably one of the most important decisions that can be made with respect to the ultimate capacity of a system. If you take a cross-section of individuals with varying developmental levels and medical and behavioral needs, then skills will spread and budgets will grow in a steady, competent fashion. For example, if two individuals with severe behavioral disorders are placed in an agency for 1 year, a core of staff (let's say four) can be trained to work with and support those individuals as they learn and adjust to community living. At the same time, staff will develop further confidence and skills as they design programs and adapt environments intended to enhance the success of the persons with whom they work. The following year, you could take an additional four individuals with behavioral needs, as the original core of four staff persons trains eight additional staff to work with those new persons. As time passes, individuals who were once seen as extremely difficult to serve become a routine challenge to staff who are confident of their ability to adapt behaviors. In a similar manner, you can efficiently develop staff ability to support other people with specialized needs in areas such as medical supports or skill enhancement. Technology is shared as individuals who were once seen as "residual institutional populations" become integrated into the community.

Another advantage of taking individuals with wide-ranging needs for support in the community is that budgets will grow steadily over time rather than peaking when more "difficult" populations are finally served. There is no doubt that some individuals will need more intensive staffing patterns and therefore cost more than other, less involved persons. If, over the years, you build those staffing costs into your budget, people with mental retardation will not have to bear the burden of "being too expensive to serve." Averaging costs over numbers of individuals with varying needs generally makes for a cost that can be justified to boards and legislators. In contrast, averaging costs over a group of individuals who have only high needs seems to stimulate calls for conservative fiscal restraint and larger institutions for "those" people. It is our job, as administrators, to act responsibly so that groups of individuals don't get set up to fail on fiscal issues they cannot possibly control.

Integrated environments and role models are critical. I would state clearly that clustering persons with like needs, as we did in Fairbury, is not the way it should be done. A cross-section of people with developmental needs should not only be taken into the program but should be placed together. Segregation of any kind should be avoided. That goes for segregating persons with high needs from persons with low needs. Role models are lost and inappropriate behaviors are shared and modeled.

Use the changing technology. With the explosion in computer technology and the advances in bio-engineering, great strides are being made in the area of services to persons with severe or profound mental and physical disorders. There are many tools that can be used today to make learning and improvement much easier for both the worker and the staff. We would be remiss if we did not take advantage of technological advances.

Consistent, structured programming is a must. Programs will have to be designed and run based on seconds, not minutes. The tasks analysis will have to be broken down into much smaller steps. More thought will have to be given to the small things that make it possible for specific individuals to function in the community, for example, the jigs used to compensate for severe physical impairments.

Use community resources. Rather than repeat what has already been gone over in this chapter, I would summarize by stating that the vision you have of what you are will, to a large extent, be embraced by the community. If you view yourself as an industry, then use community organizations, mayors, and city councils as industry would and let them do the groundwork for you if you are just coming into that community. If you are already established, use community organizations as a means of doing some public education, marketing, employee training, thus cultivating a group from which support can be mustered. Community colleges, technical colleges, and universities are a tremendous resource for us and someday may become the training sites, as our workshops close down. Medical services, in many instances, have improved in the rural communities where we have established programs. Where some communities did not have access to an anesthesiologist, we have joined with the local medical community to bring one in. The entire area benefits. Use the media like anyone interested in enhancing the image of a business would. As you elevate the status of your business, you also elevate the status of your staff and employees. Give the media legitimate stories, geared to meet your image (industry) or to tell your story (training workers) or to get your employees jobs outside your worksites.

Conclusion: Providing Services to Individuals

Decision making regarding program design and service system supports for any person is an undertaking of critical importance. In the final analysis it is a process that hinges not only upon technical competence and creativity within the service delivery system, but upon the fundamental beliefs, assumptions, and philosophic aims of a society as well. Accordingly, any attempt to define service options, programmatic models, or lifestyle choices must ultimately address the foundation principles underlying the service network. It is inherently more reasonable to *address these assumptions initially, rather than ultimately,* in order to promote an orderly development of services and resources that is in harmony with a desirable conceptual framework.

It is critically important for any system to *clearly articulate its mission and philosophy.* That mission and philosophy must be conveyed to, understood by, and, most important, embraced by all staff. Staff, at all levels of the system, must be committed to the mission and principles of the system.

If there is one prevailing belief that permeates all of the managerial and programmatic activities of Region V, it is respect for the individual. That respect is not only directed toward persons with mental retardation but also to their family members, staff, and the public. Clearly, the idea that we are all people first applies to everyone. Consequently, the mission statement and the principles endorsed by the region refer only to "people" and the principles are applied to persons with handicaps and to staff.

Region V's Mission Statement reads as follows: "Region V helps people gain the knowledge and experience to increasingly use and benefit from the resources and settings available to everyone." To fulfill its mission, Region V relies on six principles that guide decision making at every level of the system:

1. Every person has value.
2. Every person should be treated with dignity and respect.
3. Every person is capable of growth and learning through community experiences.
4. Every person should experience life in the most natural settings.
5. Every person has the right to be the primary decision maker in his or her life and carries the responsibility for the direction it takes.
6. Every person is protected by the full weight of the Constitution and its amendments.

Put simply, if all levels of staff believe that *everyone will be served and integrated into the community,* all persons, regardless of the severity of their handicapping condition, will be. Then, only time will be the determining factor.

References

Paolini, M. (1980). *The Nebraska model: A system of values.* Lincoln, NE: Region V Mental Retardation Services.

Powell, D., Humphrey, M. J., & Rucker, L. (1983). *Status of Nebraska mental retardation services—1983.* Lincoln, NE: The Association for Retarded Citizens/Nebraska.

Part III

WITH THE PEOPLE

7

Beyond Caregiving

A Reconceptualization of the Role of the Residential Service Provider

JAMES KNOLL
ALISON FORD

When Kenneth* was an infant he was dependent on others for many of the necessities of life. He was bathed. He was fed. He was carried. He was diapered and clothed. Today, in adulthood, Kenneth is still bathed, fed, carried, diapered, and clothed. Needless to say, these caregiving activities are no longer viewed in the same manner as they were during infancy when they were the responsibility of his parents. Then they were considered short-term necessities; now they are carried out by service providers who work in the community residence where he lives, and they are regarded as long-term management needs. Kenneth is among an increasingly large number of individuals who reside in homes supported and operated by human service agencies. The charge to his service providers is to assist him in becoming an active participant in home and community life. To date, however, little more has been accomplished than the day-to-day management of his basic needs. Thus the status of Kenneth, and many others like him, has essentially remained unchanged. He continues to assume the role of a recipient of caregiving services, much as he did during infancy.

The purpose of this chapter is, first, to explore the role that individuals like Kenneth might assume within their homes and community settings. This role will extend far beyond that of a care receiver. Second, we will offer a reconceptualization of the role of direct-service providers. Specifically, we will focus on those providers who are serving *adults* with multiple disabili-

*All names used are pseudonyms.

ties.[1] Finally, we will provide a series of practical strategies designed to maximize the integration of adults with severe disabilities within our communities.

Beyond Care Receiving

In recent years significant efforts have been made to demonstrate that disabled individuals can acquire the skills necessary to performing meaningful work in nonsheltered settings (Brown et al., 1983; Wehman & Hill, 1982); performing housekeeping and cooking tasks in their homes (Livi & Ford, 1985); preparing basic meals (Schleien, Ash, Kiernan, & Wehman, 1981); using public transportation systems (Coon, Vogelsberg, & Williams, 1981; Neef, Iwata, & Page, 1978); shopping in grocery stores (Wheeler, Ford, Nietupski, & Brown, 1980); and demonstrating social and recreational skills (Wuerch & Voeltz, 1982). Such accomplishments have fueled the expectation that, with appropriate education and support, persons with severe disabilities can enjoy "normalized" lifestyles as adults. Indeed, there are more and more examples of severely disabled individuals who experience lives much richer than those they might have expected not so long ago.

Terry is one such example. He is a young adult with severe disabilities, yet the activities that comprise his daily routine could easily typify the routines of many of his nonhandicapped peers. Terry takes care of his personal needs. He prepares his own meals. He works. He occupies his leisure time by going out to the movies, playing computer games, and socializing with friends. Perhaps a difference between Terry and some of his nonhandicapped peers lies in the amount and nature of the support that he receives as he engages in his daily routine. Since he is not able to perform all of these routines independently, he relies on ongoing support, which is provided by human service workers. For example, during work hours, Terry is "coached" by a vocational specialist. During nonwork hours, Terry and his roommates receive ongoing support from a residential service provider.

For many of us, it may not be difficult to envision how Terry might be supported within his daily routine. But what about an individual with multiple disabilities? What about someone like Kenneth, whose learning difficulties are attributed to severe mental retardation as well as pronounced motor, sensory, and health-related difficulties? Do we envision Kenneth functioning in an adult routine similar to Terry's?

To respond to this question, we might outline a hypothetical daily

[1]The distinction between adults and children is an important one. We concur with the view of Taylor, Racino, Knoll, and Lutfiyya (Chapter 3 of this volume) and others who have taken the position that all children, including those with the most severe disabilities, should live with families where "parenting" is the primary support provided.

schedule for Kenneth. (See Ford et al., 1982, for a complete discussion of this process.) Projections could be made about the specific routines that would (or should) comprise his day. We could easily project that Kenneth will be involved in eating, dressing, toileting, and grooming routines, since, by their very nature, some level of participation would be required on his part. If Kenneth does not do them, he would at least have to allow someone else to do them *to him*. For example, if his arm is not sufficiently relaxed while dressing, he may have little choice but to participate in the relaxation techniques that ultimately allow the sleeve of a sweater to be maneuvered over his arm. In other words, he will be "acted upon."

Although involvement in self-care activities may demand a substantial portion of Kenneth's time, it certainly will not fill his entire day, nor should it. Imagine functioning in a daily routine in which one's involvement is limited to eating, dressing, and grooming. This restrictive vision leads to many unsettling observations. First, it relegates Kenneth to the role of a passive observer within his home. He is expected to sit back and watch while others assume responsibilities for cooking, house cleaning, and doing laundry. These tasks are done *for him,* as they might be done for a child. Instead, Kenneth might be expected to assume his share of the household responsibilities and receive the necessary support to carry them out. Second, the projected daily routine lacks recreational activities. In order to reduce dead time and maximize the constructive use of leisure time, Kenneth should receive the support necessary for him to engage in a variety of recreational activities when he is alone or with a friend. Third, our restrictive vision of Kenneth's daily routine is confined to one setting—the house. The limited range of stimulation and social contact that could be derived from one setting would surely have a negative effect on his growth and development. Thus, we might consider Kenneth's involvement in community activities such as walking or "wheeling" around the neighborhood, mall, and city park; seeing a movie with a friend; going to the library; swimming at the YMCA; eating in restaurants; and so forth.

Finally, an obvious omission from Kenneth's projected routine is a job. Few would question the benefits that can be accrued from a daily work experience. Yet many would point to the intensity of support that may be required and the minimal "production" that would reasonably be expected of someone with Kenneth's difficulties. However, a vocational routine must not be rejected on such a basis. Indeed, there are many compelling reasons for envisioning a lifestyle that includes meaningful work in a community setting. First, if we deny people the opportunity to participate in an activity as highly valued as work, then we deny them the respect and dignity that are usually afforded workers in our society. Second, a daily vocational routine would provide adults with multiple disabilities with a purpose for leaving their houses each day. Third, a work environment can provide one of the most stable and predictable settings in which people function throughout the day. This predictability is a necessary ingredient for active participation. Fourth, the workplace provides a setting in which people can develop sustained relationships with nonhandicapped adults. Fifth, if workers are compensated according to their contribution, then production limitations need not be used as a rationale for exclusion. Finally, supported work options, which are now becoming available, will enable adults who still require a great deal of supervision to work in community settings.

In our attempts to understand what the typical day of an adult with severe multiple handicaps should be like, we have recognized that there are some activities in which an individual must engage in order to maintain reasonable health and well-being (eating, grooming, getting from one place to another, and so forth). There is a tendency to view such activities in the context of caregiving. Consequently, the service provider may expect very little participation by the individual. Furthermore, because these caregiving needs seem so great, they can easily become the sole focus of service provision, at the expense of involving an individual in various opportunities within the community. In order to achieve a better quality of life, Kenneth's role within his home and community must extend far beyond that of a care receiver. It is our view that the lifestyle envisioned for him need not differ from that depicted for his nonhandicapped or less handicapped peers, once proper supports are in place. That is, the degree to which adults with severe multiple handicaps become actively involved in their home and community depends largely on our vision and the supports necessary to turn visions into reality.

The Direct-Service Role

As it stands now there is very little mesh between the vision we propose for the life of people with multiple disabilities and the day-to-day realities of their living situations. In many service systems only the most sophisticated people have received the supports necessary to live in small, normalized community settings. In the meantime, large numbers of people with more extensive service needs have continued to live in traditional institutions, nursing homes, and large "institutional" community settings (Hauber et al., 1984). As a result, many community providers and agencies have had little or no experience serving "the most severely disabled" individuals.

In such a service system, with a primary focus on the needs of mildly and moderately handicapped people, the direct-service provider has been defined as roughly analogous to a house manager in a large boarding house or a residential counselor in a college dormitory. That is, the staff member makes sure the house runs smoothly, mediates disputes between housemates, acts as a source for referrals to community resources, and provides personal counseling (Humm-Delgado, 1979; Slater & Bunyard, 1983).

In reviewing a number of materials designed to train staff to work in this system (Bernstein, Ziarnik, Rudrud, & Czajkowaki, 1981; Ebert, 1979; Fanning, 1975; Fiorelli, 1979; Gage, Fredericks, Johnson-Dorn, & Lindley-Southard, 1982; Holland, 1974; Living Resources Corporation, 1984; McCarthy, 1980; Provencal & Evans, 1977; Tjosvold & Tjosvold, 1981; Youngblood & Bensberg, 1983), we found that when people with severe and profound mental retardation or multiple disabilities are discussed it is usually in terms of their needing a relatively restrictive type of setting and specialized care. In all of the materials a clear distinction is drawn between the needs of individuals with severe handicaps and other "clients." Some staff-development materials even go so far as to give the impression that the community is not an appropriate place of residence for some of these individuals. When the relationship of community residence staff to these people is described, the emphasis is almost exclusively on meeting their personal care needs—caregiving—and the use of applied behavior analysis in managing their behavior. There is no indication in any of these materials that the lifestyle that we envision for Kenneth is even a remote possibility.

Nevertheless, we are convinced that the individuals in the front lines of residential services are in a position to have considerable impact on the lives of people with severe disabilities. But this potential will be realized only if these providers come to see themselves as significant in the lives of the people they serve and are given the knowledge and support needed to work out the substantial challenges they will face. That is, direct-service providers must have a clear understanding that the primary goal of their services is home and community participation, and they must see themselves as facilitators of that goal.

Community Participation as a Goal

In residential staff-training materials we found a myriad of specific strategies for managing behavior, making menus, or running a "facility" but almost no clearly articulated statements of general principles or goals to guide the direct-service worker. The few statements of general principles that did exist were (1) usually contained in a *brief* discussion of the principle of normalization, (2) often de-emphasized by minimal coverage, and (3) lost in the sea of minutiae that the worker-in-training is told to remember (e.g., the names of various drugs, the proper number of servings required each day from the major food groups). Nowhere was the goal of residential services outlined at the beginning of a training manual with the caveat that all other training and practice should be measured against it.

So what does it mean to say that the primary aim of services for individuals with severe disabilities is community participation? To begin with, community participation is very different from deinstitutionalization. The latter can be accomplished by the simple relocation of services into smaller, less isolated settings (Blatt, Bogdan, Biklen, & Taylor, 1977). It carries with it a minimal mandate for programmatic changes, as can be seen in how it has been actualized in many areas (cf. Bercovici, 1983). Community participation or integration as an organizing concept for services represents a quantum leap from deinstitutionalization, which sought merely to relocate services. When integration is the guiding principle for services, the emphasis is on how people with severe disabilities are like everyone else. An individual's limitations are not ignored, but the focus is on how best to bridge the gap between the demands of the environment and the ability of the person. From this perspective services concentrate on the support and adaptations needed to insure the individual's participation in the life of the community.

In the area of residential services, community participation means people with disabilities share a fundamental need with everyone else—the need for a stable, secure *home*, not a residential facility (see Chapter 3 of this volume). In all of its elements this home should blend into its neighborhood. The people living in the home should participate in the life of their community in the same manner as their neighbors. Within the walls of the house the disabled members of the household should be actively involved in the functioning of the house, to the maximum extent possible. After all, the life of a home revolves around the people who live there; people's lives are not defined by their houses.

Tensions Created by New Roles

Reconceptualizing their primary role as "facilitators" of home and community participation should help service providers to focus clearly on several tensions that are inherent in the dichotomy between a community residence being simultaneously an individual's home and a human services "setting." Service providers might find themselves asking, "I have to manage so much of what goes on in this person's home; can I be both a central figure and a facilitator?" "Should home and community participation be defined as gradual movement toward independence, or is it interdependence?" "With all the learning needs this person has, shouldn't I provide a highly structured learning environment, rather than simply give support within a home?" It is essentially impossible to resolve these 3 tensions fully, but how an individual provider attempts to deal with these issues will have a significant impact on the quality of life of the people served. In the following discussion we examine the implications of these tensions.

Central Figure or Facilitator? As we have pointed out already, residential workers are generally seen as falling into one of two groups: caregivers who have strong relationships with "their" residents, a good heart, and few skills; or residential technicians who are characterized by having the skills to carry out efficiently the interventions designed by professionals. In both of these roles residents are asked to view the service provider as a central figure in the home, someone to depend on for caregiving or directions. Moreover, the service provider works for the agency instead of the individual, in the role of managing the *agency's* house instead of facilitating functioning within the *resident's* home.

A focus on the goal of community integration does not mean that the service provider is relegated to the role of servant. Neither does it mean that the quality of the relationship between residential service worker and resident has to be reduced to one characterized by a detached clinical manner. What we are talking about is the definition of a new type of role that really has no parallel in our culture. This demands that we state right up front that the places of residence, regardless of the "model" of service, are people's homes and direct-service workers are employed in those homes as aides, educators, and facilitators of relationships. In other words, workers are to a certain extent prostheses meant to aid the functioning of the individuals for whom they work and not to act as ward attendants. These are highly personalized—indeed, intimate—relationships. Nonetheless, it must be kept in proper perspective that workers are there as resources, not as substitutes. In the end the highest achievement of effective direct-service providers is to realize that they are no longer needed during a particular time of the day because the persons they are serving have enough skills and enough enduring relationships to function on their own or without the services of paid personnel.

In this role as facilitators, residential service workers in the future will see their job expand beyond the direct provision of service. They will have to serve as consultants and resources for natural families, specialized foster families, neighbors who have agreed to go to disabled people's homes and help support them, and other people who are in a quasi-service-provider role for people with disabilities in the community. This means that people in the formal role of residential service providers have to be effective in communicating some of the basic principles of service provision and some strategies for supporting people with severe disabilities, to people who are not part of the world of human services. Closely allied with this consultative function is the unique demand for fostering the growth of relationships that is placed on workers who serve people with very severe disabilities. In other words, some people will need help to learn how to negotiate and share household responsibilities as well as to build supportive friendships with members of the community.

Independence or Interdependence? The dominant model of residential services is conceptualized as a continuum of "options" ranging from institutionalization on one extreme to independent living on the other. This model has a number of basic flaws (see Chapter 2 of this volume). Two of the problems with the continuum have a particularly strong influence on how residential service providers define their role: First, if an individual is seen as being incapable of attaining a higher level of independence, she or he will be confined to the more restrictive end of the continuum. Such settings, whether called institutions, skilled nursing facilities, or ICF/MRs, tend to be highly professionalized facilities—hardly what anyone would call a home. Second, the continuum of service operates on the assumption that as people gain skills they are required to move on to the next less restrictive environment. By pushing people toward some mythical goal called independence this type of service system undercuts the possibility of developing enduring relationships. The residents of this system are robbed of a sense of stability. They are always in a state of flux; someone in the house is always going or coming.

In a system of residential services that aims at supporting individuals in their homes, service providers need to consider that the fostering of community participation demands a balancing of independence and interdependence. First, the lack of skills cannot be used to rationalize keeping people in restrictive settings. Second, the development of skills cannot be considered in isolation from an individual's network of relationships. Very rarely can *any* person assert that they accomplished something without support or assistance from someone else. Certainly, any home where there is more than one person either functions on an interdependent model or soon finds itself torn asunder. This principle has important implications for life within residential settings, for example, for residents mutually supporting each other socially and in various activities, or for homes where nondisabled people may help support their neighbors with disabilities.

Highly Structured Learning Environment or a Home? Much of the literature on community residences gives the impression that these settings are intended as community classrooms in which people will develop the skills needed to live more independently. Yet, for most adults in our culture, home seems to be defined by ownership and control of the environment. The designation of a place as a person's home—whether rented or owned—carries with it a sense of intrinsic inviolability. This very fact is codified in our laws, which require a hearing before a judge to show cause that there is some essential police function of the state that demands a specific overriding of this fundamental right.

If a person is severely disabled, however, and lives in a setting that may be owned or leased by a service agency, this right is given little or no reflection, since in reality the setting is a service facility and not a home. Every minute is likely to be duly accounted for on an activity schedule; there may be special periods of the day designated as "goal time"; all of the residents will be on an individualized program plan; the staff will be seen conspicuously collecting data on clipboards and charts in every room; and visits with friends may have to be scheduled in advance so they do not conflict with the program.

It is true that home is a primary learning environment for the people living there, so one part of community integration is assisting people to develop the skills necessary to increase their control of their environment. Nevertheless, the fact remains that a home is not a school. Learning in the home is usually in context and determined by personal preference and mutual support of household members. Every aspect of home life, whether it is "charted" or not, is a potential learning experience. Who makes the rules? Who picks the furniture? Who plans the menus? How are disputes between housemates handled? Who picks the TV shows? How do people with limited communication skills participate in decisions? The point is that in a home the real demands of daily life define the "program," the program does not define daily life.

These and other tensions will always exist in residential services. It should be apparent, however, that the goal of community integration offers service providers some clear guidelines on the approach to take in attempting to resolve them. If errors in judgment are to be made, perhaps they should be in the direction of viewing oneself as facilitator of life within the home rather than a central figure, of supporting interdependence rather than independence, and of maintaining a subtle instructional presence rather than being an obtrusive "programer."

Principles and Strategies for the Direct-Service Provider

To support the integration of people with severe disabilities into the natural flow of home and community life, residential service providers must operate from sound principles and a strong commitment to the individual. To date, training manuals have dealt primarily with whether residential service providers are prepared to administer first aid, manage a household and a budget, and "control" aberrant behavior. With the reconceptualization of the service provider as a decision maker, an additional set of concerns becomes prominent: Providers must demonstrate a commitment to a philosophy of home and community participation and have a solid value base for grappling with the tensions that might arise when attempting to achieve this goal.

Principles

Direct-service workers need some specific sign posts to help them gauge the degree to which the desired ideal of community integration is being realized in their service to people with disabilities. The following are among the important guiding principles of home and community participation that providers can use in developing residential services and making day-to-day decisions.

Relationship Building and Natural Supports. This is simultaneously both the primary indicator and essential aim of integration. The supports provided within a residential setting should be geared toward insuring the growth of new nonpaid relationships (Perske, 1980; Strully & Strully, 1985). Certainly the service provider has to be sure that nothing about the home interferes with existing relationships with family and friends or with the potential for the residents to form new relationships. But providers must also be prepared to take an active role, perhaps as a temporary intermediary, to aid the growth of a relationship.

Community Involvement. This term is used to capture the sense that the walls of a person's home should be just that and not the impenetrable barriers that surround a total institution. In other words, there should be nothing about the home or its routines that will interfere with the residents' interactions outside the house. We must remind ourselves that we are speaking about people with some serious limitations. Their service providers must consciously reflect on how to foster their involvement outside the walls of the house. This will entail the routine use of public resources, visibility in the community, participation in the life of the community, and membership in community organizations.

Active Participation. People with severe disabilities have traditionally been excluded from many activities because it was assumed they could never perform them independently. While a person with a severe disability may not ever be able to carry out a whole skill sequence, accommodations can be made so that some control can be exercised over the activity (cf. Baumgart et al., 1982). This principle is based on the assumption that it is better to participate at least partially in a task rather than just watch someone do it for you. In this way people with severe disabilities are seen by others and by themselves as integral parts of their home or community activities.

Nonintrusive Interventions. This principle affirms that no intervention should be used with people with severe disabilities that would not be used with any other person or would not be acceptable for use in any public setting (The Association for the Severely Handicapped, 1981; also see Chapter 8 of this volume). Just as people should be served in a nonrestrictive environment (see Chapter 3 of this volume), the interventions used in these environments should be nonintrusive. This should lead service providers to replace with a positive alternative any behavioral, physical, or chemical intervention that they would find personally offensive.

Access to Privacy and Personal Space. Most people value the opportunity just to get away by themselves for a while. Unfortunately, since they are in the service system and usually under someone's watchful eye, many people with severe disabilities find such opportunities unavailable to them. Intrinsic to the definition of an adult's home seems to be the right to go into your room or somewhere else and say, "Don't bother me!" So, it remains the responsibility of sensitive direct-service workers to know the people they are serving well enough to realize that alone time is what they want or need. The obvious corollary of this is to be left alone, if at all possible, in those areas of life where our culture generally expects privacy, such as while bathing or using the toilet.

Natural Routines. There should be nothing about a community residence that speaks of the tight scheduling, regimentation, and routine that are often seen in settings that are exclusively focused on the development of specific skills. A person's home should be just that and not a "community classroom." The routine—the program—in someone's home has to be managed so that it is indistinguishable from daily life because the "program" is just that—living everyday life.

Age-appropriateness. In all aspects of home life, including home furnishings, room decorations, and leisure activities, efforts should be made to minimize any characteristics that serve to distinguish a person with severe disabilities from nondisabled individuals of the same age. Age-appropriateness should be reflected in the daily activities of persons with severe disabilities. For example, adults usually work an 8-hour day, not a 6-hour, 9:00 to 3:00 schedule, and they are able to make their own decisions about what time they need to go to bed at night or get up in the morning.

Real Choices. Somewhere in every manual of practices and policies, there is the statement that the resident will have direct input into the development of an individualized program plan. At the quarterly planning meeting this policy often translates to the following two sentences: "Well, do you agree that's a good goal for you to work on?" and "Ok, that's about it, but before we finish up, is there anything that you wanted to work on in the next quarter?" Sometimes, the fortunate resident has a parent or advocate present who can transform this exercise into more than a charade of personal choice. If people are to make real choices, the people working with them have to be very sensitive to their methods for expressing themselves. But they also have to provide the residents with experiences on which to base real choices; train them in self-assertiveness so they know how to express choice (if they are able); and support self-advocacy, which has a real impact on the service system.

Minimal Dead Time. "Dead time" refers to those periods of the day when a person is engaged in no constructive or true recreational activity and so can engage in maladaptive, inappropriate, and counterproductive behaviors. Although it is certainly appropriate for people to have time within their own homes when they just do nothing, a direct-service worker may have to make a conscious decision that in the case of some people with severe disabilities such "free time" or "TV time" may merely reinforce some counterproductive behaviors. It might, at certain times in a person's life, be better to err on the side of "overguidance," with an eye toward helping a person develop the skills to use free time in the future in a more constructive or truly leisurely manner.

Personalization of the Full Experience. In the past many human service settings have been judged solely on the degree of client change they have effected. Answers to questions like, "Did the therapy work?" "Was the skill learned?" "Was the maladaptive behavior decreased?" were the measures of the quality of service provided. When the service is essentially assisting people to live the fullest possible lives in their own homes, a much broader line of questioning seems appropriate: "Would I, myself, like living here under these circumstances? If not, why not? Why should a person with a severe disability be subjected to this if I would not tolerate it for myself?" This principle is basically an assertion that one primary criterion for judging a residential service is one's personal reaction to the full experience of life within a particular house.

Strategies

When the direct-service role is reconceptualized as focusing primarily on integration, the essence of the residential worker's job can be captured in a relatively small set of strategies. However, it is crucial for the provider to keep in mind that strategies cannot be separated from the principles that guide them. When divorced from sound principles of community integration, the most effective practical strategies can degenerate into nothing more than one more way of managing people's lives. The strategies listed here are intended to give direct-service workers a practical, systematic framework within which to work out the day-to-day problems of assisting a specific individual to become more fully integrated into the community.

1. *Envision the routines that should characterize the day-to-day functioning of the individual with a disability; consider the broadest array of choices*. A useful approach to accomplishing this objective is to conduct a "life space analysis" for the disabled person of concern and a parallel analysis for same-age, same-sex, nondisabled peers. One version of a life space analysis would entail listing the routines typically encountered by nondisabled persons throughout the day (Brown et al., 1979). The envisioned routine, for example, might be directed in a manner similar to that used to discuss Terry's day, presented in the introductory section of this chapter. The inventory for the nonhandicapped person provides a basis for comparison and a concrete model against which to judge the routine of the handicapped person.

2. *Describe the unique constellation of strengths, weaknesses, preferences, communication modes, and personality characteristics of the person with a disability.* To make informed decisions about the life of an individual, it is necessary for the people who know that person to pool their knowledge. In this process service providers may find that their most effective role is as active listeners who attempt to synthesize what others know about their family member or friend. Their intent is to develop an in-depth profile of the person, which will guide them in deciding on the appropriate level of support that will be needed at various times during the day. This process is particularly crucial for individuals who have severe multiple disabilities and very limited ability to express their own preferences.

3. *Identify the needs of the person based on his or her current lifestyle in comparison to the lifestyle envisioned.* After having envisioned the routines that should characterize day-to-day functioning, draw comparisons between the resident's current lifestyle and that of a nonhandicapped person. A useful guide for evaluating the quality of a person's present routines has been offered by O'Brien (in press). He presents a series of statements and questions under 5 essential areas: community presence, choice, competence, respect, and community participation. The questions prompt us to evaluate the current lifestyle of the focal person (e.g., "Identify the people who are the person's friends and allies.") and to devise strategies for improving the quality of life (e.g., "What would it take to increase the number of nonhandicapped people, including age-peers, who know and spend time with the person as an individual?"). Based on this type of analysis, a service provider can target the areas where the greatest and most crucial needs exist.

4. *Make an informed decision that a particular activity is a legitimate caregiving function for a particular person.* The life space analysis may lead to the identification of activities that are presently done "for" the person with a disability. Some of these activities may have legitimate caregiving functions. For example, it is conceivable that a person's extensive disabilities may preclude his or her participating in washing windows, cleaning the bathroom, or vacuuming the carpet. In some situations it would be appropriate to enter into negotiations with roommates (e.g., "Jerry will participate in dusting and straightening-up, and Suzanne has agreed to vacuum and clean

the bathroom"). In other cases, it may be best to hire a housekeeper or cleaning service. It is important that these trade-offs on legitimate caregiving functions be negotiated in a conscious manner. The goal is to avoid situations where caregiving functions unnecessarily limit the household participation of persons with severe disabilities or where the service providers find their role defined as a servant rather than an aide.

5. *Prioritize and set goals accordingly.* It is likely that the life space analysis will lead to the identification of many areas of a person's life that require attention. It may not be possible to address immediately all of the areas targeted for an improved quality of life. Thus, prioritization becomes an important component of the planning process. The service provider, the person with a disability, and parents or others who are closest to the person should all meet together to identify priority areas and set goals accordingly. The principles outlined in the preceding pages should guide this decision-making process. For example, one of the most important principles to keep in mind is relationship-building and natural supports. Oftentimes service providers limit goals because of perceived staff limitations (e.g., "This art class would really help to expand Sarah's leisure repertoire, but we simply don't have the staff to support her."). This principle should stand as a reminder that a central part of the service provider role is to facilitate strong natural support systems so people are not limited by paid employees' schedules. When this view is taken, creative efforts can be made to strengthen the network of relationships and natural supports available to people with severe disabilities (e.g., "This art class will increase Sarah's leisure skills and provide a good vehicle for fostering her relationship with her friend Jean, who would like to go with her.").

6. *Devise and implement a plan to achieve priority goals.*

- Determine the level and type of support needed in order for the person to participate in the targeted activity. Use natural supports whenever feasible.
- Arrange for the support to be provided at the most natural time, in the most natural location, and for the necessary length of time.
- Ascertain if there are any environmental or attitudinal constraints that may interfere with the realization of the targeted goal; act to remove them.
- Manage logistical factors such as accounting for other individuals to whom you should be providing services, transportation, finances, and so forth.
- Analyze the activity in a manner that will allow the determination of the skills typically required in order to engage in the activity, the skills that are missing from the repertoire of the disabled person, the specific skills that will need to be adapted or developed for the person to become competent in the activity, and the natural supports available within the

setting. This step in the process entails the application of the principle of partial participation and the development of the individualized adaptations to the resident's daily home and community routines.

- Facilitate the learning of individuals within the context of the naturally occurring activity.
- Fade services when the individual demonstrates desired competencies and when sufficient natural supports are in place.

7. *Balance the demands of formal goals and objectives with skills that are addressed in an informal manner.* This serves as a reminder that residential services present a highly complex situation, where the service provided is inseparable from the boundaries of a person's life. In other words, all aspects of the day are part of the "program," every minute presenting another learning opportunity. Of course it is impossible to devise a formal approach to all aspects of every day and still maintain the essential qualities that define a home. So, good residential service workers must develop within themselves an attitude that naturally uses the spontaneity of daily life to foster individual development, regardless of whether the concern at hand is written up in behavioral terms and duly recorded in someone's case file. In many ways the skill with which this unobtrusive and thorough integration of "the program" into all aspects of a person's life is accomplished will be what distinguishes truly effective service providers. Where this is most effectively accomplished the person with a disability will cease to be perceived as the client of an agency, because the services being received will be totally integrated into a typical lifestyle.

8. *Evaluate the effectiveness of the supports provided, to determine whether they have had a noticeable impact on the quality of life of each person served; decide upon the next steps.* All of the preceding strategies have been outlined with an underlying premise in mind; that is, residential service providers can make a difference. Persons in this role can facilitate movement toward greater home and community participation. To do so, however, will require frequent evaluation of the supports provided. How effective have they been? Have they had a noticeable impact on the quality of the focal person's life? Of course, the best evaluations of effectiveness are not made by residential providers alone; rather, they come from the person with a disability, others close to her or him, and those who share the same community settings and have had the opportunity to notice change over time.

These strategies summarize what is central to the direct-service provider's job, but there are also a number of ancillary skills that the direct-service workers will need to have in order to be able to see effectively to the social, health, safety, and learning needs of people they serve. For example, a large number of the activities that the recipients of services will be involved in will revolve around home management. It seems obvious that direct-service workers need to have good common-sense knowledge and ready access to additional information in this area. Basic knowledge in the area of health and safety as well as a certain degree of specialized knowledge concerning the specific medical and physical needs of the people served are also necessary job requirements. Although these ancillary skills are necessary, they must be seen in perspective, not as the primary focus of a residential agency but as supportive of the primary goal of facilitating an individual's full social integration. The current administrative and training practices of service agencies should be scrutinized to determine the extent to which they reflect a reconceptualized role.

Admittedly, the vision of the residential service worker's role that we have presented here is substantially more challenging and perhaps more complex than what we see in place in most of our community residences today. Is this reconceptualized role a pipe dream? We hope not, particularly if the alternatives are the stagnant models of caregiving and the residential technician, neither of which serves people with severe disabilities or their service providers very well.

References

The Association for the Severely Handicapped. (1981, November). Resolution on intrusive interventions. *TASH Newsletter,* 7(11), 1–2.

Baumgart, D., Brown, L., Pumpian, I., Nisbet, J., Ford, A., Sweet, M., Messina, R., & Schroeder, J. (1982). Principle of partial participation and individualized adaptations in educational programs for severely handicapped students. *Journal of the Association for the Severely Handicapped,* 7(2), 17–27.

Bercovici, S. M. (1983). *Barriers to normalization: The restrictive management of retarded people.* Baltimore: University Park Press.

Bernstein, G. S., Ziarnik, J. P., Rudrud, E. H., & Czajkowski, L. A. (1981). *Behavioral habilitation through proactive programming.* Baltimore: Brookes.

Blatt, B., Bogdan, R., Biklen, D., & Taylor, S. (1977). From institution to community: A conversion model. In E. Sontag, J. Smith, & N. Certo (Eds.), *Educational programming for the severely and profoundly handicapped* (pp. 40–52). Reston, VA: Council for Exceptional Children.

Brown, L., Branston, M. B., Hamre-Nietupski, S., Pumpian, I., Certo, N., & Gruenewald, L. (1979). A strategy for developing chronologically age appropriate and functional curricular content for severely handicapped adolescents and young adults. *Journal of Special Education, 13*(1), 81–90.

Brown, L., Shiraga, B., Ford, A., Nisbet, J., VanDeventer, P., Sweet, M., & Loomis, R. (1983). Teaching severely handicapped students to perform meaningful work in nonsheltered vocational environments. In L. Brown, A. Ford, J.

Nisbet, M. Sweet, B. Shiraga, J. York, R. Loomis, & P. VanDeventer (Eds.), *Educational programs for severely handicapped students* (Vol. 13). Madison, WI: Madison Metropolitan School District.

Coon, M. E., Vogelsberg, R. T., & Williams, W. (1981). Effects of classroom public transportation instruction on generalization to the natural environment. *Journal of the Association for the Severely Handicapped, 6*(2), 46–53.

Ebert, R. S. (1979). A training program for community residence staff. *Mental Retardation, 17*, 257–259.

Fanning, J. W. (1975). *A common sense approach to community living arrangements for the mentally retarded.* Springfield, IL: Charles C. Thomas.

Fiorelli, J. S. (1979). *A curricular model for preservice training of alternative living arrangement direct service personnel* (ERIC No. ED 202 984). Philadelphia: Temple University, Developmental Disabilities Center.

Ford, A., Davis, J., Messina, R., Ranieri, L., Nisbet, J., & Sweet, M. (1982). Arranging instruction to ensure the active participation of severely multihandicapped students. In L. Brown, J. Nisbet, A. Ford, M. Sweet, B. Shiraga, & L. Gruenewald (Eds.), *Educational programs for severely handicapped students* (pp. 31–80). Madison, WI: Madison Metropolitan School District.

Gage, M. A., Fredericks, H. D., Johnson-Dorn, N., & Lindley-Southard, B. (1982). Inservice training for staffs of group homes and work activity centers serving developmentally disabled adults. *Journal of the Association for the Severely Handicapped, 7*(4), 60–70.

Hauber, F. A., Bruininks, R. H., Hill, B. K., Lakin, C., Scheerenberger, R., & White, C. C. (1984). National census of residential facilities: A 1982 profile of facilities and residents. *American Journal of Mental Deficiency, 89*, 236–245.

Holland, J. F. (1974). *Operating manual for residential services personnel.* Columbus, OH: Nisonger Center for Mental Retardation and Developmental Disabilities.

Humm-Delgado, D. (1979). Opinions of community residence staff about their work responsibilities. *Mental Retardation, 17*, 250–251.

Livi, J., & Ford, A. (1985). Skill transfer from a domestic training site to the actual homes of three moderately handicapped students. *Education and Training of the Mentally Retarded, 20*, 69–82.

Living Resources Corporation. (1984). *Mandatory Training Schedule.* Albany, NY: Author.

McCarthy, T. J. (1980). *Managing group homes: A training manual.* Nashville, TN: TMAC Behavior Development.

Neef, N. A., Iwata, B. A., & Page, T. J. (1978). Public transportation training: In vivo versus classroom instruction. *Journal of Applied Behavior Analysis, 11*, 331–344.

O'Brien, J. (in press). A guide to personal futures planning. In G. T. Bellamy & B. Wilcox (Eds.), *The activities catalog: A community programming guide for youth and adults with severe disabilities.* Baltimore: Brookes.

Perske, R. (1980). *New life in the neighborhood.* Nashville, TN: Abingdon.

Provencal, G., & Evans, D. (1977). *Resident manager education: A curriculum model for educating foster parents and group home personnel.* Mt. Clemens, MI: Macomb Oakland Regional Center.

Schleien, S. J., Ash, T., Kiernan, J., & Wehman, P. (1981). Developing independent cooking skills in a profoundly retarded woman. *Journal of the Association for the Severely Handicapped, 6*(2), 23–29.

Slater, M. A., & Bunyard, P. D. (1983). Survey of residential staff roles, responsibilities, and perception of resident needs. *Mental Retardation, 21*, 52–58.

Strully, J., & Strully, C. (1985). Friendship and our children. *Journal of the Association for Persons with Severe Handicaps, 10*(4), 224–227.

Tjosvold, D., & Tjosvold, M. M. (1981). *Working with mentally handicapped persons in their residences.* New York: Free Press.

Wehman, P., & Hill, J. (1982). Preparing severely handicapped youth for less restrictive environments. *Journal of the Association for the Severely Handicapped, 7*(1), 33–38.

Wheeler, J., Ford, A., Nietupski, J., & Brown, L. (1980). Teaching moderately and severely handicapped adolescents to shop in supermarkets using pocket calculators. *Education and Training of the Mentally Retarded, 15*, 108–122.

Wuerch, B. B., & Voeltz, L. M. (1982). *Longitudinal leisure skills for severely handicapped learners: The Ho'onanea curriculum component.* Baltimore: Brookes.

Youngblood, G. S., & Bensberg, G. J. (1983). *Planning and operating group homes for the handicapped.* Lubbock, TX: Texas Tech University, Research and Training Center in Mental Retardation.

8

Gentle Teaching

An Alternative to Punishment for People with Challenging Behaviors

JOHN J. McGEE
PAUL E. MENOUSEK
DANIEL HOBBS

The purpose of this chapter is to give caregivers a guide for helping persons with mental retardation and severe behavioral needs to participate in the confluence of community life. This includes those with severe or profound mental retardation with highly aggressive or self-injurious behaviors and those with mild or moderate mental retardation who have difficulty in maintaining their emotional well-being.

Some children and adults with mental retardation present significant challenges to caregivers. Persistent behaviors such as hitting, biting, kicking, screaming, self-injury, and self-stimulation tend to distance these persons increasingly from family and community life, as well as from their caregivers. Furthermore, these types of behaviors often result in punishment. Caregivers frequently become administrators of punishment because there is little insight into the nature of severe behavioral problems and the interactional nature of human behavior. The current technology of applied behavioral analysis fails to recognize the fundamental need for caregivers literally to teach persons with these special needs the value inherent in human presence, participation, and reward—cornerstone factors that lead to mutual bonding.

In this chapter we will present an option to the punishment practices prevalent in the care and teaching of individuals with severe behavioral problems (Azrin, Gottlieb, Hughart, Wesolowski, & Rahan, 1975; Azrin & Wesolowski, 1975; Barkley & Zupnick, 1976; DeCatanzaro & Baldwin, 1978; Duker & Seys, 1977; Rusch, Close, Hops, & Agosta, 1970; Singh, Dawson, & Manning, 1981; Solnick, Rincover, & Peterson, 1977; Winton & Singh, 1983). For many researchers and professionals the axiom is, "If it works, use it." This leads caregivers to use such repugnant and torturous instruments as cattle prods (Corbett, 1975; Corte, Wolfe, & Locke, 1971; Horner & Barton, 1980; Lichstein & Schreibman, 1976; Lovaas, Schaeffer, & Simmons, 1965; Lovaas & Simmons, 1969; Prochaska, Smith, Marzilli, Colby, & Donovan, 1974; Sherman, Swinson, & Lorimer, 1984; Singh, 1977; Tate & Baroff, 1966), as well as to engage in common practices such as time-out (Bean & Roberts, 1981; Bostow & Bailey, 1969; Calhoun & Matherne, 1975; Foxx & Shapiro, 1978; Harris & Ersner-Hershfield, 1978; Lutzker, 1978; White, Nielsen, & Johnson, 1972), overcorrection (Epstein, Doke, Sajwaj, Sorrell, & Rimmer, 1974; Foxx, 1976; Foxx & Azrin, 1972, 1973), and a dehumanizing array of aversive practices like squirting ammonia in the person's face (Gross, Berler, & Drabman, 1982; Tanner & Zeiler, 1975).

In contrast, our focus is based on the centrality of a humanizing social attachment between the caregiver and the person with severe behavioral problems, which we call bonding. We will delineate a personal posture and allied techniques that preclude punishment as a treatment option and focus on the teaching of bonding between mentally retarded persons with severe behavioral problems and their caregivers. This posture involves the recognition that persons who hit, bite, kick, scratch, or self-stimulate have actually not bonded with their caregivers, nor have the caregivers bonded with them. It is necessary to teach bonds of affection with the person.

Gentleness implies that there must be a central focus on the development of a range of affectionate and respectful techniques that can help the behaviorally involved person move from a state of emotional confusion to one of meaningful human engagement, so that persons with mental retardation will find it unnecessary to express their needs through primitive or harmful responses. We believe that caregivers need to look upon these behavioral needs from a pedagogical perspective. It is crucial to redirect maladaptive behaviors toward meaningful human engagements. This redirection is essentially a teaching process. It is a process that results in bonding—a liberating and humanizing process for all involved. It is, indeed, a liberatory pedagogy—a teaching process that focuses on the nurturance of human solidarity, mutuality, and interdependence.

In *gentle teaching* there is no room for traditional punishment strategies. The use of punishment implies submission. Gentle teaching focuses on both alternatives to punishment and the actualization of bonding. Recent research clearly validates this focus. For example, Barrett (1977), Jansen (1980), and Touchette (1978) emphasized the unacceptability of behavioral interventions that focus solely on the deceleration of inappropriate behaviors. There is no doubt that punishment can eliminate inappropriate behaviors, at least for short periods of time. The key consideration is that we "therapeutically" produce submissive, oppressed, crouching, and fearful persons, rather than persons engaged in joyful human interactions. There are some who say that "mild" punishment is permissible, but we question even this. For example, Azrin, Sneed, and Foxx (1973) reported a "positive" practice procedure for bedwetting that involved awakening the resident, reprimanding him, having him replace the linen on the bed, having him lie down for 3 minutes, awakening him, and then directing him to the toilet. The final 3 procedures were repeated about 9 times. This may eliminate bedwetting, but it is too toxic for the creation of bonding, for teaching the value inherent in human presence, or for gaining interactional control.

Since persons with severe behavioral needs are often voiceless and defenseless, they tend to isolate themselves from meaningful human interactions. If caregivers further isolate them through punishment practices, then the value of both the caregiver and the person in need is diminished. Yet many current "treatment" practices for this complex population tend to fight violence with violence. For example, Foxx, Foxx, Jones, and Kiely (1980) reported one of their cases in which social isolation was used with a retarded person. Whenever Paul became aggressive he was "instructed" in a neutral tone to go to his bed and lie down. If he did not, he was immediately "escorted" to his bed. If he refused to lie down, he was physically "guided" into a supine position. If he resisted, he was forcefully held down. He was informed that he would be denied all social contact for 24 hours. He was then instructed to remove his outer clothing and put on a hospital gown. All his personal effects were removed from his living area, and he was left alone. Such an authoritarian and mechanistic approach can achieve obedience, but not bonding.

We advocate for the primacy of bonding through gentle and respectful teaching techniques, rather than the submission of a person through punishment. A few behaviorists have begun to point toward the interactional nature of behaviors (e.g., Bijou & Dunitz-Johnson, 1981). Bonding is the first goal of gentle teaching—moving the person away from aggressive, self-injurious, avoidant, or self-stimulatory behaviors and toward relationships at first with direct caregivers and eventually with the community at large.

We assume that it is possible and necessary to teach bonding (Combs & Slaby, 1977; Hopkins, 1968; Hops, 1982; Larsen, 1975; Strain, Shores, & Kerr, 1976; Strain & Wiegerink, 1976) through teaching the value inherent in human presence and reward. Bonding unites the caregiver and the person with these needs.

Caregivers who punish assume that the person with mental retardation cannot be redirected toward meaningful human engagements, but rather needs to be "taught" a lesson: "Don't do this or else!" This is a fatalistic view of human development. We assume that it is essential to teach the person that there is a value and goodness inherent in human interactions, human presence, and human participation. Teaching the value and goodness of human presence and participation leads to bonding. The use of punishment precludes this learning, since it results in submission, not bonding.

Interactionalism

The majority of caregivers who work with mentally retarded persons take a behavioral approach in their treatment process. This often takes the form of focusing on the presenting of maladaptive behaviors and seeking "consequating conditions" for modifying them. There is often little attention or significance given to underlying factors. For example, persons with severe behavioral problems who "live" in oppressive back-ward environments (external factors) have little chance to improve behaviorally within a setting that is intrinsically dehumanizing. Punishment might bring submission, but not the fullness of human development.

The principles of applied behavioral analysis have contributed a great deal to our understanding of how persons learn, in that caregivers can pinpoint behaviors and measure behavioral change over time. When applied to persons with severe behavioral problems, they often result in failure or the use of punishment and restraint. This failure centers on a lack of insight into the needs of persons with severe behavioral problems. Any primary focus on the elimination of maladaptive behaviors, rather than the teaching of bonding, is destined to fail.

The principles of applied behavioral analysis help caregivers pinpoint and define measurable behaviors, as well as the antecedents to and consequences of those behaviors. These insights into the human learning process are important and useful; yet in practice this analysis breaks down when applied to persons with severe behavioral patterns. A basic principle in applied behavioral analysis is that of the power of consequences; that is, reward increases the probability of behaviors occurring and punishment decreases the probability. It is true that if negative behaviors are punished strongly enough those behaviors will disappear. Yet this disappearance is not learning. It is simply submission to powers stronger than ourselves. It offers little in the form of liberation or humanization for either the caregiver or the person with special needs. Beyond this, persons with histories of strong, entrenched maladaptive behaviors learn that punishment is a way of life, a way to respond to an otherwise absurd, meaningless, and unresponsive world. Punishment becomes their reward in that it is a means for the person with severe behavioral needs to gain control over such a world. Persons with these needs find that there is more meaning in the punishment placed on them, since it draws people to them or away from them. Opportunities for reward are few. When they occur they are given in a nonjoyful manner. Reward loses its power.

For example, the story of Maria symbolizes the despair of many persons with mental retardation. Maria is a 28-year-old woman who lives in the back ward of a state institution. According to her caregiver, "She is in constant restraint (straitjacket and a masked, locked helmet) because of self-abuse. She hits her face and her head with her fist when she is not restrained." Staff further reports that after three years of such "care" she is now "restraint dependent." In addition, she has been subjected to a variety of psychotropic medications. Her record also indicates that at one time the use of cattle prods was effective in decreasing her self-abuse. Based on these data, a six week trial use of "electrical stimulation" was recommended and approved. Three months later, at the time we met Maria, they were still using cattle prods on her. Reward in the form of decent, kind, loving interaction is meaningless to Maria. The cattle prod has become her reward.

A major conceptual flaw in the application of the principles of applied behavioral analysis is that reward is given rather than taught. If reward is given and there is no response, then the pathway to punishment is opened. Most caregivers would surely prefer a positive response to reward, but when none is given, they rarely question why. If they do, the questioning centers on the person's supposed weaknesses rather than the environments that probably created such behaviors. We believe that the meaning of reward needs to be taught to persons with these special needs. The caregiver has to look upon reward-teaching as a primary pedagogical objective. This necessarily precludes the use of punishment.

The fundamental element in all human development is bonding. Punishment and submission are the antithesis of bonding. Bonding has to be seen as the goal of all initial human interventions. This connectedness that we advocate between the caregiver and the person with a behavioral problem is somewhat different from the bonding that Bowlby (1967, 1974, 1980) described as so crucial in the human development of infants. We are generally discussing persons who are older, many of whom are likely to have been bonded once but have lost these human connections. With these differences in mind we can define bonding as the establishment of reciprocal lines of communication, affectional ties between the caregiver and the person. Initially, the caregiver must impose demands on the person so that the value of human presence, interaction, and participation can be learned. As this relationship develops there are fewer superimposed demands and the interaction becomes more equitable and interdependent.

The caregiver uses the daily activities of the person as a vehicle for teaching the value of human relationships. In this effort the caregiver can apply some of the most basic principles of applied behavior analysis as a guide during this intense period of active teaching. In the first hours the person may throw objects, hit, scream, and so forth. The caregiver prevents such behavior from occurring as much as possible and continuously redirects the person back to the task. The need for tolerance, warmth, and affection is absolutely crucial at this point. It is particularly important that the caregiver find ways to express affection, gentleness, respect, and human solidarity even while the person is attempting to withdraw or attack. This process of ignoring the inappropriate behavior and redirecting it serves to begin to teach the person that the caregiver will remain present, will not punish, and will continue to seek and nurture humanizing interactions.

By this total unconditional acceptance of the person, the caregiver teaches the values of human presence, interaction, and participation, and lays the foundation for mutual bonding. Thus, the first steps are taken toward liberating the person with mental retardation from the oppression of restraints, punishment, and psychotropic medications that have filled the void left by the absence of meaningful human contact. To summarize, the three basic principles of interactionalism are: (1) bonding is the goal, (2) the value of human presence and participation must be taught, and (3) the posture that the caregiver brings to the interaction is more important than any technology.

Behavioral Assumptions

Gentle teaching is based to a large degree on basic behavioral principles; however, its posture and practices often differ considerably from strategies currently employed in settings with persons with mental retardation. This difference results from a different posture, within the principles of applied behavioral analysis, toward persons with severe behavioral needs, rather than from a difference in technical perspectives. Behavioral analysis is a neutral tool, as is all technology. The humanizing value of any technology, if it is to have one, must arise out of our personal values and beliefs, that is, our posture toward ourselves and others. Like any tool in human hands, behaviorism can be used to bring people into submission or raise them to a liberated state. It should be noted that our use of the word *liberation* is not taken lightly. It is based on a critical analysis of the dehumanized state in which we find people with these special needs and on the noncritical questioning of their oppression. Mutual liberation is at the very roots of gentle teaching strategies.

A traditional behavioral assumption revolves around the "functionality" of behaviors. According to this assumption, all behaviors serve some function in our lives. Behaviors are learned because they allow us to obtain some control over our environment. People with mental retardation often display behaviors that are easy to label "abnormal" from that perspective. However, a review of developmental histories and previous environments and experiences suggests more basic rationales for such behaviors. Limited support, non-nurturing social interactions, minimal developmental stimulation, limited language abilities, and other intrinsic and extrinsic factors can result in behaviors that are very adaptive for some environments, even though considered inappropriate in other environments. For example, people placed in a sterile, institutional back ward may develop self-injurious behaviors such as head-banging. This would be regarded as highly inappropriate in the noninstitutionalized world, yet in reality it is a logical response to an absurd world in which people with severe or profound mental retardation find themselves among large numbers of other people with similar needs, a world in which they are unable to communicate verbally and have been taught no alternative means of communication, and in which they spend the majority of time in a "warehouse" atmosphere. Head-banging can easily be interpreted as a logical response to such a world and a powerful means of distancing oneself from others or avoiding meaningless, often hurtful human interactions.

The purposefulness of such behaviors may be interpreted as "functional"; however, a much more basic interpretation is that of the quest for human survival. In other words, such behaviors are very purposeful in that they serve to communicate, "I don't want to do this," "I don't understand or know how," or "I'm tired of doing this, and I want to stop."

If inappropriate behaviors are seen as purposeful because of the role they play in previous or current environments, the teaching or treatment objective becomes that of teaching alternative forms of behaviors that are more appropriate or more adaptive in the present situation. The major focus becomes that of the replacement of behaviors. Yet, more central to the point is the need to teach bonding as the prelude to other forms of learning, using these alternate behaviors and interactions as vehicles for teaching the value of human presence, participation, and reward. Current practices of suppression or elimination of inappropriate behaviors before more socially acceptable alternatives can be taught fail to lead to bonding. Even nonpunitive approaches fail if they do not recognize that bonding is at the core of all human development and that it must be taught.

Another behavioral assumption is that social reinforcement is the most natural form of reward available and that, when given, it should increase the probability that positive behaviors will occur. Social reinforcement in the form of touching, stroking, pats on the back, smiles, verbal praise, or other pleasant social interactions are the most "normal" and readily available forms of reinforcement. More important, they represent the type of contact-seeking behaviors that nurture bonding.

However, while social reinforcement is normalizing and readily available, it must not be assumed that it is always the most immediately effective, particularly for people who have learned to avoid human interaction. The value of social interactions must be taught to persons with these complex needs. It initially has no power, for it has no meaning. In this sense, reward must be learned. Interdependent relationships must evolve over time between caregivers and people with these needs. The nurturing aspects of these relationships then develop their inherent value as reinforcing human interactions. The types of social reinforcement just cited are not only important as consequences but also as concrete, mutual signs of bonding. As people learn the value of verbal and tactile praise through their frequent use by caregivers, they begin to reciprocate. This learned consequence spirals into an ongoing set of human interactions—the process of bonding.

A basic postulate in gentle teaching is that considerable change in behavior can result from a focus on antecedent conditions, as opposed to consequences. The current and popular approach in behavior management is to focus almost solely on the consequences of a behavior: Appropriate behaviors that occur are consequated positively; inappropriate behaviors that occur are consequated negatively. Gentle teaching presupposes the need to teach the value inherent in human presence, as well as the value of reward. It is assumed that the caregiver's presence is the primary antecedent to all human behaviors. It becomes necessary to teach people that their caregivers signal safety, consistency, and reward. Any use of punishment counteracts these feelings. It is fatalistic to believe that human behavior is solely a result of what we receive. Since there are no positive consequences for inappropriate behaviors, the "treatment" of choice in the traditional behavioral approach becomes time-out, overcorrection, seclusion, restraints, electric shock, and the like. Punishment cannot teach more appropriate and acceptable behavioral alternatives, let alone bonding.

Once a behavior occurs, nothing can be done that will help to replace the behavior. Learning to clean up spilled milk does not help to teach drinking without spilling. Neither does time spent in seclusion or restraint help develop more appropriate and acceptable behavioral responses. The solution can more readily be found in the prevention of maladaptive behaviors through preventive strategies. This enables caregivers to focus their attention on teaching bonding rather than punishment. In the vast majority of instances, aggressive or self-injurious behaviors can be prevented.

Interactional Objectives

The first pedagogical objective in gentle teaching is reward teaching—systematically and consciously teaching the goodness and reinforcing power inherent in verbal and tactile praise. Adaptive or cognitive behaviors that are taught (e.g., assembling a puzzle, performing job tasks, identifying survival words) are at the start vehicles by which to teach the consequences—verbal and tactile praise. The consequences become the behavior taught. For example, if a person is continuously hitting himself and a caregiver is attempting to teach an adaptive skill, the particular task is the vehicle or instrument for teaching reward. If the caregiver only *gives* reward, it is quite possible that the reward will have little or no reinforcing meaning to the person. On the other hand, if the caregiver recognizes that the task is an instrument for *teaching* reward, she will do everything possible to prevent the self-hitting (antecedents), increase the likelihood that the particular task will be performed successfully (teaching method), and then use the successful performance on the task as an instrument for teaching reward.

Along with reward-teaching—and equally critical—is the need to teach the power of the caregiver's presence and interaction with the person. This is the most basic initial behavioral antecedent—human presence and interaction. These also must often be taught. Many persons with severe behavioral challenges have learned to distance themselves from others through their behaviors. Screams, hits, and kicks are astute ways of repelling caregivers. Such behaviors are actually logical ways of distancing caregivers and avoiding interaction.

If caregivers punish (which is common) for any of the array of maladaptive behaviors, they are doing one of two things: teaching people to submit to others or teaching people that their maladaptive behaviors are strong means for distancing others from them. The caregivers' punishment thus becomes a reward—a means of gaining control over a world that is confusing, unresponsive, and absurd.

Hence, the interactional analysis of behavior involves the following sequence of events: (1) insuring and teaching the value of human presence by preventing as much as possible the maladaptive behaviors from occurring, (2) using adaptive tasks as the instrument upon which attention is focused, and (3) using this focus to teach reward. The interactions involved in this sequence transcend any specific skill teaching. Focusing on a barren stimulus-response mechanism ("You do this, you receive that . . .") is far too removed from the human interactions that people need to learn. Such a mechanistic approach reduces people to a robotlike level and fails to cultivate mutually humanizing interactions. It also allows caregivers to "hide" behind impersonal consequences, preventing their involvement in the bonding process and fostering human distancing.

Thus, the 3 major principles of applied behavioral analysis that have an impact on gentle teaching are: (1) the value of reward must be taught, (2) the value of human presence must be taught, and (3) the tasks presented to people form the bridge across which interactions gain their meaning.

The Critical Questioning of Postures

As we have emphasized, technology is a tool that can be used for good or evil, for submission or bonding, depending on our value system. We have delineated a value system that is built on gentleness, respect, and solidarity with the person with mental retardation. Our posture toward the person with behavioral problems should shape how we will use behavioral technology.

Caregivers have several choices relative to their attitude toward persons with these special needs. Caregivers need to reflect on and move away from cold, distancing, and dependency-provoking postures, toward ones that enhance human interdependence. In using the phrase *gentle teaching,* we do not wish to imply an attitude that fosters pity or low expectations. Although not blatantly or consciously cruel, such a posture also leads to human subjugation. On the other hand, although gentle teaching implies structure and discipline, we do not wish to foster an authoritarian relationship devoid of tolerance and affection. Caregivers need to reflect on and actualize a posture that brings full acceptance of the humanity of the person, in spite of oftentimes repulsive behaviors. This means cultivating a true solidarity with the person, protecting her or him from harm, redirecting her or him toward bonding. This posture is at the core of gentle teaching.

Dimensions of Gentle Teaching

To teach bonding it is important to understand the basic dimensions through which people with special needs and their caregivers pass. At the core of these dimensions is an evolving relationship. At the start the caregiver superimposes this relationship upon the person with severe behavioral problems. For mentally retarded persons with behavioral problems there are likely no affectional ties. There is fear, rebellion, and avoidance. Caregivers give but receive nothing. They prevent aggressive and/or self-injurious behaviors as much as possible and continuously redirect people toward tasks or interactions that are used as vehicles for teaching the value of human presence and reward in a gentle, tolerant, respectful manner. As the minutes wear on, people with special needs begin to respond better to the tasks and interactions. This is good, but not the primary focus. This improved redirectability to on-task participation provides multiple opportunities to teach reward. Gradually people begin to catch on to the meaning of human presence, reward, and participation. Simultaneously, caregivers fade these supports, allowing people with special needs to assume more self-directed control. As this interactional equity sets in and takes hold, bonding begins to emerge.

The gentle teaching process has as its goal the teaching of bonding as rapidly as possible. Several dimensions can be delineated through which people with mental retardation and their caregivers typically pass on the way toward bonding:

- The caregivers' awareness and actualization of a gentle and respectful posture toward people with mental retardation
- An initial brief phase in which caregivers superimpose their values on the people they help such that distancing behaviors will be ignored (while ensuring that no harm comes) and almost simultaneously redirected so that reward can be taught
- A phase in which caregivers work intensely with people and gain the beginnings of interactional equity; that is, where people with mental retardation begin to accept the caregivers' presence and reward and then gradually begin to reciprocate reward
- A catch-on phase in which caregivers and those they help gradually begin to share reward
- A generalization phase in which the bonding carries over into many of the people's major life transactions

The fact is that each caregiver creates this bonding process. The first 3 phases in this process should generally take no longer than 10 to 20 days, though this may vary with the nature of the behavior, the quality of the environment, and the skill and posture of the caregivers.

First Dimension: The Caregiver's Posture toward the Person

Gentle teaching is based on the belief that all people, regardless of their bio-psychosocial condition, are able to develop and actualize their human potential. It is held that every person's value is intrinsic, simply because she or he is a unique human being. This value does not depend on any other characteristics or measurements—neither cognitive nor behavioral. This value must be felt in spite of the person's maladaptive behaviors.

Caregivers need to develop, internalize, and put into practice such a posture, using it to model all interactions with people with these special needs. On the one hand, this posture is based on values that emphasize mutual human needs; on the other hand, it will lead to the means by which caregivers will discover ways to teach bonding.

This posture embraces two interrelated factors: tolerance and affection. As we have stated, the process of bonding is at the heart of gentle teaching. It requires the creation of affectional ties between the caregiver and the person with special needs—contact-seeking behaviors rather than aggression, self-injury, or avoidance. As bonding develops, it signifies that the person is learning to reach out, to seek out, to respond, to smile, to touch. More is required than that caregivers merely treat the person decently, although this is part of it. We must be careful that demands are not put on the person in need, although there is an ebb and flow of interactional requests and redirection to tasks, depending on the intensity of the person's aggression, self-injury, or avoidance. This ebb and flow initially requires a great deal of tolerance toward the person. Often the natural tendency is to become indignant when retarded people do not "comply" to the norm and to view them as engaging in "manipulation." Caregivers need to teach themselves to tolerate certain behaviors while retarded people are learning interactional equity.

To teach bonding, caregivers cannot overprotect, although at times people will need protection when they seek to harm themselves or others. Even at these times caregivers need to avoid smothering people. Caregivers most certainly cannot be authoritarian, although they initially need to set limits and teach people who do not want to be taught. The antithesis of caregivers who teach bonding are caretakers who present a cold, dehumanizing, detached attitude.

At first this interdependence is superimposed; that is, when confronted by a person who does not want to learn, the caregiver sets limits, presents tasks, and teaches the value of his or her presence and of reward. We call the initial steps in the teaching process *interactional equity* (more on this later). Caregivers assume full responsibility at the beginning. People with special needs are likely to display a full range of aggressive, self-injurious, or avoidant behaviors. Caregivers should remain serene, ignoring the maladaptive behaviors while simultaneously redirecting these people to their tasks and teaching reward.

Behaviorally, caregivers focus on reward-teaching to cultivate bonding; that is, they teach the value of their presence and of verbal and tactile praise. At the worst moments of aggression or self-injury, good caregivers remain calm, protect themeselves and others, and redirect people to tasks where reward can be taught. The caregiver has to be at his or her best as a teacher during the special needs person's worst moments.

Second Dimension: Superimposition of Self

The Critical First Hours. In this second dimension, caregivers spend brief amounts of time interacting with people on tasks in order to determine the correct blend of teaching techniques to use in gaining interactional equity as rapidly as possible. Caregivers focus on ways to prevent self-injurious and aggressive behaviors, ways to direct and redirect people to their tasks, ways to teach the tasks with minimal errors so that reward can be given, and ways to teach the value inherent in human presence and reward. Within these first hours it is important to develop the blend of gentle teaching techniques that initially will be used. It is crucial that caregivers constantly reflect on and discover ways to show tolerance and affection. In the initial sessions, people with these special needs may throw materials, attempt to hit or kick, spit at the caregiver, scream continuously, and so forth. Even when caregivers prevent a large part of such behaviors from happening, it is a natural tendency for them to feel insulted and threatened. To tolerate does not mean to permit harm or damage; it means to prevent it as much as possible and at the same time to ignore disruptive or destructive behaviors.

Thus, from the very start the three-pronged technique of ignoring, redirecting, and rewarding becomes the basic teaching strategy that encompasses both the technical-behavioral dimension of gentle teaching and the humanizing-liberating dimension that is so essential to the entire process. Technically, this strategy focuses on avoiding any reinforcement of maladaptive behaviors while at the same time redirecting the person toward structured tasks so that multiple opportunities are created for teaching the value of human presence and reward. From a humanizing-liberating perspective this technique forms a framework in which bonding eventually develops.

The caregiver should regard the first session with the person as their chance to select techniques for preventing maladaptive behaviors from happening and to interact with the person while trying out a personalized mixture of gentle techniques that may be helpful. Generally, caregivers spend an hour or two on this process.

At this point the caregiver formulates a tentative personalized plan centering around factors such as environmental management (ways to arrange the environment and external stimuli to prevent maladaptive behaviors), the degree of assistance required by the person to perform a task, and the person's responsiveness to verbal and/or tactile praise so that reward can be taught as the primary pedagogical objective.

The first sessions are a key time during which caregivers continuously adapt the personalized plan to fit the actual needs of the moment. This plan, reformulated as interactional equity, is gradually developed, enabling people to enter into and remain in the mainstream of residential, vocational, and/or educational services.

Staffing Ratios. Caregivers need to consider—based on the responsiveness of the person at the very moment—ways to give the least amount of "staffing" possible, in order to avoid teaching learned helplessness. They also must aim for the most integration possible, in order to teach maximum interdependence from the very start.

It has been our experience that most persons with severe behavioral problems do not require one-to-one staffing, since most severe behavioral problems can be prevented and avoided from the start by analyzing factors such as (1) the events that lead up to self-injury or aggression; (2) how encouragement and redirection can be given to the person as these events begin to appear; (3) how to present tasks to the person so that successful task completion is facilitated; (4) the most supportive groupings of persons (e.g., not placing 2, 3, or more persons with aggressive or self-injurious behaviors in the same proximity); (5) how to initiate sessions with a high degree of assistance and reward for a few moments and then fade away such support as rapidly as possible; and (6) how to arrange the environment and tasks in such a way as to increase the probability that interdependent interactions will occur.

With a few persons, one-to-one staffing is necessary for the first several days to weeks, due to high-frequency, self-injurious or aggressive behaviors. Even this intensive staffing level should not need to occur for over 2 to 3 weeks. It should be noted also that most aggressive or self-injurious behaviors occur when requests are made of the person.

Finding the Proper Mix of Techniques. To find the right mix of gentle teaching techniques:

- Formulate a tentative plan focused on the prevention of the behavioral problem.
- Set up the environment and the task so as to prevent as many behavioral problems as possible.
- Spend an hour or two adapting this plan by interacting with the person on tasks.
- Use errorless learning techniques to ensure success.
- Remember that the goal is to teach the value and goodness of human presence, participation, and reward.
- Carry out this personalized plan in the normal flow of the day.
- Modify the plan from moment to moment. A gentle posture is at the core of gentle teaching. It requires ongoing reflection. Without this posture caregivers will not critically question their treatment or teaching strategies.

Through this process the caregiver quickly moves from superimposition of the self to a more spontaneous interactional equity. Initially caregivers need to prevent aggressive and self-injurious behaviors from occurring as much as possible, but when they do occur caregivers need focus on redirection, not punishment. In the actual teaching process caregivers should focus on offering as much assistance as may be necessary so that people can successfully complete tasks and thereby receive reward.

Lastly, caregivers need to focus on affection. It is crucial to understand that we are teachers of bonding and that working with people with severe behavioral needs can be done with gentleness if we assume that human interactions are the foundation of all learning. In assuming this, from the very first session caregivers will seek nonpunitive ways to interact with behaviorally complex mentally retarded people and will teach the value of human presence and interactions.

Third Dimension: Interactional Equity

The third dimension involves the implementation of a full-day, active program centered around teaching interactional equity. Caregivers have already worked with the person for a brief period of time. The first 5 to 10 days generally are very intense; this intensity lessens as interactional equity takes hold.

The person's day is structured into time modules that afford numerous opportunities for caregivers to teach equitable interactions. The modularized day follows the normal flow of the day, taking advantage of all of the normal activities, tasks, and interactions that make up the day. As people distance themselves via maladaptive behaviors, caregivers ignore those behaviors, simultaneously redirecting people to appropriate tasks and interactions so that the value of human presence and participation can be learned. It is necessary to recognize that, for many people, much assistance will initially have to be given so that they can succeed in the tasks, activities, and interactions. These extra supports should be rapidly withdrawn as gains are made, allowing more and more equity to emerge.

Too much assistance is as detrimental as too little. These decisions need to be made situationally, sometimes from moment to moment. For example, a classroom teacher working with a child with severe behavioral problems might work closely with the child to gain the beginning of interactional equity. There would likely be several one-to-one modules in the classroom during the first several days, as well as some programs conducted by the parents at home. However, any one-to-one attention, exaggerated rewards, management, and the like should be faded out as quickly as possible. A pragmatic objective in this phase is to expect that the child or adult should be focused on a task without the immediate presence of a caregiver for at least 30 to 60 minutes at a time, with only intermittent reward and redirection required. During this time the caregiver should only have to redirect and reward the person occasionally, depending on the ebb and flow of the behaviors. There should only be minimal, nondisruptive behaviors displayed as interactional equity is established.

Thus, to gain initial interactional equity in this stage:

- Teach intensely for 5 to 10 days.
- Set as your target on-task behaviors for 30 to 60 minutes at a time, with minimal redirection and reward.
- Make a point to move quickly from maximum assistance to minimal assistance and from one-to-one staffing to lesser staffing.

- Coordinate the day program with residential programs.
- Teach reward repeatedly.
- Be ready to provide occasional extra reward or redirection as necessary.

Fourth Dimension: The Catch-on Phase

By the end of phase 3, people should display minimal, preventable, and redirectable behavioral problems. However, this interactional equity will not necessarily have transferred to other peers or caregivers. In the fourth stage the focus is on the transfer of the interactional equity, developing, as it expands, bonding across persons and settings. In the previous phase a small number of caregivers will have gained interactional equity and will have bonded with the people they teach. In this phase those who have gained interactional equity need to teach all significant others to interact in the same manner. More important, in this phase people begin to reciprocate reward on their own, by bringing about self-initiated appropriate personal and social interactions. Those who have already gained interactional equity should:

- Coach co-caregivers so that all will be able to apply it in a very consistent way.
- Critique one another honestly, openly, and joyfully, as well as give one another support.
- Meet frequently (and informally) to modify the teaching plan.
- Ensure the people they teach of only the degree of support absolutely necessary to maintain and/or improve interactional equity. The more minimal the assistance is, the more maximal the interdependence. That is, if caregivers leave the interactional equity at the point where only a few caregivers know how to maintain it, they essentially leave people in a very dependent position. The goal is for caregivers to bond, to develop almost rhythmic lines of communication with those they help, placing social demands, backing off, and expecting self-initiated social interactions.

Fifth Dimension: Generalization Phase

As immediate caregivers gain interactional equity and as people adapt well within a structured program, the next step centers on "unstructuring" the day, integrating people into the mainstream of family and community life with as little supervision as necessary. The objective is to see to it that people can live in as full a manner as possible. Structure remains to the degree necessary, but people are given increasingly complex opportunities to interact personally and socially with others and vice versa.

Perhaps the greatest challenge in mental retardation is the goal of generalizing learning from familiar (bonded) persons and surroundings to unfamiliar ones. In this phase caregivers should begin to increase the number of complex and normalizing activities and interactions in which people participate, with decreasing assistance on the part of the caregivers. From the very start the plan has involved using normal tasks, activities, and interactions as the vehicles for teaching the value of human presence, participation, and reward. As interactional equity has been gained over time, these tasks, activities, and interactions should have been socially valuable and useful in relation to adaptive skills. Even though bonding has been the main goal and other learning has been secondary, adaptive learning will have been occurring, many skills will have been acquired, and many social opportunities will have been experienced. However, at this point the master plan should involve broadened experiences in relation to where people live, go to school, or work. Staffing ratios should be normalized, self-care skills should be performed at least with supervision, and the person should be experiencing multiple socialization opportunities.

Gentle Teaching: Techniques and Their Application

Gentle teaching techniques are based on the humanizing and liberating posture we have discussed in this chapter. This posture shapes the use of technology; without it, the techniques are meaningless. Each technique should be studied and used from the perspective of this value system.

The techniques focus on the prevention of aggressive, self-injurious, or avoidant behaviors whenever possible. They provide the means for gently and respectfully dealing with aggression or self-injury when these occur. They provide a mechanism for developing and actualizing a teaching structure through which caregivers can create multiple opportunities to teach the value of human presence and reward. These techniques are not a recipe for the teaching of bonding. They are techniques we have found useful in our daily work with persons with these needs. There is no uniform formula with which to determine which of these techniques to use or how to use them, since people bring their own histories, caregivers, developmental potentials, and personal learning characteristics. However, if caregivers develop highly personalized mixtures of these techniques for a particular person, they will likely have at least the framework for teaching bonding. Using the posture we have discussed, caregivers should be able to develop a much broader range of gentle teaching techniques.

Specific Techniques

We have adapted a number of techniques that enable caregivers to teach interactional equity and avoid the use of punishment. None of these techniques are new; rather, they are time-tested, common-sense approaches that have been used by other caregivers for years. What is new is that mixtures of these techniques enable us to avoid using punishment and, more important, teach interactional equity, which leads to bonding. The principle techniques are as follows.

1. *Ignore–Redirect–Reward* (Berkson & Mason, 1964; Favell, McGimsey, & Schell, 1982; Gaylord-Ross, Weeks, & Lipner, 1980; Horner, 1980; Mulick, Hoyt, Rojahn, & Schroeder, 1978). Do not speak to or look at people as they engage in maladaptive behaviors. Simultaneously, redirect them to a task in order to minimize any attention given to maladaptive behaviors and, more to the point, in order to maximize reward-teaching.

2. *Interrupt–Ignore–Redirect–Reward* (Azrin, Besalel, & Wisotzek, 1982; Azrin & Wesolowski, 1980; Peterson & Peterson, 1968; Tarpley & Schroeder, 1979). Intervene in the least conspicuous and most gentle manner possible to protect self, the person, or others. Interruption should be a last resort. Even then, it can and should be done in a gentle, respectful, and minimal manner. In our experience interruption too often occurs once people have been allowed to work themselves into a fury. It is preferable to avoid this. On the few occasions when it happens, caregivers need to protect themselves and others. Generally, this is accomplished by backing off. Occasionally it is necessary to protect the person physically, but in an ignoring and calming manner.

3. *Environmental management* (Boe, 1977; Hewitt, 1967; Murphy & Zahm, 1978; Rago, Parker, & Cleland, 1978). Set up the physical setting in such a way as to increase the chances of learning reward by preventing maladaptive behaviors from occurring through consideration of such factors as seating arrangements, safety precautions, the grouping of persons, and so forth.

4. *Stimulus control* (Bellamy, Horner, & Inman, 1979; Gold, 1972; Irvin, 1976; Panyan & Hall, 1978; Striefel & Wetherby, 1973; Striefel, Wetherby, & Karlan, 1978; Terrace, 1963; Walls, Zane, & Ellis, 1981). Set up the tasks while people watch, so as to insure on-task success through the consideration of factors such as the arrangement of the tasks, control of materials, concreteness of the task, teaching methods, and so forth.

5. *Errorless learning* (Becker & Engelmann, 1976; Coon, Vogelsberg, & Williams, 1981; Cronin & Cuvo, 1979; Foxx & Azrin, 1973; Lambert, 1975; Terrace, 1966; Touchette, 1968; Walls, Zane, & Thvedt, 1980; Weeks & Gaylord-Ross, 1981). Break learning skills into a sequence that facilitates their acquisition, and provide adequate assistance in order to avoid errors. In this way, structured tasks can serve as vehicles for teaching reward throughout the day.

6. *Shaping and fading* (Becker & Englemann, 1978; Horner, Colvin, & Bellamy, 1981; Horner & McDonald, 1981; Sprague & Horner, 1981; Stokes

& Baer, 1977). Use the caregiver's initial intense presence, necessary assistance, and reward-teaching as ways of insuring, as much as possible, the person's on-task attention. Remove the external assistance and reward as rapidly as possible so that the person will remain on-task and be able to receive sufficient regard.

7. *Teaching quietly* (Gold, 1972). Initially use minimal verbal instructions, in order to maximize the power of verbal reward, and gradually use more language as the reward-learning takes hold. This requires using nonverbal means of communication (e.g., gestures or signs) along with teaching quietly to facilitate correct responses and to maximize the power of verbal reward.

8. *Assistance* (Brown, Holvoet, Guess, & Mulligan, 1980; Heads, 1978; Kazdin, 1980). Initiate learning with a degree of assistance high enough to ensure success. Systematically and rapidly decrease the degree of assistance. Be ready at any given time to offer higher degrees of assistance for purposes of redirection or reward-teaching.

9. *Reward envelope* (Koegel & Williams, 1980; Saunders & Sailor, 1979; Williams, Koegel, & Egel, 1981). Initiate learning, with a degree of reward-teaching sufficient to ensure that the person learns the power of verbal and tactile praise. Systematically and rapidly decrease the degree of reward. Be ready at any given time to offer higher degrees of reward for the purpose of redirection.

Making Decisions in Gentle Teaching

At any given moment caregivers need to know how much assistance to provide, what combination of techniques to use, and how much interruption or ignoring should occur. Too much assistance can lead to learned helplessness, too little to constant failure. Too much interruption can lead to punishment, too little to harm. Too much ignoring can lead to missed opportunities to redirect, too little to frustration.

A key factor in decision making is to define the seriousness of various inappropriate behaviors at various times and then to develop general intervention strategies for those moments in an ebb-and-flow fashion, ever ready to give more support when necessary and sensitive to the moment when it should be withdrawn. There are 3 broad categories of inappropriate behaviors: distractive, disruptive, and destructive. In this section we will examine each of these and offer intervention strategies.

Distracting Behaviors. These are minimal off-task behaviors that occur during the teaching–learning process. They often occur during structured activities, especially when interactional control and bonding have not yet been established. The first decision that must be made when inappropriate behaviors occur is whether teaching can continue in spite of such behaviors.

That is, are the behaviors simply distracting, or do they interfere with learning? Often behaviors such as rocking in one's seat, talking, or inappropriate vocalizations are not distracting enough to detract from teaching. Such behaviors can simply be ignored while easily redirecting the person back to teaching activities with a simple gestural cue. Nonattending behaviors such as not looking at task materials, talking to others, and so forth also often fit the category of distracting behaviors and are best ignored as long as on-task behaviors continue. This is especially true when caregivers are teaching tasks or interactions where eye contact may be helpful but is not essential to participation or success on the task. Again, a simple verbal or gestural cue is enough to redirect the person to the task at hand. Caregivers need to give persons with distracting behaviors the freedom to engage in such behaviors as long as they do not interfere with learning or social interactions.

Disruptive Behaviors. Many behaviors encountered may accurately be considered disruptive to learning in the sense that they temporarily prevent the continuation of the teaching process. In these circumstances several strategies are available. The first strategy is to ignore the behavior and redirect the person back to the task. It is important to note that the meaning of *ignore* is somewhat different in this situation than in the previous strategy of continuing teaching with a simple verbal or gestural redirection. Caregivers cannot "ignore" such behaviors as attempting or actually hitting, kicking, biting, or scratching, in the sense of allowing them to continue. These behaviors should be ignored in the sense that they should not be consequated per se. That is, we do not recommend such typical interventions as verbal reprimand, restitution, physical restraint, overcorrection, and time-out. Because the essence of gentle teaching is to teach the power of human presence, participation, and reward, it is counterproductive to use any consequences, besides actions to protect self or others, that might reinforce the maladaptive behaviors or reinforce any human distancing. While some precautionary or protective measures such as blocking a hit or avoiding a scratch or a kick might occasionally be necessary, the basic strategy is to redirect people back to their tasks. This can be accomplished by physically assisting them back to the task, physically or verbally prompting them on the next step of the task, providing verbal instructions, modeling the appropriate response, or a combination of these techniques.

In some cases it is not possible to redirect an individual back to the task immediately. A flurry or cluster of behaviors may occur that prevent return to the task, such as teaching materials being thrown or scattered, or scratching or hitting occurring each time the person is approached with materials. In these instances it is often appropriate to avoid immediate redirection and simply wait until the disruptive behaviors have subsided to some extent. Again, these behaviors are ignored in the sense of protecting self or others and not consequating. Nothing is said in the way of a reprimand. The basis of this strategy is to shape the return to task involvement by gradually rewarding successive approximations to appropriate on-task behavior. Typically this involves periods of attending/rewarding alternated with periods of ignoring. Calm, nonaggressive, cooperative behaviors are usually rewarded first, even if they do not result in on-task behavior. It is often just an approximation of cooperation. The cooperation behavior leads to task completion (or substep completion). The key is to be able to teach reward for cooperative behavior. Indeed, caregivers need to understand that at this point rewarding cooperative participation (e.g., the person allowing the caregiver to give hand-over-hand assistance) is more important than task completion. Caregivers need to seek out any behavior for reward that is incompatible with the disruptive behavior.

Another strategy that can be employed involves a variety of tactics that modify the environment in an attempt to increase the probability of successful responses. While this strategy can be effective in managing disruptive behaviors during a particular teaching session, its primary focus is preventive and it therefore can be contained through each additional training session with the person. This involves adjusting either the teaching method or the environment, to increase the likelihood of success.

Destructive Behaviors. In some cases these strategies are not successful in managing disruptive behaviors and another decision must be made. This involves an assessment of the "direction" of the person's behavior; that is, is the behavior escalating to an out-of-control phase that could result in behaviors that could be harmful to self or others? Has it already escalated to that point?

There are various phases in the evolution of assaultive or explosive behavioral episodes, starting with a triggering phase during which caregivers can see precursors to an eventual crisis. This is followed by a crisis phase and a calming phase. In general the previous strategies constitute an attempt to defuse this cycle in the initial, precursor phase. Caregivers must immediately decide whether the strategies employed were successful in defusing or avoiding a behavioral crisis or whether the behaviors are going out of control. If the latter situation occurs, the most appropriate decision often is to interrupt activities.

When the decision to interrupt is made, there are 3 strategies that can be employed, again individually or in various combinations. The first is a prevention strategy. While the behaviors may be in the escalation phase, sometimes the interruption of the demands of the teaching situation are sufficient to defuse the escalation process. Often simply taking a break from teaching is sufficient to avoid a major behavioral crisis. With some persons the verbal cue that a break will occur can have a similar effect. This can often be done by asking and helping the person complete one more task so that the caregiver can terminate the task while the person is still in control.

Engaging in a nondemanding activity such as taking a walk can help avoid or decrease an aggressive outburst. This is essentially a soothing and calming redirection. In essence this time (as brief as possible) serves as an exaggerated form of redirection by taking people, either physically or psychologically, out of an overly stimulating situation. As people calm down, caregivers should give concrete, goal-oriented redirection so that people return knowing what the expectations are. Caregivers should not fear that they are giving in or are being manipulated by people. By the time people are approaching a behavioral outburst, they are virtually irrational, knowing neither the nature nor the consequences or their behaviors. It is much more preferable to focus on decelerating the outbursts and redirecting people, rather than focus on punishment or retribution.

In some cases the escalation phase progresses to the crisis or "outburst" phase, and in these situations the only strategy is often one of protecting the person, others, and (least important) property. Separating the person from others, either by moving to another room or by maintaining separation with objects (tables, chairs, etc.) can help protect others. Removing dangerous or valued objects from the area is another example of a protective strategy. In rare instances this involves physically restraining the person by using an open-handed, nonthreatening approach. Calming in a nonpunitive manner is the goal. This should be done in as nonreinforcing a manner as possible and for as short a time as possible. Although possibly reinforcing, these strategies are done only to protect the person and others from harm. Any strategies that focus on force should be avoided.

A third strategy that is often effective involves a calming approach. Talking in a soothing, reassuring voice can help de-escalate an outburst as it is about to or is occurring, and deep breaths exhaled can have a relaxing effect that also helps avoid crisis situations. These techniques are helpful in the recovery phase if a crisis cannot be avoided.

The major purpose of this decision-making process is to allow the caregiver to decide upon several strategic paths that all have the objective of engaging the learner in an interactionally controlled instructional activity. The goal in a sense is to come full circle, through several teaching strategies, to manageable, nondestructive learning situations. The basic model for this process is a problem-solving approach of identifying, selecting, and implementing strategies; evaluating the results; and modifying strategies accordingly. While the strategies identified here are valuable, the importance of the feedback loop cannot be overemphasized. Without the fine tuning that occurs with the observation of the effects of a particular strategy, the strategies described here are not likely to be successful. It is the exponential effects of this feedback process (both minute-by-minute and day-by-day) that increase interactional equity and allow for success in dealing with the most challenging individuals.

Gentle Responses to Common Questions

It is impossible to cover all of the questions and situations that arise when attempting to gain interactional equity and teach bonding. People vary; circumstances vary. However, some common questions and general strategies can shed light on the decision-making process in gentle teaching.

We have found that direct-care providers want to treat those with whom they work with gentleness and respect but are often thwarted in this by policies that encourage punishment. Once asked to reflect on a posture that encourages bonding and solidarity, we have found that direct-care providers accept this challenge. The issue then becomes one of applying gentle teaching techniques in day-to-day practice.

The following pages contain the questions we have received most frequently from direct-care workers, as well as our responses. Bear in mind that these are general rules of thumb.

If the person tries to hit you:

Protect yourself as nonintrusively as you can, for example, by blocking the hit with your arm.
Generally say nothing about the hit.
Firmly, calmly, and fairly redirect the person to the task.
Help the person return to the task with cues, physical assistance, and the like.
Give concrete goals to the person.
Give strong reward.

If the person who is in a fury is beyond redirection at the moment:

If possible, in a firm but fair manner, try to redirect the person.
If redirection fails, protect yourself, the person, and others through environmental or physical control until the fury subsides.
During the fury's peak, do not chastise the person; remain calm and soothing.
As the fury subsides, gently redirect the person to a task or activity.
As the person redirects, focus on gaining interactional control.
Henceforth focus on prevention by identifying the precursors that led up to the fury.
In the future redirect the person as these precursors begin to appear.

If the person is working up to a fury:

Identify the behavioral and physiological signs (precursors) that lead up to a possible fury and look for preventive measures.
Give concrete instructions to the person in the form of a goal: "Let's do one more."
Remove unnecessary stimuli from around the person.
Help the person meet the goal through verbal or physical assistance.
Take a short break with the person.
As the signs subside, gently redirect the person back to the task.

If the person is self-stimulating:

If it does not interfere with learning, ignore it.
If it interferes, find a way to prevent it or block it.
If it involves hand- or arm-waving, use tasks that require the use of both hands.
Use tasks that require a relatively fast pace.
If the person rocks, arrange the seating or table position to reduce it.
Perform the task standing up if necessary.

If you are afraid to have the person go to school, work, or live with others:

Teach sharing to all who live, work, or go to school together.

If the person refuses to participate:

Make sure there is a structured flow to the day.
Make sure caregivers are not reinforcing such behavior.
When a refusal is made, try to take the person gently by the hand or arm.
If the person is cooperative, proceed with the person, reinforcing the cooperative behavior.

If the person still refuses to participate:

Give the instructions again.
Make the task easy and reward any approximation toward participation.
Do not get into a "tug-of-war."
Remain near the person, giving no eye contact or verbal input other than periodic gestural or verbal redirection.
Use a visual cue representative of the task or activity.
Be prepared to do this for 30 to 60 minutes.
Make sure no one else interferes.

If the person runs from the classroom, workshop, or home, into a dangerous situation:

Quickly catch up with the person in as nonconspicuous a manner as possible.
Attempt to block further progress unless this were to result in a physical confrontation.
Redirect—"Let's sit down," "Let's go for a walk," "Let's look at . . .."
If necessary, hold the person by the hand or wrist in a reassuring manner.
As soon as the fury subsides, return to the appropriate place.
Establish a concrete goal, for example, "I will help you do five, then we will take a break."

If the person throws objects:

Prevent these actions through environmental and stimulus control in the future.
Proceed with the task, ignoring the thrown objects on the floor.
Don't make the person pick them up.
Have enough materials available to you so you can proceed.
Avoid using such punishing consequences as overcorrection and retribution.

If the person ruminates food:

Keep a towel handy.
Ignore it, while redirecting the person to the task.
Clean yourself or the person as necessary.
Watch your seating arrangement to avoid being spat on.
Emphasize tactile praise.

If the person tries to eat dangerous objects (engages in pica):

Be cautious, through stimulus control.
Present tasks initially shadowing the person's hand movements, to block the possibility of objects being put in the mouth.
Emphasize tactile praise.
Use stimulus control and shadowing techniques.
Fade these as interactional control emerges.

If the person bangs his or her head:

If previously used, eliminate helmets, masks, straitjackets, and so forth.
Focus on intensive developmental programing.

Position yourself and the person to prevent head-banging, keeping away from walls, table tops, arms of chairs, and the like, if necessary.
Work quickly for interactional control.
Gradually lessen the environmental control.

If the person punches his or her face:

Initially sit face-to-face with the person, with their legs between you, while teaching a task.
Carry out programs in this position.
If possible, gently redirect the person physically to the task as she or he attempts to strike a blow.
If this causes a tug-of-war, shadow the blows, allowing the person to strike your hand.
Say nothing, while gesturally redirecting.

If a person wets or soils his or her pants:

Always have an extra set of clothing available.
Accompany the person to the bathroom.
Assist him or her in changing clothes as necessary, in silence.
Redirect to the task.
If necessary, develop a daily toileting schedule to prevent wetting or soiling in the future.

If the person talks incessantly or inappropriately or screams:

Ignore it; say nothing; do not look at the person.
Redirect the person to the task, verbally or gesturally.
Indicate when you will speak with the person; at that time, direct the conversation.
Reward the person for appropriate conversation.

If the person talks disassociatedly but at the appropriate time and place:

Politely break into the conversation.
Indicate that you will not talk on the disassociated topic.
Reinforce conversation that is appropriate to the time and place.
Make sure others are consistent in this approach, for it is easy to reinforce "funny" conversation.

If the person is depressed—withdrawn, slovenly, possibly regressing, crying, or nonverbal:

Be especially gentle.
Become the person's emotional structure, scheduling the day; setting up concrete, attainable goals; and so on.
Use verbal and tactile rewards.
If necessary, use exaggerated verbal and tactile rewards.
Use necessary physical assistance as a way of soothing and reassuring the person.
Avoid delving into the causes of the depression with the person.
Examine causes with significant others.
Ensure supportive stability in the person's life.

If the person is "high functioning," that is, functionally capable of independence but a danger to self and others:

Take a firm posture.
Structure the day, setting rules and limits.
Give adequate supervision.
Expect 3 to 5 years of such structure and supervision.

If you think your work is in the poorest setting in the world and that gentle teaching is impossible:

Examine the needs of all the persons whom you serve.
Prioritize the individuals according to who more readily needs interactional control.
Provide whatever number of minutes per day of gentle teaching on the living unit that you can.
Make sure the person is in a day program if possible.
Teach interactional control, one person at a time.
Envision your most difficult person bonding.
Over time, publicly advocate for gentle teaching.
Organize residents, other caregivers, and parents to bring about social change.

If the interdisciplinary team wants to use punishment:

Come prepared with data and videotapes to show that gentle teaching works.
Focus on teaching reward through a structured day.
If necessary, refuse to sign the program plan; include a note stating why.
Persevere.
If punishment used is particularly torturous, work with the local parent association to make the torture public.

If you are responsible for a person in restraint:

Untie him or her.
Spend as much time as possible for 5 to 10 days working with the person.
Be concrete and soothing.
Do your work with this person at the same time as you work with others.

If the person is on psychoactive medications:

With the supervision of a psychiatrist, see what the person is like when medication free.
Concurrently engage the person in an active developmental program to determine the need for drugs.
Use drugs only to make the person initially more available and responsive to learning.
If drugs are used, reduce the dosage as the person gains interactional control.
Eliminate the drug whenever possible, as the person gains "redirectable" behavior.

If nothing has worked:

Examine the tasks in which the person is involved and question their functionality and meaningfulness.
Question whether you might be inadvertently reinforcing inappropriate behaviors with attention or by withdrawing demands.
Examine the "power" of your teaching methods, especially your degree of assistance for successful task completion.

If you are short-staffed:

Start with less complex tasks, to lessen instructional time.
Provide frequent praise to all persons.
Set up groupings that are positively self-reinforcing.
Use modeling of appropriate behaviors if persons go off task.

If one person fights with another:

Give attention and praise to the person attacked.
Ignore the attacker.
Use your body or furniture to protect others.
Separate and redirect the attacker.
Avoid future attacks through better environmental control.

If the person fails to respond at all or responds only minimally:

Give physical assistance; if necessary, work hand-over-hand.
Simplify the task to ensure success.
Use prosthetic devices to help the person.
Seek tasks that are within the person's ability.
Gradually fade assistance.

If the person lies on the floor:

Verbally or gesturally redirect the person to a seat.
Say nothing and give no eye contact.
If the person does not return to a seat, give a physical prompt.
Avoid a tug-of-war.
If necessary, work on the floor until the person becomes responsive.
When on-task, redirect the person to a seat.

If the person interacts with you age-inappropriately or sexually inappropriately:

If a child, expect behaviors of a child.
If an adult, expect behaviors of an adult.
Model appropriate behaviors: "Give me a handshake (instead of a hug). . . ."
Redirect the person to a task.
Consider ongoing teaching of appropriate behaviors in the personalized plan.

If the person does not display cooperative behaviors:

Subdivide tasks and activities so that sharing has to occur.
Orchestrate two or more persons so that sharing behaviors can be rewarded.

If the person continuously jumps out of his or her seat:

Analyze seating placement.
Place the person in the least distractable position.
Heavily reward on-task behaviors.
If necessary, control the chair and table.

If you fear the client:

If you think the client's anger stems from on-task frustration, reanalyze the task, set concrete goals, and give mini-breaks as a reward.

Recognize signs leading up to anger.
Take clear, calm control at this time: "Let's do one more."
Examine whether the person is overstimulated or understimulated.
If necessary, remove a sufficient amount of stimuli or increase the challenge of the task.

If fellow staff members do not know how to carry out this approach:

Spend time working "hands-on" with the person; have staff watch and ask questions.
Coach staff in working with the person.
If necessary, seek outside help.

If the person is disruptive in a classroom or workshop:

Look for prevention techniques for the future. Notice where the person sits and with whom, the types of work contracts or materials used, and so forth.
At the moment of disruption, apply the range of techniques described previously.
Interrupt and protect when necessary.

If the person is not learning the task:

Reanalyze the task.
Try to simplify the task.
Use a layout board to sequence the tasks in steps.
Provide initial assistance.
Focus on reward as the primary teaching/training goal in the first phase of learning.
See if the task or work itself might be boring.

If the person gets into fights:

Structure the person's day.
Avoid sudden (and confusing) changes in the routine of the day.
Focus on group work, to teach socialization as well as educational or work skills.

If there is no way to structure the group home:

Look at the natural flow of the day.
Understand that much of the home's structure can be found in ordinary transactions.

Focus first on self-care and daily living skills.
Determine how much teaching or supervision you have to do.
Recognize these ordinary activities as potential vehicles for teaching reward.

If this is not enough:

Invent "sit-down" programs that give, especially in the beginning, more structure and insight into the person's needs, fast run-around time in terms of interactional control, and some carry-over in other areas of living.
Use the insight and practical techniques that you learn in these programs as the basis for your techniques in less structured times and settings.

If you feel that the person will be too disruptive in a group home:

Place the person with a compatible mix of other persons.
Avoid placing persons with similar needs in the same setting.
Mix and match people's needs and strengths.

"What can you try if . . ." can be posed in hundreds of ways with thousands of responses. We have given only a few questions with general responses. What caregivers need to remember is that creativity is the key in any challenging situation.

Conclusion

Many issues that impact significantly on the well-being of persons with severe behavioral problems have little to do with clinical treatment or teaching challenges, but rather the creation of new structures to meet the needs of these persons. We refer to structures in the sense of new, creative approaches toward using current programs (residential, educational, and vocational) to serve as the environments within which bonding can occur. It is doubtful that caregivers can gain interactional equity or bonding in settings in which there is little hope; poor staffing ratios that allow only for custodial, rather than developmental, care; the widespread use of punishment; the use of medications as chemical straitjackets; and so on. Issues such as the number of people who live together, their range of needs, and their involvement in active day programs all must be considered.

Many communities around the world are not yet able to offer respectful residential, educational, and vocational alternatives to mentally retarded persons with behavioral challenges. This can change. It must change if persons with severe behavioral disorders are to be served with dignity and respect in the mainstream of family and community life.

Persons with these needs are too often locked in the back wards of our world's institutions or are hidden away in closed community settings. There is no need for punishment, nor the seclusion of persons with these needs. Community-based programs need to open their classrooms, their group homes, and their workshops to these persons. These are the settings in which personal change and, more important, social change can come about as we teach all people to learn to live together.

Persons with severe behavioral problems tend to be the last to be served, the least likely to be served, and the most subject to abuse. It is our challenge to break this vicious cycle of despair. Besides the clinical issues that we have pointed out thus far, caregivers need to be advocates of social change. Many community programs still refuse to serve persons with severe behavioral problems. Children are kicked out of public-school classrooms in spite of national mandates written into law. Adults are often refused entry to workshops because they will be "too disruptive" or harm staff, themselves, or others. Many agencies say that they are not adequately prepared to serve persons with these needs or that another agency should serve them. The end result is that mentally retarded people with behavioral problems are not served. Their behaviors worsen. Punishment becomes the rule.

Gentle teaching is not simply "being nice" to persons with severe behavioral problems. It is a posture that refuses to punish and focuses instead on teaching the value of reward, human presence, and participation. It requires not only intense, personal work and effort but also social change. This then is our challenge—to support persons with severe behavioral challenges into the mainstream of family and community life; to base this support on a gentle and respectful posture; and to create an atmosphere in which we are teachers of bonding rather than administrators of punishment. Thereby, we will all be liberated.

References

Azrin, N. H., Besalel, V. A., & Wisotzek, I. E. (1982). Treatment of self-injury by a reinforcement plus interruption procedure. *Analysis and Intervention in Development Disabilities, 2*(1), 105–113.

Azrin, N. H., Gottlieb, L., Hughart, L., Wesolowski, M. D., & Rahan, T. (1975). Eliminating self-injurious behavior by educative procedures. *Behavior Research and Therapy, 13,* 101–111.

Azrin, N. H., Sneed, T. J., & Foxx, R. M. (1973). Dry bed: A rapid method of eliminating bedwetting (enuresis) of the retarded. *Behavior Research and Therapy, 11,* 427–434.

Azrin, N. H., & Wesolowski, M. D. (1975). Eliminating habitual vomiting in a retarded adult by positive practice and self-correction. *Journal of Behavior Therapy and Experimental Psychiatry, 6,* 145–148.

Azrin, N. H., & Wesolowski, M. D. (1980). A reinforcement plus interruption method of eliminating behavioral stereotypy of profoundly retarded persons. *Behavior Research and Therapy, 18,* 113–119.

Barkley, R., & Zupnick, S. (1976). Reduction of stereotyped body contortions using physical restraint and DRO. *Journal of Behavior Therapy and Experimental Psychiatry, 7,* 167–170.

Barrett, B. H. (1977). Behavior analysis. In J. Wortis (Ed.), *Mental retardation and development disabilities: An annual review* (Vol. 9). New York: Brunner/Mazel.

Bean, A. W., & Roberts, M. W. (1981). The effect of timeout release contingencies on changes in child noncompliance. *Journal of Abnormal Child Psychology, 9,* 95–105.

Becker, W. C., & Engelmann, S. (1976). *Analysis of achievement data on six cohorts in the Direct Instruction Follow Through model.* Technical Report 76-1. Eugene, OR: University of Oregon.

Becker, W. C., & Engelmann, S. (1978). Systems for basic instruction: Theory and applications. In A. Catania & T. Brigham (Eds.), *Handbook of applied behavior analysis: Social and instructional processes.* New York: Irvington Publishers.

Bellamy, G. T., Horner, R. H., & Inman, D. P. (1979). *Vocational habilitation of severely retarded adults: A direct service technology.* Baltimore, MD: University Park Press.

Berkson, G., & Mason, W. A. (1964). Stereotyped movements of mental defectives: IV. The effect of toys and the character of the acts. *American Journal of Mental Deficiency, 68,* 511–524.

Bijou, S. W., & Dunitz-Johnson, E. (1981). Interbehavior analysis of developmental retardation. *The Psychology Record, 31,* 305–329.

Boe, R. B. (1977). Economical procedures for the reduction of aggressions in a residential setting. *Mental Retardation, 15*(5), 25–28.

Bostow, D. E., & Bailey, J. B. (1969). Modification of severe disruptive and aggressive behavior using brief time-out and reinforcement procedures. *Journal of Applied Behavior Analysis, 2,* 31–37.

Bowlby, J. (1967). *Attachment and loss* (Vol. 1). New York: Basic Books.

Bowlby, J. (1974). *Attachment and loss* (Vol. 2). New York: Basic Books.

Bowlby, J. (1980). *Attachment and loss* (Vol. 3). New York: Basic Books.

Brown, F., Holvoet, J., Guess, D., & Mulligan, M. (1980). The individualized curriculum sequencing model (III): Small group instruction. *Journal of the Association for the Severely Handicapped, 5,* 352–367.

Calhoun, K. D., & Matherne, P. (1975). The effects of varying schedules of time-out on aggressive behavior of a retarded girl. *Journal of Behavior Therapy and Experimental Psychiatry, 6,* 139–143.

Combs, M., & Slaby, D. A. (1977). Social skills training with children. In B. B. Lahey & A. E. Kazdin (Eds.), *Advances in clinical child psychology* (Vol. 1). New York: Plenum Press.

Coon, M. E., Vogelsberg, R. T., & Williams, W. (1981). Effects of classroom public transportation instruction on generalization to the natural environment. *Journal of the Association for the Severely Handicapped, 6,* 46–53.

Corbett, J. (1975). Aversion for the treatment of self-injurious behavior. *Journal of Mental Deficiency Research, 19*, 79–95.

Corte, H. E., Wolfe, M. M., & Locke, B. J. (1971). A comparison of procedures for eliminating self-injurious behavior of retarded adolescents. *Journal of Applied Behavior Analysis, 4*, 201–213.

Cronin, K. A., & Cuvo, A. J. (1979). Teaching mending skills to mentally retarded adolescents. *Journal of Applied Behavior Analysis, 4*(12), 401–406.

DeCatanzaro, D., & Baldwin, G. (1978). Effective treatment of self-injurious behavior through a forced arm exercise. *American Journal of Mental Deficiency, 82*, 433–439.

Duker, P. C., & Seys, D. M. (1977). Elimination of vomiting in a retarded female using restitutional overcorrection. *Behavior Therapy, 8*, 255–257.

Epstein, L. H., Doke, L. A., Sajwaj, T. E., Sorrell, S., & Rimmer, B. (1974). Generality and side effects of overcorrection. *Journal of Applied Behavior Analysis, 7*, 385–390.

Favell, J. E., McGimsey, J. F., & Schell, R. M. (1982). Treatment of self-injury by providing alternate sensory activities. *Analysis and Intervention in Developmental Disabilities, 2*(1), 83–104.

Foxx, R. M. (1976). The use of overcorrection to eliminate the public disrobing (stripping) of retarded women. *Behavior Research and Therapy, 14*, 53–61.

Foxx, R. M., & Azrin, N. H. (1972). Restitution: A method of eliminating aggressive disruptive behavior of retarded and brain-damanged patients. *Behavior Research and Therapy, 10*, 15–27.

Foxx, R. M., & Azrin, N. H. (1973). The elimination of autistic self-stimulatory behavior by overcorrection. *Journal of Applied Behavior Analysis, 6*, 1–14.

Foxx, C. L., Foxx, R. M., Jones, J. R., & Kiely, D. (1980). Twenty-four hour social isolation. *Behavior Modification, 4*, 130–144.

Foxx, R. M., & Shapiro, S. T. (1978). The timeout ribbon: A nonexclusionary timeout procedure. *Journal of Applied Behavior Analysis, 11*, 125–136.

Gaylord-Ross, R. J., Weeks, M., & Lipner, C. (1980). An analysis of antecedent, response and consequent events in the treatment of self-injurious behavior. *Education and Training of the Mentally Retarded, 15*(1), 35–42.

Gold, M. W. (1972). Stimulus factors in skill training of the retarded on a complex assembly task: Acquisition, transfer and retention. *American Journal of Mental Deficiency, 76*, 517–526.

Gross, A. M., Berler, E. S., & Drabman, R. S. (1982). Reduction of aggressive behavior in a retarded boy using a water squirt. *Journal of Behavior Therapy and Experimental Psychiatry, 13*, 95–98.

Harris, S. L., & Ersner-Hershfield, R. (1978). Behavioral suppression of seriously disruptive behavior in psychotic and retarded patients: A review of punishment and its alternative. *Psychological Bulletin, 85*, 1352–1375.

Heads, T. B. (1978). Ethical and legal considerations in behavior therapy. In D. Marholin II (Ed.), *Child behavior therapy*. New York: Gardner Press.

Hewitt, F. M. (1967). Educational engineering with emotionally disturbed children. *Exceptional Children, 33*, 459–467.

Hopkins, B. L. (1968). Effects of candy and social reinforcement, instructions, and reinforcement schedule learning on the modification and maintenance of smiling. *Journal of Applied Behavior Analysis, 1*, 121–129.

Hops, H. (1982). Social skills training for socially withdrawn/isolated children. In P. Karoly & J. Steffen (Eds.), *Enhancing children's competencies*. Lexington, MA: Lexington Books.
Horner, R. D. (1980). The effects of an environment "enrichment" program on the behavior of institutionalized profoundly retarded children. *Journal of Applied Behavior Analysis, 13*(3), 473–491.
Horner, R. D., & Barton, E. S. (1980). Operant techniques in the analysis and modification of self-injurious behavior: A review. *Behavioral Research of Severe Developmental Disorders, 1*, 61–91.
Horner, R. H., Colvin, G. T., & Bellamy, G. T. (1981). *Responding in the presence of non-trained stimuli: An applied analysis of "generalization."* Unpublished manuscript. Eugene, OR: University of Oregon, Division of Special Education and Rehabilitation.
Horner, R. H., & McDonald, R. S. (1981). A comparison of single instance training versus general case training on the acquisition of a generalized vocational skill by four severely handicapped high school students. Unpublished manuscript. Eugene, OR: University of Oregon, Division of Special Education and Rehabilitation.
Irvin, L. K. (1976). General utility of easy-to-hard discrimination training procedures with the severely retarded. *Education and Training of the Mentally Retarded, 11*, 247–250.
Jansen, P. E. (1980). Basic principles of behavior therapy with retarded persons. In L. S. Szymanski & P. E. Tanguay (Eds.), *Emotional disorders of mentally retarded persons*. Baltimore: University Park Press.
Kazdin, A. E. (1980). Acceptability of alternative treatment for deviant child behavior. *Journal of Applied Behavior Analysis, 13*, 259–273.
Koegel, R. L., & Williams, J. A. (1980). Direct vs indirect response-reinforcer relationships in teaching autistic children. *Journal of Abnormal Child Psychology, 8*, 537–547.
Lambert, J. L. (1975). Extinction by retarded children following discrimination learning with and without errors. *American Journal of Mental Deficiency, 80*, 286–291.
Larsen, J. M. (1975). Effects of increased teacher support on young children's learning. *Child Development, 46*, 631–637.
Lichstein, K., & Schreibman, L. (1976). Employing electric shock with autistic children: A review of the side effects. *Journal of Autism and Childhood Schizophrenia, 1*, 163–173.
Lovaas, O. I., Schaeffer, B., & Simmons, J. Q. (1965). Building social behaviors in autistic children by use of electric shock. *Journal of Experimental Research in Personality, 1*, 99–109.
Lovaas, O. I., & Simmons, J. Q. (1969). Manipulation of self-destruction in three retarded children. *Journal of Applied Behavior Analysis, 2*, 143–157.
Lutzker, J. R. (1978). Reducing self-injurious behavior by facial screening. *American Journal of Mental Deficiency, 82*, 510–513.
Mulick, J., Hoyt, R., Rojahn, J., & Schroeder, S. (1978). Reduction of a "nervous habit" in a profoundly retarded youth by increasing toy play: A case study. *Journal of Behavior Therapy and Experimental Psychiatry, 9*, 381–385.
Murphy, M. J., & Zahm, D. (1978). Effects of improved physical and social

environment on self-help and problem behaviors of institutionalized retarded males. *Behavior Modification, 2,* 193–210.

Panyan, M., & Hall, R. V. (1978). Effects of serial versus concurrent task sequencing on acquisition, maintenance and generalization. *Journal of Applied Behavior Analysis, 11,* 67–74.

Peterson, R. F., & Peterson, L. R. (1968). The use of positive reinforcement in the control of self-destructive behavior in a retarded boy. *Journal of Experimental Child Psychology, 6,* 351–360.

Prochaska, J., Smith, N., Marzilli, R., Colby, J., & Donovan, W. (1974). Remote control aversive stimulation in the treatment of head banging in a retarded child. *Journal of Behavior Therapy and Experimental Psychiatry, 5,* 285–289.

Rago, W. V., Parker, R. M., & Cleland, C. C. (1978). Effect of increased space on the social behavior of institutionalized profoundly retarded male adults. *American Journal of Mental Deficiency, 82,* 554–558.

Rusch, F., Close, D., Hops, H., & Agosta, J. (1970). Overcorrection: Generalization and maintenance. *Journal of Applied Behavior Analysis, 9,* 498.

Saunders, R., & Sailor, N. (1979). A comparison of three strategies of reinforcement on two-choice language problems with severely retarded children. *AAESPH Review, 4,* 323–333.

Sherman, J. S., Swinson, R. P., & Lorimer, W. P. (1984). On the importance of reliable equipment in the shock punishment of self-injurious behavior. *Analysis and Intervention in Developmental Disabilities, 4,* 81–84.

Singh, N. N. (1977). Behavioral control of self-injury in the mentally retarded. *New Zealand Psychologist, 6,* 52–58.

Singh, N. N., Dawson, M. J., & Manning, P. J. (1981). The effects of physical restraint on self-injurious behavior. *Journal of Mental Deficiency Research, 25,* 207–216.

Solnick, J. V., Rincover, A., & Peterson, C. R. (1977). Some determinants of the reinforcing and punishing effects of timeout. *Journal of Applied Behavior Analysis, 10,* 415–424.

Sprague, J. R., & Horner, R. H. (1981). Experimental analysis of generalized vending machine use with severely handicapped students. Unpublished manuscript. Eugene, OR: University of Oregon, Division of Special Education and Rehabilitation.

Stokes, T. F., & Baer, D. M. (1977). An implicit technology of generalization. *Journal of Applied Behavior Analysis, 10,* 349–367.

Strain, P., Shores, R., & Kerr, M. (1976). An experimental analysis of "spillover" effects on the social interaction of behaviorally handicapped preschool children. *Journal of Applied Behavior Analysis, 9,* 31–40.

Strain, P., & Wiegerink, R. (1976). The effects of sociodramatic activities on social interaction among behaviorally disordered preschool children. *The Journal of Special Education, 10,* 71–75.

Striefel, S., & Wetherby, B. (1973). Instruction-following behavior of a retarded child and its controlling stimuli. *Journal of Applied Behavior Analysis, 6,* 663–670.

Striefel, S., Wetherby, B., & Karlan, G. (1978). Developing generalized instruction-following behavior in the severely retarded. In C. Meyers (Ed.), *Quality of life in severely and profoundly mentally retarded people: Research foundations for improvement.* Washington, DC: American Association on Mental Deficiency.

Tanner, B., & Zeiler, M. (1975). Punishment of self-injurious behavior using aromatic ammonia as the aversive stimulus. *Journal of Applied Behavior Analysis, 8,* 53–57.
Tarpley, H. D., & Schroeder, S. R. (1979). Comparison of DRO and DRI on rate of suppression of self-injurious behavior. *American Journal of Mental Deficiency, 84,* 188–194.
Tate, B. G., & Baroff, G. S. (1966). Aversive control of self-injurious behavior in a psychotic boy. *Behavior Research and Therapy, 4,* 281–287.
Terrace, H. S. (1963). Discrimination learning with and without errors. *Journal of the Experimental Analysis of Behavior, 6,* 1–27.
Terrace, H. S. (1966). Stimulus control. In W. K. Honig (Ed.), *Operant behavior: Areas of research and application.* New York: Appleton-Century-Crofts.
Touchette, P. E. (1968). The effects of graduated stimulus change on the acquisition of a simple discrimination in severely retarded boys. *Journal of the Experimental Analysis of Behavior, 11,* 39–48.
Touchette, P. E. (1978). Mental retardation: An introduction to the analysis and remediation of behavioral deficiency. In D. Marholin II (Ed.), *Child behavior therapy.* New York: Gardner Press.
Walls, R. T., Zane, T., & Ellis, W. D. (1981). Forward chaining, backward chaining, and whole-task methods: Training assembly tasks in vocational rehabilitation. *Behavior Modification, 5,* 61–74.
Walls, R. T., Zane, T., & Thvedt, J. E. (1980). Trainer's personal methods compared to two structured training strategies. *American Journal of Mental Deficiency, 84,* 495–507.
Weeks, M., & Gaylord-Ross, R. J. (1981). Task difficulty and aberrant behaviors in severely handicapped students. *Journal of Applied Behavior Analysis, 14,* 449–463.
White, G. D., Nielsen, G., & Johnson, S. M. (1972). Timeout duration and the suppression of deviant behavior in children. *Journal of Applied Behavior Analysis, 5,* 11–120.
Williams, J. A., Koegel, R. L., & Egel, A. L. (1981). Response-reinforcer relationships and improved learning in autistic children. *Journal of Applied Behavior Analysis, 14,* 53–60.
Winton, A. S. W., & Singh, N. N. (1983). Suppression of pica using brief-duration physical restraint. *Journal of Mental Deficiency Research, 27,* 93–103.

9

Achieving Success in Integrated Workplaces

Critical Elements in Assisting Persons with Severe Disabilities

JAN NISBET
MICHAEL CALLAHAN

Substantial efforts have been made to change traditional sheltered approaches to service delivery. New vocational models for persons with severe disabilities that emphasize community integration and supported employment have been developed (Brickley, Browning, & Campbell, 1982; Kraus & MacEachron, 1982; Revell, Arnold, Taylor, & Saitz-Blotner, 1982; Wehman et al., 1982). The underlying assumption of these new models is that all people with severe disabilities should have the opportunity to work in integrated community environments.

Integration does not mean only physical proximity to nondisabled workers or only performing work in the same environments as nondisabled workers. Instead, integration means working alongside and sharing responsibilities with nondisabled co-workers; taking breaks, having lunch, and attending a happy hour with their nondisabled peers; receiving instructions from the company supervisors; learning from their nondisabled co-workers; and being valued employees of the company.

The definition of *supported work* includes references to pay, supervision, and levels of integration. However, this definition does not provide sufficient guidance for vocational service providers to develop or evaluate service delivery models.

How can maximal integration be achieved in community work environments? What guidelines can service providers use when developing and evaluating vocational services? Wehman and Kregel (1985) describe program components critical to a supported work approach. These include job placement, job site training and advocacy, ongoing monitoring and follow-up, and retention. In addition to these, the following sections will list and describe the elements that positively affect the integration and success of workers with severe disabilities, related to individualized job placements, systems coordination, instruction, and technology.

These features represent the movement away from segregated models and practices and toward integrated employment opportunities for all persons with severe disabilities. This chapter identifies the practices that have inhibited successful placements and then contrasts them with alternative means of achieving integration.

Elements Related to the Development of Individualized Job Placements

Social Aspects

Working in integrated community businesses and industries increases the likelihood that persons with severe disabilities will develop meaningful relationships with nondisabled persons. The importance of these relationships cannot be underestimated. Environments and jobs that are selected for convenience rather than the opportunity for interactions may result in a person with a disability working at night, alone and isolated from others. Although the job may be lucrative, it may not allow for meaningful interactions. Merely selecting an environment and a job without attention to social interactions and relationships may result in segregation of persons with severe disabilities from their nonhandicapped peers.

The size of the business or operation may be important. Generally small businesses where bureaucratic mechanisms are minimal may be preferable over large, potentially impersonal enterprises, because of the ability to negotiate directly and easily with management. While large businesses are not necessarily unwilling to provide flexible opportunities and work schedules, more time may be required to develop individualized opportunities.

Individualization in Job Selection

Effective matching of the conditions and requirements of a particular job site with the individual characteristics of potential employees is a vital component of a successful integrated vocational service. It remains a common practice, however, in many adult service programs that, when a community job is secured, the staff have a person in mind who should be "the next one to go," regardless of the kind of job available. This practice has resulted in the placement of many persons in jobs that are not suited to their needs.

The traditional response to problems created by ineffective job matches has been to reevaluate the employee's skills and potential and to administer standardized assessments that are designed to determine the types of jobs best suited for the particular individual (Foss, Bullis, & Vilhauer, 1985). Instead of accomplishing this, most assessments determine that people with severe disabilities are not ready for employment or are unemployable.

Following the emergence of a variety of powerful instructional approaches in the late 1970s (Gold & Ryan, 1980; Snell, 1978) and due to the distrust of traditional vocational assessment and evaluation, training was considered the single most important variable in insuring job success for persons with severe handicaps. While systematic training is a powerful tool, it must be used in conjunction with information obtained through an individual vocational profile and an ecological assessment of a person's life space and the targeted job. Job matches based on specific information derived from an ecological analysis of the prospective employee's home and neighborhood, combined with a thorough inventory of the work and social skills required on the job site, should help to eliminate many of the hidden reasons that cause people to return to sheltered programs. Decisions concerning appropriate placements should be made based on the individualized needs, demands, and supports of the workplace, rather than on who is next in line or whose assessment indicates readiness.

Use of a Variety of Payment Mechanisms

The opportunity to receive pay based upon productivity, especially if that pay is less than the minimum wage, is a common reason given for the continuation of sheltered vocational programs for adults with severe disabilities (L. Brown et al., 1985). Job developers frequently have taken an all-or-nothing approach when facilitating integrated work opportunities. Following this reasoning, if potential employees cannot produce at a rate that merits minimum-wage pay, they may have to remain in sheltered employment. This attitude ignores two important considerations: (1) there are many legal ways, through the Department of Labor, to provide pay based upon productivity in integrated settings, and (2) many employers are willing to pay minimum wage to workers who produce with quality and offer other competencies such as loyalty, enthusiasm, and dependability.

The advent of the concept of integrated supported employment for people with severe disabilities has raised issues not faced in sheltered settings. A direct result of the supported work movement is the question, "Does the opportunity for integration *or* the wages one earns contribute most importantly to quality of life?" (Bellamy et al., 1984; Brown et al., 1984). Most people would agree that integration *and* wages are equally important considerations and that supported work services should strive for both.

To address the wage issue, agencies must identify some form of payment mechanism for reimbursing the employees for their work. A least-preferred option for wages might be a short-term training opportunity that leads to paid employment at a specified date. A better option is immediate pay commensurate with quality and quantity of work. Other options might include training stipends, piece-rate pay arranged through an agency's sheltered work or work activity certificate, subminimum hourly wage, minimum wage, and commensurate pay. Persons with the most severe handicaps should not arbitrarily receive the least acceptable payment options. Rather, decisions about payment of wages should be made individually and depend a great deal upon the ability of the job developer and the employer's needs.

Elements Related to Coordination of Services

Effective Use of Resources to Maximize the Number of Persons Receiving Supported Work Opportunities

Some of the most progressive work activity centers and sheltered workshops have provided opportunities for integrated employment on a one-person-at-a-time basis. Staff persons assigned to provide on-site training in employment settings often devote 100 percent of their time to each newly placed worker for 2 to 3 months or more. Additionally, most programs that provide integrated employment have only 1 staff person assigned to perform the training and support necessary for success (Banzhaf, 1985). Since the average adult day program has over 50 "clients" (Bellamy, Sheehan, Horner, & Boles, 1980) and it is not unusual to find programs serving 150 to 200 persons, such slow-moving approaches can deny persons with severe disabilities the opportunity for integrated employment.

A response to this problem has been the increasing proliferation of large-scale work stations or enclaves in local businesses. In an enclave, as many as 10 to 15 people perform work under the supervision of an agency staff person. Payment for the work performed is typically based on piece-rate or on a subminimum-wage hourly rate. The workers in an enclave are not employees of the company in which they work and are paid through the agency. Additionally, they are often segregated from the nondisabled employees during work and breaks.

The formation of community work crews represents another attempt to provide employment opportunities outside of work activity centers for more than one person at a time (Mank & Rhodes, 1983). These crews, which can consist of 5 to 10 workers, usually perform jobs such as grounds maintenance and janitorial work under the supervision of an agency staff person. While enclaves and community work crews offer adults with severe disabilities greater opportunity for integrated work than do day activity centers or sheltered workshops, both models fall short of the potential for the real integration available through individualized, supported employment. The challenge for agencies that want to offer quality integrated employment is to identify and then implement strategies that will serve the maximum number of people in settings that maximize the potential for integration.

Although it may seem unrealistic to suggest that any agency could deliver such an ideal-sounding outcome, there are several strategies that can be implemented. There are ways, however, to maximize the efficient use of staff in training and support. For example, close cooperation between the job developer and the employment trainer, if they are separate individuals, can result in a clustering of employment sites in a given area (Shiraga, 1985). This strategy can allow one trainer the ability to move quickly among several sites and manage the needs of as many as three or four employees at one time. This approach involves no more than one or two employees at a given work site, maximizes integration, and efficiently uses staff resources.

Coordination with Life Space Areas: Vocational, Recreation/Leisure, Domestic/Residential, and Community Functioning

Persons with severe disabilities often lead very fragmented lives. The various persons and agencies responsible for their vocational, domestic living, recreation/leisure, and community functioning are frequently unaware of one another's intentions or services. Unfortunately, this leads to disruptions in community vocational functioning. In a study in progress, Romans and Nisbet analyzed residential providers' knowledge of vocational services. They found that the majority of providers knew little about an individual resident's vocational program and therefore were not able to coordinate programs or address problems or deficiencies. For example, a person with a disability frequently may be late for work. Rather than seeing this solely as a vocational problem and addressing it within this context, the residential provider could facilitate moving through the morning routine at a faster rate.

Changes in where a person lives may affect transportation to and from a job, relationships, and recreation/leisure activities. However, residential changes are frequently made independent of the vocational program and can result in placement decisions favoring sheltered vocational settings. For example, an agency bus might be available to bring the person to the sheltered workshop, since public or alternative forms of transportation to an integrated work environment are now difficult to arrange.

Recreation/leisure functioning must also be included in a vocational service plan. Persons with severe disabilities may be unable to occupy their time appropriately during a break or lunch; as a result, a sheltered workshop might be considered to be more appropriate than an integrated setting. Staff time initially allotted to teach recreation/leisure skills and other break-time skills could prevent unnecessary placement in workshops.

Interaction and Coordination with Educational Programs

When students with severe disabilities graduate from the public educational system they should have the necessary skills and experience to function in integrated work environments. To achieve this goal, individualized educational plans (IEPs) must contain objectives related to work skills, behaviors, transportation, communication and social skills, and appropriate leisure skills necessary to function in community businesses. The last 1 or 2 years of education, referred to as the transition phase, should be devoted to preparing students to function in a specific work environment subsequent to graduation (Bellamy, Sowers, & Bourbeau, 1983). This should include individualized transition plans (ITPs). Upon graduation a transfer of responsibility should occur from the public school to an adult service agency that is responsible for maintaining the graduate (Nisbet et al., 1982). The involvement of the adult work agency during this transition phase is critical in the development of vocational curricula and the ITPs.

Inattention to the nature and content of the educational programs designed for students with severe disabilities can result in serious transition difficulties and enhance the likelihood of segregated work environments. Some educational programs are replete with nonfunctional vocational objectives directed at the performance of sheltered workshop tasks. In order to assess the impact that these objectives have on the attainment of nonsheltered employment, school systems should carefully evaluate the outcomes of their graduates. The majority of follow-up studies (Brody-Hasazi, Salembier, & Finck, 1983; Brown et al., 1984; Wehman, Kregel, & Seyfarth, 1985) indicate that actual performance in integrated work environments during school years is positively correlated with vocational success in nonsheltered adult environments.

This correlation should be recognized and adult vocational agencies must work closely with school systems in the identification of placement and training opportunities. This effort, in conjunction with educational interventions that inform parents/guardians and consumers of integrated vocational opportunities, will help to assure success in business and industry.

Relationships with Employers

Of all the major players in the effort to provide adults labeled severely disabled with meaningful, integrated work, employers are probably the most crucial. They will provide the settings where opportunities exist for workers with severe disabilities to interact with nondisabled persons, to be productive, and to earn wages. It is also fair to say that employers, for the most part, are unaware of their vital role. While there have been advances in the expectations and technologies for people with the most severe handicaps, the ultimate success of the concept of integrated work depends on employers. The good news is that employers are responding to the challenge when approached in a rational, businesslike manner and clearly informed as to the goals and needs of integration (Banzhaf, 1985; Garner, Zeiter, & Rhodes, 1985; Gordon, 1979).

In the past, rehabilitation professionals approached employers to market sheltered workshops as viable sources for subcontract labor and, less frequently, to provide employers with "job-ready" workers. Employers were approached within the framework of a "hard-nosed" business relationship. This strategy did little to promote employment in community jobs for the majority of people in the sheltered workshops and work activity centers. Unfortunately, employers were led to believe that if people were not "ready for work" they should remain in sheltered settings. The effort to legitimize sheltered workshops as meaningful and necessary places resulted in employers believing that sheltered workshop employees could not work in integrated settings.

Traditional efforts to provide integrated employment for workshop employees have often resulted in confusing situations for employers and, potentially, the loss of opportunity for employment for the person with a disability. In job development, typically the job facilitator learns the requirements for a job that has been secured and then selects a potential employee who supposedly can meet those requirements. The agreement with the employer usually involves a guarantee by the job facilitator that production standards will be met. This type of "all-or-nothing" guarantee is because of the erroneous assumption that productivity is the only important requirement of most employers. Some job developers will not consider any type of relationship with employers that does not focus on meeting the existing productivity requirements of the job (Hearne, 1985). The strict adherence to this approach excludes most people with severe handicaps (Brown et al., 1983). Ultimately, opportunities for integration are hindered when employees are not able to meet strict, inflexible productivity requirements.

Many studies describe in detail the requirements that employers feel are necessary for employment (Baxter & Young, 1982; Rusch, 1984; Wilms, 1984). Items that consistently appear near the top of any list include communication skills, ability to read and follow simple directions, ability to perform basic addition and subtraction, and desire to work. Except for the last item, people with severe disabilities might never master such requirements. Rather than focusing exclusively on either training people to perform these supposed requirements or on choosing people who already possess the skills, the traditional relationship with employers should be redefined by meeting certain needs rather than all of the existing job requirements. Some of the needs that most employers have are for quality, safety, the performance of work that meets a real need of the employer, and satisfactory relations with customers and co-workers. These are needs that can typically be met by all persons with disabilities through effective training, representation, and careful matching of individuals with jobs (Callahan et al., 1981).

Successful negotiations with employers on these and other essential needs can result in flexible, tailor-made opportunities for persons who might not reach production standards quickly. Employers can view employees individually, based upon the needs identified by the job developer. This approach should result in enhanced relations with employers and increased integrated opportunities for persons with severe disabilities.

Elements Related to Instruction and Technology

Training, Placement, and Follow-Up that Are Not Time-Referenced

Time-referenced training, placement, and follow-up strategies refer to those approaches that require that an individual meet productivity requirements within a set number of days or weeks. In many states, under vocational rehabilitation guidelines, 60 days is the designated period of time for placement and training in community environments. Most of the funding mechanisms and accompanying strategies designed to provide employment for persons with disabilities have traditionally involved these time-limited approaches. The practice of vocational rehabilitation services throughout this country has focused on the closure of individual cases rather than on a commitment to providing the necessary amount of training and intensity of placements and follow-up techniques to those individuals in jobs. Similarly, federal employment projects such as the Comprehensive Employment and Training Act (CETA) and, more recently, the Job Training Partnership Act (JTPA) allow training and follow-up support only within a set of strict, time-limited guidelines. Using parallel guidelines, many work activity centers and sheltered workshops have designed employment services based on readiness and time-referenced rationales. Even the initiative for the Employment of Developmentally Disabled Persons, sponsored by the Office of Human Development Services, U.S. Department of Health and Human Services (1984), encourages systems that match individuals who are "ready" for jobs with available jobs rather than finding ways of supporting all persons with disabilities in the workforce.

The concept of insuring work readiness through the provision of training in preparatory, worklike settings such as sheltered workshops is the cornerstone of time-limited strategies. Other strategies, such as the job clubs, provide preparatory experiences outside of sheltered environments. However, the persons who benefit from this approach have been identified as mildly disabled. If people with severe disabilities can be "made ready" for work in settings that are typically segregated and not time referenced, then, logically, the resources necessary for providing integrated employment can be estimated and placed within time limits; at least, that is the theory. Unfortunately, this approach has produced dismal results. Only about 5,000 of the more than 95,000 students with mental retardation who leave special education programs each year find employment (Elder, 1984). The figures for adults with mental retardation are no better. Most studies (Crites, Smull, & Sachs, 1984; M. Hill et al., 1985) indicate that only about 5 percent of adults who are mentally retarded are employed in integrated settings.

Several emerging viewpoints recognize the ineffectiveness of transitional approaches for facilitating the employment of persons with severe disabilities. One viable approach is to take the nontime-referenced services available in sheltered settings and provide them in integrated workplaces (Shelton & Lipton, 1983). This strategy requires a reconceptualization of readiness for work that acknowledges that persons with severe disabilities need to learn tasks and skills in the places where they will perform them (Brown, Nietupski, & Hamre-Nietupski, 1976; Ford & Mirenda, 1984). More important, the provision of training and support that is not time referenced should help agencies to embrace the goal that all the people receiving services can and should work in integrated environments.

Although this approach will eventually involve a basic restructuring of the sheltered workshop concept and job funding mechanisms, some employment programs are discovering creative ways of using existing funding mechanisms (M. Hill et al., 1985). Services such as work activity centers, vocational rehabilitation, job service, the local school district, and JTPA can each provide vocational training, placement, and follow-up for the same individual, resulting in an open-ended support model of service. This type of innovation provides immediate opportunities for people who are currently in segregated settings and creates guidelines for the restructuring of funding to support integrated placement, training, and follow-up.

Use of Job-Site Inventories and Job-Related Ecological Inventories

By 1980 a body of information regarding systematic instructional procedures had been developed and determined to be effective for teaching persons with severe disabilities to perform in segregated work sites (Gold & Ryan,

1980; Hunter & Bellamy, 1976). Although this information arose from research in segregated environments, many job trainers began providing for community-based employment opportunities by using systematic training on specific job skills as designated by the *Dictionary of Occupational Titles* (U.S. Dept. of Labor, 1977) or traditional job descriptions. The narrow application of this strategy resulted in the often-heard expression "the reason he was fired was not because he could not do the job, but rather because of social skills, behavior problems, and difficulties with communication." Specific job skills were often learned without much difficulty because the systematic procedures provided were sufficiently powerful. However, the other related skills and routines typically not included in traditional job descriptions were often ignored or perceived as not teachable. This oversight resulted in the loss of integrated opportunities for many persons with severe disabilities. The ecological inventory (Belmore & Brown, 1978) has emerged as an organizational and conceptual tool used to help insure that all the skills and routines that are necessary for job success are identified and analyzed. The use of ecological inventories also assists job trainers to match the skills and needs of the employee with the demands of various work sites.

The effectiveness of ecological inventories in facilitating vocational opportunities for persons with severe disabilities is well documented (Falvey et al., 1979; Ford & Mirenda, 1984; Sweet et al., 1982; Wehman, 1981). Inventories have been used as tools (1) to develop individual profiles with information relevant to employment; (2) to determine the characteristics of vocational training sites; (3) to provide critical information to be used in securing vocational opportunities; (4) to write an agreement outlining the responsibilities and duties of the employer, the vocational agency, and the person with a disability; and (5) to develop a comprehensive training plan, including goals, to insure success at the job site (Sweet et al., 1982).

After the ecological inventory is compiled, the employment trainer can then conduct a discrepancy analysis. This is an on-site evaluation of the worker that compares actual performance with the skills identified in the ecological inventory. The discrepancies are then target areas for intervention. The power of the inventory and subsequent discrepancy analysis is that they are tools entirely devoted to facilitating participation in the targeted job.

Emphasis on Social Skills and Communication

One of the keys to a successful vocational service is attention to the acquisition of job, social, and communication skills. Supported work services, which serve adults who potentially may have had previous social and communication skills training in the community, may simply have to maintain the person in an environment previously selected for the integration benefits. However, if the person has not had the benefit of working in an integrated environment, close attention should be paid to social and communication skills. Greenspan and Shoultz (1981) reported that the majority of workers labeled mentally retarded lose their jobs because of poor social and communication skills. Likewise, Rusch (1984) found that employers prioritized important job skills. This provides an important message to persons attempting to develop meaningful vocational options for persons with severe handicaps. First, social and communication skills must be targeted and should be considered as important as job skills. Second, because social and communication skills are frequently dependent upon the specific role context, it is not a professionally sound practice to teach them in isolated, simulated, and sheltered environments and expect them to generalize to integrated community jobs (Stokes & Baer, 1977). Finally, the provision of instruction in a sheltered environment may facilitate the acquisition and maintenance of inappropriate social and communication skills (Brown et al., 1983; Nisbet & Vincent, 1986), which will ultimately interfere with job retention. Therefore, to minimize the potential for failure, direct instruction of social and communication skills in the workplace is the most promising practice.

Use of Natural Supports

The professional literature in the area of vocational preparation is replete with training and supervision models. Most of the models rely on the use of professionals to develop placement opportunities for persons with severe disabilities and then provide the necessary training, advocacy, and follow-along services (Wehman, 1981). The reliance on this trainer/advocate model presumes that individuals with severe disabilities will eventually learn skills of sufficient quality and produce at an acceptable rate, so that supervision can be almost or completely faded. With the advent of the supported work movement, many are recognizing the need for ongoing supervision and intervention in the workplace (Brown et al., 1983; Rusch, 1984). Shelton (1984) has presented a model that relies on co-workers and employers rather than agency personnel to provide long-term support. This model relies on "social bonding" between the co-worker or employer and the person labeled severely disabled. Without this social bonding, the worker may never become an integral part of the workplace and may not be retained in the job.

The use of natural supports in the workplace appears to be one answer to the growing dilemma of how to provide consistent and ongoing training and follow-along services in integrated work environments. Co-workers frequently become involved with persons with disabilities, through the process of day-to-day contact in the workplace. While co-workers may not have all the skills needed to train a person to perform a job, they may be able to provide support and supervision.

The job trainer has the responsibility for facilitating relationships among co-workers and assisting with the transfer of the supervision and support. Depending on the nature and intensity of the support, co-workers may assume the supervision as part of their typical work responsibilities. If, however, the support requires co-workers to perform additional tasks, some type of reimbursement may be warranted. For example, if a co-worker spends 25 percent of her time supervising a worker with a disability who is currently being remunerated at 25 percent of the prevailing wage, then the vocational service agency must reimburse the co-worker for the 25 percent of wages lost. Regardless of the intensity, natural supports must be recognized as a critical element of successful integrated work opportunities for persons with severe disabilities.

When natural supports are not used, several problems arise. First, sole reliance on agency personnel may make fading of external supervision difficult and hence result in a one-to-one supervision model for an extended period of time. Second, because of the documented need for long-term follow-along (Hanley-Maxwell, Rusch, Renzaglia, & Chadsey-Rusch, 1986), vocational agencies must have the resources to provide those services. This may reduce the number of people that can be served if only an external supervision model is used. Third, unpredictable events that involve workers with severe disabilities may occur after supervision has been faded. If a co-worker is not involved, the event may not get the attention it deserves and the individual may be fired. Finally, lack of co-worker and employer involvement may limit the degree to which integration can be achieved. If workers are seen as part of the agency rather than as part of the business, efforts may not be made to integrate them physically and socially. Co-workers and employers are typically seen as primary natural supports.

Natural supports must also extend beyond the employment environment. Some of these may include a friend, neighbor, or family member assisting with transportation and after-work recreation/leisure activities. Family and friends can also be involved in problem solving if there is a temporary layoff or difficulty in the workplace. Reliance on persons other than primary vocational service providers enhances the consistency and level of integration in and out of the workplace.

Use of Systematic Instruction

Once an integrated vocational site has been developed and all the components of the job have been analyzed, systematic instruction is the initial strategy most trainers use to teach an employee to perform the job. The use of systematic instruction represents both an indispensable component of integrated vocational activity and a possible deterrent. One key distinction to be made is whether training is viewed as a means to a valued end or as an end in itself. Too often in adult services, the provision of expensive, well-organized, data-based training on tasks that are not required in integrated settings has been considered to be meaningful. Energies and resources often seem to be directed more at writing plans, securing release time for individualized training, and taking copious data than at providing opportunities in valued, integrated vocational settings. Systematic instruction thus has been seen as an end in itself rather than a means of achieving integrated employment opportunities. Systematic instruction is vital when meaningful opportunities are available; however, training as an end in itself is meaningless for persons with severe disabilities. Systematic instruction must be used after a meaningful job in the community has been secured and the required skills have been delineated.

Use of Job Creation/Modification Strategies

Traditional orientations to job development and placement rely on identifying situations that parallel the performance requirements of nondisabled persons. The *Dictionary of Occupational Titles* (U.S. Dept. of Labor, 1977) is used to identify the skills necessary for specific jobs. For example, lifting, mobility, use of numbers, and knowledge of product codes are required for working in a warehouse. This traditional strategy of job analysis is appropriate for some persons with disabilities. People labeled severely disabled, however, may require a more precise and sequential delineation of skills, the modification of sequences, the reconceptualization of a job, or even the creation of a job. In such situations, an employment trainer surveys a vocational environment and assesses the jobs being performed by a variety of workers. A decision is then made whether to modify a job already being performed or develop a job that combines required skills. For example, combining the filing responsibilities of 6 secretaries into a new job for a person with a severe disability permits the secretaries to spend the majority of their time transcribing and typing. When job-creation strategies are not considered, persons with severe disabilities become victims of structural unemployment (Brown, Hibbard, & Waters, 1985) and may be seen as incapable of performing a designated job. Consequently, they are relegated to quasi-integrated or segregated work, work activity, or day treatment.

Use of Adaptive Devices

Although many persons with severe disabilities receive instruction designed to prepare them to function in nonsheltered vocational environments, some, because of severe physical and/or learning deficits, require adaptive devices or personal supervision to function at acceptable standards. Previously, adaptive devices were viewed as cumbersome, costly, and appropriate only for people who were the most severely disabled. Now adaptations are also assisting persons with memory difficulties and sensory impairments. The emphasis on maximal participation has facilitated the further examination of a variety of jigs, sequential booklets, quality checklists, electrical switches, and mechanical devices.

More important is the relationship of integrated work environments to the development of adaptive devices. The need to perform work and the variety of related skills that exist in integrated work environments have been incentives to the development of adaptations. Many of these adaptations would not have been developed if integration were not a high priority and a job could have been brought to the person. Benchwork tasks, those typically performed in sheltered work settings, eliminate many of the necessary routines and sequences that persons with severe disabilities may have difficulty completing and that therefore require the use of adaptations.

Adaptive devices are now enabling large numbers of persons with severe disabilities to access environments and jobs from which they were formerly excluded (Nisbet et al., 1984). For example, one person was taught to prepare mailings at a local office building. Because of motoric and visual deficits, he was unable to fold the letters into the necessary thirds for insertion into the envelopes. To compensate for this, a device was created with a metal flap that allowed the individual to fold one end of the letter, then the other, toward the center. When both ends were folded over the metal flap, the letter was removed and inserted into the envelope. This increased the productivity and quality and therefore permitted the worker to receive a greater wage.

In some situations, deficits in performance are not related to physical disabilities. Many persons with severe disabilities require additional information or an instructional cue to perform specific skills within a sequence. For example, in a hospital, a person who packaged pills was required to return the supplies to a specific shelf. After several months of instruction, the person continued to have difficulty locating the shelf without verbal and physical cues. In consultation with the employer, the trainer attached a pill package to the appropriate shelf in order to provide a cue to where the supplies should be placed. While these examples seem simple, if time had not been devoted to developing these adaptations, these persons could have been relegated to sheltered or nonwork environments. Perceptions on unemployability and inconsequential work can often be changed and modified through the use of adaptive devices.

Summary

The 14 critical elements discussed in this chapter are not only challenges to service providers who are presently providing segregated vocational services, but also to those service providers who are developing integrated vocational alternatives for persons with severe disabilities. As new models are developed, important new features will evolve and old ones will be refined. In the final analysis, each model can be evaluated only by the success of workers with disabilities who are integrated into community businesses and industries. Researchers and service providers must continue to develop measures of success in order to strengthen systematic approaches to the placement and training of these workers.

References

Banzhaf, K. (1985). Personal communication.

Baxter, M., & Young, J. (1982). What do employers expect from high school graduates? *NASSP Bulletin, 66,* 93–98.

Bellamy, G. T., Horner, R. H., & Inman, D. P. (1979). *Vocational habilitation of severely retarded adults: A direct service technology.* Baltimore: University Park Press.

Bellamy, G. T., Rhodes, L. E., Bourbeau, P. E., & Mank, D. M. (1982). *Mental retardation services in sheltered workshops and day activity programs: Consumer outcomes and policy alternatives.* Paper presented at the National Working Conference on Vocational Services and Employment Opportunities, Madison, WI.

Bellamy, G. T., Rhodes, L. E., Wilcox, B., Albin, J. M., Mank, D. M., Boles, S. M., Horner, R. H., Collins, M., & Turner, J. (1984). Quality and equality in employment services for adults with severe disabilities. *Journal of the Association for Persons with Severe Handicaps,* 9(4), 270–278.

Bellamy, G. T., Sheehan, M., Horner, R., & Boles, S. (1980). Community programs for severely handicapped adults: An analysis. *Journal of the Association for the Severely Handicapped,* 5(4), 307–324.

Bellamy, G. T., Sowers, J., & Bourbeau, P. E. (1983). Work and work-related services: Post-school options. In M. Snell (Ed.), *Systematic instruction of the moderately and severely handicapped* (2nd ed.) (pp. 490–501). Columbus, OH: Charles E. Merrill.

Belmore, K., & Brown, L. (1978). Job skills inventory strategy for use in a public school vocational training program for severely handicapped potential workers. In N. Haring & D. Bricker (Eds.), *Teaching the severely handicapped (Vol. 3).* Seattle: American Association for the Education of the Severely/Profoundly Handicapped.

Brickley, M., Browning, L., & Campbell, K. (1982). Vocational histories of sheltered workshop employees placed in Projects with Industry and competitive jobs. *Mental Retardation, 19,* 113–116.

Brody-Hasazi, S., Salembier, G., & Finck, K. (1983). Directions for the 80's: Vocational preparation for secondary mildly handicapped students. *Teaching exceptional children, 15,* 206–210.

Brown, L., Nietupski, J., & Hamre-Nietupski, S. (1976). The criterion of ultimate functioning and public school services for severely handicapped children. In M. A. Thomas (Ed.), *Hey, don't forget about me!* (pp. 2–15). Reston, VA: Council for Exceptional Children.

Brown, L., Shiraga, B., Ford, A., VanDeventer, P., Nisbet, J., Loomis, R., & Sweet, M. (1983). Teaching severely handicapped students to perform meaningful work in nonsheltered vocational environments. In L. Brown, J. Nisbet, A. Ford, M. Sweet, B. Shiraga, R. Loomis, & P. VanDeventer (Eds.), *Educational programs for severely handicapped students,* Vol. 13 (pp. 1–100). Madison, WI: Madison Metropolitan School District.

Brown, L., Shiraga, B., York, J., Kessler, K., Strohm, B., Rogan, P., Sweet, S., Zanella, K., VanDeventer, P., & Loomis, R. (1984). Integrated work opportunities for adults with severe handicaps: The extended training option. *Journal of the Association for Persons with Severe Handicaps,* 9(4), 262–269.

Brown, R., Hibbard, M., & Waters, B. (1985). The transition of people with mental retardation from school to work: The implication of structural unemployment. In M. S. Gould and G. T. Bellamy (Eds.), *Transition from school to work and adult life* (pp. 2–24). Eugene, OR: Specialized Training Program.

Callahan, M., Balicki, P., Guardanapo, E., McBride, H., Pelmonter, C., & Rutherford, K. (1981). *The Mississippi project: The process of employing.* Urbana, IL: Marc Gold and Associates.

Crites, L., Smull, M., & Sachs, M. (1984). *Demographic and functional characteristics of respondents to the mentally retarded community needs survey: Persons living at home with family.* Unpublished manuscript. Baltimore: University of Maryland School of Medicine.

Elder, J. K. (1984). Job opportunities for developmentally disabled people. *American Rehabilitation, 10*(2), 26–30.

Falvey, M., Ferrara-Parrish, P., Johnson, F., Pumpian, I., Schroeder, J., & Brown, L. (1979). Curricular strategies for generating comprehensive longitudinal and chronological age appropriate functional individual vocational plans for severely handicapped adolescents and young adults. In L. Gruenewald (Ed.), *Strategies for teaching chronological age appropriate functional skills to adolescent and young adult severely handicapped students* (Vol. 9, Part 1) (pp. 102–309). Madison, WI: Madison Metropolitan School District.

Ford, A., & Mirenda, P. (1984). Community instruction: A natural cues and corrections decision model. *Journal of the Association for Persons with Severe Handicaps,* 9(2), 79–88.

Foss, G., Bullis, M. D., & Vilhauer, D. A. (1985). Assessment and training of job-related social competence for mentally retarded adolescents. In A. S. Halpern & M. J. Fuhrer, *Functional assessment in rehabilitation* (pp. 145–159). Baltimore: Brookes.

Garner, J., Zeiter, S., & Rhodes, N. (1985). *Training and employment for persons labeled mentally retarded: A project with industry.* Syracuse, NY: Marc Gold and Associates.

Gold, M. C., & Ryan, K. M. (1980). Vocational training of the mentally retarded. In Marc Gold (Ed.), *Did I say that? Articles and commentary on the Try Another Way System* (pp. 207–225). Champaign, IL: Research Press.

Greenspan, S., & Shoultz, B. (1981). Why mentally retarded adults lose their jobs: Social competence as a factor in work adjustment. *Applied Research in Mental Retardation, 2,* 23–28.

Hanley-Maxwell, C., Rusch, F., Renzaglia, A., & Chadsey-Rusch, J. (1986). Reported factors contributing to job terminations of individuals with severe disabilities. *Journal of the Association for Persons with Severe Disabilities, 11*(1), 45–52.

Hearne, P. B. (1985). Reviewer comment. A marketing approach to job placement. *Rehab. Brief: Bringing research into effective focus* (Vol. 8) (p. 4). Washington, DC: National Institute of Handicapped Research.

Hill, J., Seyfarth, J., Orelove, F., Wehman, P., & Banks, D. (1985). Parent/guardian attitudes toward the working conditions of their mentally retarded sons and daughters. In P. Wehman & J. Hill (Eds.), *Competitive employment for persons with mental retardation: From research to practice* (pp. 285–325). Richmond, VA: Research and Training Center.

Hill, M., Hill, J. W., Wehman, P., Revell, G., Dickerson, A., & Noble, J. (1985). Time-limited training and supported employment: A model for redistributing existing resources for persons with severe disabilities. In P. Wehman & J. Hill (Eds.), *Competitive employment for persons with mental retardation: From research to practice* (pp. 134–169). Richmond, VA: Rehabilitation Research and Training Center.

Hunter, J., & Bellamy, G. T. (1976). Cable harness construction for severely retarded adults: A demonstration of training technique. *AAESPH Review, 1*(7), 2–13.

Kraus, M., & MacEachron, A. (1982). Competitive employment training for mentally retarded adults: The supported work model. *American Journal of Mental Deficiency, 86*, 650–653.

Nisbet, J., Shiraga, B., Ford, A., Sweet, M., Kessler, K., & Loomis, R. (1982). Planning and implementing the transitions of severely handicapped students from school to post-school environments. In L. Brown, J. Nisbet, A. Ford, M. Sweet, B. Shiraga, & L. Gruenewald (Eds.), *Educational programs for severely handicapped students* (Vol. 12) (pp. 185–213). Madison, WI: Madison Metropolitan School District.

Nisbet, J., Sweet, M., Ford, A., Shiraga, B., Udvari, A., York, J., Messina, R., & Schroeder, J. (1984). Utilizing adaptive devices with severely handicapped students. In L. Brown, A. Ford, J. Nisbet, M. Sweet, B. Shiraga, J. York, & R. Loomis (Eds.), *Educational programs for severely handicapped students* (Vol. 13) (pp. 104–142). Madison, WI: Madison Metropolitan School District.

Nisbet, J., & Vincent, L. (1986). The differences in inappropriate behavior and instructional interactions in sheltered and nonsheltered work environments. *Journal of the Association for Persons with Severe Handicaps, 11*(1), 19–27.

Revell, G., Arnold, S., Taylor, B., & Saitz-Blotner, S. (1982). Project transition: Competitive employment services for the severely mentally retarded. *Journal of Rehabilitation, 48*(1), 31–35.

Rusch, F. R. (1979). Toward the validation of social/vocational survival skills. *Mental Retardation, 17*, 143–145.

Rusch, F. R. (1984). Competitive vocational training. In M. Snell (Ed.), *Systematic instruction of the moderately and severely handicapped* (pp. 503–523). Columbus, OH: Merrill Publishing.

Shelton, C. S., & Lipton, R. (1983). An alternative employment model. *Mental Retardation, 33*(2), 12–16.

Shiraga, B. (1985). Personal communication.

Snell, M. (Ed.). (1978). *Systematic instruction of the moderately and severely handicapped*. Columbus, OH: Merrill Publishing.

Stokes, T. F., & Baer, D. (1977). An implicit technology of generalization. *Journal of Applied Behavior Analysis, 10*, 349–367.

Sweet, M., Shiraga, B., Ford, A., Nisbet, J., Graff, S., & Loomis, R. (1982). Vocational training: Are ecological strategies applicable for severely multihandicapped students? In L. Brown, J. Nisbet, A. Ford, M. Sweet, B. Shiraga, & L. Gruenewald (Eds.), *Educational programs for severely handicapped students* (Vol. 12) (pp. 99–131). Madison, WI: Madison Metropolitan School District.

U.S. Department of Health and Human Services, Office of Human Development Services. (1984). *Employment of developmentally disabled persons*. Washington, DC: Author.

U.S. Department of Labor. (1977). *Dictionary of occupational titles* (4th ed.). Washington, DC: U.S. Government Printing Office.

Wehman, P. (1981). *Competitive employment: New horizons for severely disabled individuals*. Baltimore: Brookes.

Wehman, P., Hill, M., Goodall, P., Cleveland, P., Brooke, V., & Pentecost, J. (1982). Job placement and follow-up of moderately and severely handicapped individuals after three years. *Journal of the Association for Persons with Severe Handicaps*, 7(2), 5–16.

Wehman, P., Kregel, J., & Seyfarth, J. (1985). Transition from school to work for individuals with severe handicaps: A follow-up study. *Journal of the Association for Persons with Severe Handicaps, 10*(3), 132–137.

Wilms, W. (1984). Vocational education and job success: The employer's view. *Phi Delta Kappan, 65*(5), 347–350.

10

Living in the Community

Speaking for Yourself

MICHAEL KENNEDY
PATRICIA KILLIUS

with
DEBORAH OLSON

Who We Are

We are Michael Kennedy and Patricia Killius, two self-advocacy coordinators at the Center on Human Policy in Syracuse, New York. The following are some of the important aspects of our lives.

MIKE: I am 24 years old. I use an electric wheelchair. I lived with my family until I was 5 years old. My parents could not afford to pay for all my medical needs. They were both working and had three other children to care for. So I went into an institution and lived in three different state institutions for people with developmental disabilities and mental retardation for a total of 15 years. Today I live in a Medicaid-funded apartment with three other people. It's my home, not an institution. I have learned many skills that I didn't have the chance to learn in an institution, for example, arranging my own transportation, some budgeting, and doing my own laundry.

PAT: I lived in institutions for 18 years. I was born blind. I also use a wheelchair. In the institution I didn't have the freedom to fight for many of the things I wanted, but I was a member of a self-advocacy group that wanted to talk about ways of keeping our rights while living in the institution. Now I live in a Medicaid-funded apartment. I receive better services and better care because I fought to get out of the institution.

As self-advocacy coordinators we speak to professionals to tell them that disabled people have rights. We want them to know that we can make decisions and speak out for ourselves. We also teach people with developmental disabilities and mental retardation that they have the right to self-determination and to live as independently as is possible for them.

One way we do this is to facilitate 2 self-advocacy groups. In these groups, people like ourselves learn to speak out for themselves. People with all kinds of disabilities participate in the groups. Some of them still live in the institution, but most live in group homes, in supportive apartments, with families, and even independently.

In July 1985, we held a statewide conference in New York on self-advocacy for people with developmental disabilities, to give them the chance to speak out about their rights and the things they want to see changed. We also wanted professionals to see that we have a voice of our own. We want the same rights as everyone else; nothing more, but nothing less.

Definition of Self-Advocacy

Self-advocacy for people with developmental disabilities means speaking up and speaking out for our rights. For people who cannot speak, it means having someone to help say what we want. People with developmental disabilities should have the right to speak up and teach other people about their rights. We won't always have someone to look out for us.

People need to listen to what we want, even though they might not want to. Speaking out can be taking a risk. Sometimes we're afraid a staff person or parent might say no. In an example from the *Rights Now!* training material (National Institute on Mental Retardation), Don wants to go scuba diving, but a staff person is afraid it is too dangerous. He has to decide for himself whether he can take that risk. He talked to a lot of different people and took into account the fact that he was a good swimmer. He decided to go scuba diving and take the risks.

Some people can't speak for themselves because of their disability. Other people may be really shy or uncomfortable talking. In the institution they often get pushed aside or shut out of activities. This can happen even in the community. Just because they can't speak, it doesn't mean they can't be a part of everyday life. People with a severe disability can still live in the community, even though they can't express themselves very well. They need a friend who can speak for them. The best spokesperson for someone who can't speak is another person with a disability who can speak, maybe a friend. Another disabled person knows where that person is coming from; they've had similar experiences. Professionals may say they understand, but in reality they haven't lived as we have and haven't had the same experiences.

What Is Self-Advocacy About?

Having Choices

Living in the institution you don't have the freedom to make choices. You are told what to do, for example, when to eat, when to sleep, and when to get ready for work.

You have no choice about going places when the whole unit is going someplace. You can't go out on your own.

Self-advocacy, or speaking for yourself, is a big part of living in the community. People with disabilities who live in the community should have the right to make their own decisions, just like anyone else. For example, we should have the choice of who we want to work with us. In our apartment, the director will interview a person who wants to work with us. Then she will bring them to the apartment and have us interview the person. We ask things like, "Have you ever worked with disabled people before?" "What kind of recreational things do you like to do?" We ask this so that we can get a good idea of what they like to do and if we like the same thing. We also ask how they feel about transferring someone from one chair to another. We ask that in order to get an idea of how they feel about being with us. After these questions, the person asks questions of us. We'll give them answers about where we work and what we do. The following day we get together with the director and talk about that person. She takes our ideas to the board of the agency and the board usually approves who we recommend for hiring.

PAT: Another choice you have in the community is attending the church of your choice. At one institution they had one auditorium for Catholic and Protestant services and you couldn't go to a church in the community. At another institution you could only go to church at certain times a month because of shortages of staff. In the community I can go to the church of my choice and I can go every Sunday. I feel good about that.

In the institution you couldn't choose your own friends and you couldn't have your friends come to see you. In the community you can make your own friends and have them come to see you when you want.

Having a Say About Your Services

People with developmental disabilities can and should have an impact on services by participating in agency boards and councils. It's important that we share our ideas, because we use some of the services. Many of us have been getting services from agencies all of our lives. We know that some services are good because they try to meet our individual needs. We also recognize that some services are bad because they don't integrate people in the community and they don't provide programs to help us become more independent. We can tell agencies what kinds of things we need to live and grow in the community. But it's not enough to have just one consumer on a board. If there are several with different disabilities or different experiences, providers will know more about our needs.

When we first got our self-advocacy jobs, a lot of agencies asked us to be on their boards. They didn't seem to be aware of other people with disabilities who could also speak out on their programs.

People with disabilities might need special supports to be on a board. For example, we might need aides to help us get to the meeting, to help us with personal needs, for writing and reading, for speaking for someone who can't speak or interpreting for someone who can't hear. It's important to have this support so that we can participate on the board. Without this support we're just a token.

We just can't walk into a meeting and expect to know everything that is going on and participate. Like everyone else, we need to prepare—to know what is on the agenda, what are the issues, what we can contribute and who will be there.

Choosing Your Employment

People with disabilities have the right to choose employment different from a sheltered workshop. For example, you can make more money in an office than working in a workshop. Not everyone can go right into any work setting. They need aides for personal needs; to get to work they need transportation; or they need to learn the skills to work in the community. People need to learn to speak out for transportation or to get a new job.

> MIKE: Once I was in a sheltered workshop for a 5-week evaluation. I worked on a typing job and was told that I would receive minimum wage like everyone else. Then I found out that I would receive less than minimum wage. It was because of my disability and the fact that I typed a little slower than the others. I talked to my supervisor about it and he said that he wouldn't change the wages. Then I left the workshop, because he couldn't give me any explanation as to why I was receiving less than minimum wage.

Learning to Speak Out

All disabled people have the right to learn to speak for themselves. It's important because there will be a day when our parents won't be able to speak for us. Disabled people can teach each other how to speak for themselves. Role-playing a variety of problems or situations is a good way to learn self-advocacy.

There's more strength in forming a group. One individual speaking out is easily overlooked. If you have a group of people who want the same thing, you have a better chance of people listening.

This is what we did in Syracuse. We drew up a list of friends and other people we knew. We told them about self-advocacy and asked them if they wanted to become involved. That's how we got started. We brainstormed some issues and talked about issues at every meeting. For example, we talked about transportation problems and education.

Learning by Doing

Not very many people could get transportation to our meetings, so we decided to associate with College for Living, a program that teaches independent living skills to people with disabilities. People can always get staff to provide transportation to College for Living classes. We started a group that met once a week at night. To teach ourselves about our rights we used a tool called *Rights Now!* (National Institute on Mental Retardation). It contains cassettes, pictures, and a slide show about different people in various situations learning about self-advocacy. Issues include finding meaningful work instead of sheltered employment, finding time to be alone with your friends, or working out compromises with the people you live with.

During the second semester of College for Living, we started 2 self-advocacy groups. One group met every Tuesday afternoon and used the *Rights Now!* materials. The other group met on Thursday nights. Since some of the people in this group had used the *Rights Now!* materials in the previous semester, this group talked about other things, such as making decisions and being assertive. We spent a lot of time talking about getting people out of institutions and what we could do about it. We decided to write a letter to the editor of the local newspaper.

First we agreed to write just one letter which we would all sign. We did this so that we could all help each other with it. Then we made a list of things we wanted to say. Everybody contributed something to the list. Our helper took notes and wrote down what each person said.

Then we looked at the list and decided what we wanted to say first, then second, and third, and so on. When we got it in the order that we wanted, our helper read it back to us and we agreed on it. Our helper took it home and typed it in letter form. The following week we signed our names to it and mailed it.

We also wrote letters to Congress about some legislation to help get people out of institutions. In doing these two letters we learned one important strategy in self-advocacy: writing letters to important people.

Sometimes people in self-advocacy groups testify on important issues at public hearings.

> MIKE: For example, I testified at the hearings of the Senate Subcommittee on the Handicapped in Washington, DC. I told them about my experiences in institutions, that they are too large, and that I think they ought to be closed. It was exciting, but I was nervous. I felt good about the testimony because I had practiced a lot. Senator Lowell Weicker, chair of the hearings, was really interested in what I had to say.

It's very important to give testimony of this type because too often consumers are not heard on these issues.

When we decided to have a conference, we talked to the two self-advocacy groups and brainstormed some ideas for the conference, such as getting to meet new people, some workshop topics, having time to socialize with each other, and accessibility of the location. Almost everyone in the groups actively participated in the conference. They were guides, they helped plan and conduct the workshops, they spoke on panels, they gave press interviews, and they helped with the wrap-up session.

Ways to Start a Self-Advocacy Group

We started our groups through College for Living, but not everybody has to do it the same way. There are many ways to start a group. First you have to find a good place to meet, one that is easy for everyone to get to. Then you have to make a list of people who could be a part of the group. It's okay to start small. You have to let people know about the meeting, either by calling them or seeing them at work or where you live. You have to agree on a meeting date and time that would be good for everybody.

When you have your first meeting, you have to be sure that everyone feels comfortable. You should have people introduce themselves and maybe say why they wanted to learn about self-advocacy. You may have to explain about self-advocacy first. If you decide to use the *Rights Now!* material, you'll have to tell people about the cassettes and pictures. Or you could show a film about self-advocacy, like *People First* (Stanfield Film Associates, 1976), or a slide show like *Our Voice Is New* (Center on Human Policy, 1986), which we helped produce. After the film or slides you can talk about some issues, like speaking out, having someone speak for you if you can't speak well, or what it feels like to be labeled mentally retarded.

We and the people in our group think that it is good to form a group because:

- People aren't always going to be around to make decisions for you, so you have to learn to make your own decisions.
- You can learn about each other; everyone has different needs.
- You can work together for new opportunities for people with disabilities.
- You can learn about your rights as a citizen.
- You can help other people who can't speak.
- You can have fun by meeting other people.

By speaking for yourself you help other people—group home staff, government officials, and the general public—see that you are a person just like them, not a "disability." Self-advocacy is part of living in the community. Without it we might as well be shoved back into the institution.

References

Center on Human Policy. (1986). *Our Voice Is New* (slide show). Human Policy Press, P.O. Box 127 University Station, Syracuse, NY 13210.

Rights Now! National Institute on Mental Retardation, P.O. Box 5019, Downsview, Ontario, Canada, M3M 3B9.

Stanfield Film Associates. (1976). *The People First* (movie). James Stanfield Film Associates, P.O. Box 1983, Santa Monica, CA 90406.

11

Conclusion

The Next Wave

ROBERT BOGDAN
STEVEN J. TAYLOR

Despite the disappointments—the mini-institutions, the nursing homes, the neglectful boarding homes—no one can legitimately claim that the lives of people with developmental disabilities are not better today than when the current wave of reform began in the early 1970s. It would take a cynical and uninformed outlook to suggest that deinstitutionalization has been an utter failure, that community settings are just as abusive as institutions, that the lot of people with developmental disabilities has not improved considerably over the past 15 years or so.

Just as surely, though, it would be naive to think that the hopes and dreams of the 1970s have come to pass. Far too many people with the label of mental retardation remain segregated, isolated, and cut off from other people, both in places referred to as "institutions" and those referred to as "community facilities."

Over the past decade and a half, we have been participant observers of the mental retardation/developmental disabilities scene. We have spoken out on behalf of the rights of people with developmental disabilities to live in the community, worked with civil rights attorneys, exposed institutions, and organized with parents and consumers. Every once in a while, we have stood back and watched things from a distance—talked to people about their lives and aspirations; observed institutions, group homes, foster homes, schools, and other settings; followed the controversies and debates; listened to new ideas and reformulations of old ones. We have seen and heard much that gives us hope and much that gives us cause for reflection. The next wave of the movement to halt the exclusion of people with developmental disabilities from society will face new challenges. Let us now look at some of these.

Being in the Community Is Not the Same as Being Part of the Community. Early formulations of deinstitutionalization and community living were not clear enough in distinguishing between "being in the community" and "being part of the community." Being *in* the community points only to physical presence; being *part* of the community means having the opportunity to interact and form relationships with other community members.

People can be placed in the community and experience segregation, isolation, and loneliness. This is not to say that moving people out of institutions is an unworthy pursuit. To the contrary, for people to be part of the community, they must be in the community. We have never met a single person in an institution who was a central part of anything other than the institutional culture. What we are saying is that community placement is simply a means to an end, and not the ultimate goal.

Being Part of the Community Means Having Meaningful Relationships with Other Community Members. To be part of the community is to be a family member, neighbor, schoolmate, friend, casual acquaintance, church member, shopper, co-worker, and significant other. It means being a fellow member of clubs, organizations, and associations, and sometimes being a consumer of services as well. Being part of the community means much more than being treated nicely by staff or even having a citizen advocate or volunteer. It means being known as an individual, a unique person, and not as a label, a ward of the state, a client of an agency, or the recipient of another's altruistic acts.

We know quite a bit about the sociology of exclusion. We understand now the dynamics of labeling, stereotyping, and the self-fulfilling prophecy. We know far less about how people make friends and how those who are different come to be accepted. In the next wave, we will need a sociology of acceptance.

Being Part of the Community Means Contributing to the Community. It means being a good citizen. While this usually means holding down a job, it also means contributing in other ways, by volunteering, by celebrating when the community celebrates and grieving when it experiences tragedy, and by engaging in neighborly acts.

Being Part of the Community Requires Being Supported by Services and Agencies in Such a Way as to Become Less Dependent on Those Services and Agencies. When people with developmental disabilities have to rely exclusively on the services of a particular agency, they are destined not to become part of the community. The more an agency provides, the less others will be involved in a person's life. Only when support is spread throughout the community can people become part of their communities.

Institutionalization has been defined largely in terms of physical placement in remote facilities, but it can be more insidious. It can also be represented by the total consumption of a person's life by an agency or a program. When this happens, the person becomes the label; the client role takes over and the person becomes lost. When, however, a person has a range of contacts in the community, she or he can escape the client role and relate to people on other terms. We must begin to define deinstitutionalization not simply in terms of moving people out of public institutions, but in terms of breaking down the control that services, programs, and agencies have over the lives of people with developmental disabilities.

In the next wave, professionals and staff must view themselves not as people who are all things to their so-called clients, but as community organizers and mobilizers, people who help them become part of their communities.

Being Part of the Community Should Never Be Confused with Neglect, Indifference, or Denial of Supports. While the goal is for people with developmental disabilities to become part of their communities, this cannot be used to excuse the denial of supports and services people need to remain in or return to their communities. To be part of the community does not mean that people with developmental disabilities or their families must do without support from publicly funded agencies.

Being Part of the Community Will Ultimately Mean Doing Away with Concepts Like Normalization, Integration, and Mainstreaming. Concepts like *integration, normalization, life-sharing, mainstreaming,* and others are only vehicles for change and not the end. When we reach a state of natural acceptance and inclusion of people with developmental disabilities, we will no longer need these ideas. That we have these concepts does not mean that we have arrived; it only means that we recognize that people with developmental disabilities have been denied.

Normalization and integration carry with them a level of self-consciousness that can inhibit people becoming part of the community. Normalization is not normal. When people focus on normalization, they find it difficult to have spontaneous and unself-conscious relationships with people with developmental disabilities. Spontaneity is characteristic of mutual relationships.

We can envision a society that would perplex the most adamant believer in normalization or social-role valorization. This society would be marked by a natural acceptance of people with disabilities. Members of this society would not have the faintest understanding of normalization principles. If one asked them about normalization or integration, they would not know how to respond. The society would not operate on normalization, just spontaneous, unself-conscious acceptance. Here the use of concepts like normalization would represent a step backward.

Being Part of the Community Will Take Time. In helping people with mental retardation and developmental disabilities to become part of the community, there will be frustrations and setbacks. Communities may not always welcome people with developmental disabilities with open arms. Relationships may not always form spontaneously. Acceptance and inclusion will not be accomplished overnight.

When people with developmental disabilities are visible and involved in their communities—in schools, workplaces, and neighborhoods—good things happen. If community members do not step forward to take over for agency staff, this should not be cause for despair. Progress toward the goal will be measured in terms of kind words and subtle gestures, a greeting on the street, an offer of a ride home, an invitation to dinner or a party.

Being Part of the Community will Require Changes in the Community and Society. For people with developmental disabilities to become part of the community, the community and society will have to change. Personal relationships are the cornerstone of being part of the community; however, social policies and practices can systematically thwart opportunities for people to come together. Until vested interests, funding mechanisms, economic policies, counter-ideologies, agency policies, architectural barriers, and other forces supporting segregation are confronted and changed, people with developmental disabilities will not become part of the community.

Being Part of the Community Is an End in Itself. People with developmental disabilities who are part of their communities act in more normal and socially appropriate ways. They may indeed become more independent and productive. But the strongest argument in favor of enabling people to become part of their communities is that they lead better, more fulfilling lives.

It is important for agencies to operate under the assumption that people can change, that they can learn new skills, that the most difficult behavior problems can be overcome. Even if people do not change dramatically and become more independent and productive, however, they should be able to be part of the community. The right to lead a decent life as part of the community should not be made contingent on becoming "nondisabled" or "normal."

Being Part of the Community Cannot be Packaged. Just because an idea, model, or approach seems to work in one place at one time does not mean that it can work anywhere or at any time. To be sure, we can all learn good ideas from other people and some models are inherently superior to others.

We cannot assume, however, that every good idea can be replicated with equal success. We all know there is a difference between having a home-cooked meal and eating in a franchise restaurant. What makes the difference is not the recipe, but the care, attention, and personal touch that go into the cooking.

When people become attached to models or approaches, this can interfere with helping people become part of the community. They develop a vested interest in the model or approach; change means losing face. As we have learned not to invest in the bricks and mortar of institutions, we must not bet on a particular way.

The steadfast adherence to a particular approach can prevent new people in the field from having the opportunity to contribute their creativity and insight in developing the next wave. As more and more community programs develop, recruitment of staff is becoming more routine, not like joining a spirited movement as it has been in the past. In the next wave, we will need to find ways of helping new people develop a sense of the history of the struggles that brought us to where we are today, while at the same time being open to fresh ideas.

For people with developmental disabilities to become part of the community, what will be needed is a strong commitment, a sense of mission, and clear values. None of these things can be packaged.

It is exciting to know that people are accomplishing things today that we could not even dream about 15 years ago. We have to realize that our dreams are too much a product of what exists today and what we have been through. We can strive for change, but what is down the road is beyond our imagination. Some of what will come to pass will exceed our expectations, and some will be disappointing. We must be thoughtful about what the future might bring and committed to being a part of bringing it about. But the next wave will have its surprises that will provide the challenges for the next decade of struggle.

ABOUT THE EDITORS AND THE CONTRIBUTORS

INDEX

About the Editors and the Contributors

Douglas Biklen, Ph.D. (**editor**), is Director of the Division of Special Education and Rehabilitation at Syracuse University. He has been with the Center on Human Policy there since its founding in 1971 and has written extensively on issues of school and community integration.

Robert Bogdan, Ph.D., is Professor of Special Education and Sociology at Syracuse University. He works closely with the Center on Human Policy there and is Director of Research of the Center's Research and Training Center on Community Integration. He has published widely on qualitative research and conducted numerous studies of institutional and community life.

Michael Callahan is President of Marc Gold and Associates and is currently a doctoral candidate in rehabilitation at Syracuse University. He has also worked on community integration projects with the Center on Human Policy there and has consulted widely for educational and vocational agencies and businesses on work placements for adults with severe disabilities.

Gunnar Dybwad, J. D., is Professor Emeritus at Brandeis University and a visiting Professor at Syracuse University, where he works closely with the Center on Human Policy and teaches courses in law and policy in the Division of Special Education and Rehabilitation. Professor Dybwad was one of the earliest proponents in this country of deinstitutionalization of people with mental retardation, and is recognized nationally and internationally for his promotion of community integration, parent involvement, and self-advocacy.

Alison Ford, Ph.D., is Assistant Professor of Special Education at Syracuse University. She has extensive background in teacher training, applied research, and curriculum development activities designed to improve the quality of services provided to learners with severe disabilities.

Michael Kennedy is a self-advocacy coordinator at the Center on Human Policy at Syracuse University and works on the Center's community integration projects. He has lived in several institutions and currently lives in a community setting. He has made numerous presentations on self-advocacy and consumer involvement at professional, parent, and consumer conferences and has presented invited testimony at U.S. Senate hearings on institutions.

Patricia Killius has served as a self-advocacy coordinator at the Center on Human Policy at Syracuse University and has been actively involved in self-advocacy in New York State. Prior to moving into an apartment in the community, she lived in several institutions and helped to organize a resident government at one.

James Knoll (editor), is presently on the staff of the Community Integration Project at Syracuse University's Center on Human Policy. He has extensive experience working in residential services and as a teacher of students with severe disabilities. At Syracuse, where he is a candidate for a Ph.D. in special education, he is involved in research on disability as a social phenomenon and on practical questions of supporting community integration for people with severe disabilities.

Zana Lutfiyya is a doctoral student in the Division of Special Education and Rehabilitation at Syracuse University. Her current research interests include community living, integration, and public policy.

John J. McGee, Ph.D., is Associate Professor of Medical Psychology at the University of Nebraska College of Medicine. He has lectured throughout the Americas and Europe on issues related to community services for people with mental retardation, especially for those with severe behavioral challenges.

Paul E. Menousek, Ph.D., is Assistant Professor of Medical Psychology, and **Daniel Hobbs** is on the staff at the University of Nebraska College of Medicine. Both have been extensively involved in implementing and conducting research on *gentle teaching* techniques.

Jan Nisbet, Ph.D., is Associate Professor of Rehabilitation at Syracuse University. She has worked extensively with schools and adult services agencies to integrate people with severe disabilities into typical schools, community settings, and workplaces and has directed several vocational and transitional projects.

John O'Brien is the cofounder of Responsive Systems, Inc., which consults with public and private agencies and community groups. He has worked widely with public and private agencies throughout North America, Australia, and Great Britain, and is the author of many articles on normalization, personal futures planning, the meaning of community, and the nature of change.

Deborah Olson is the Director of the Parent Training Project operated by the Parents' Information Group for Exceptional Children in Syracuse, New York. She formerly worked at the Center on Human Policy at Syracuse University and is a doctoral candidate in special education at Syracuse University. She assists the self-advocacy movement in New York.

Gerald Provencal is Director of the Macomb Oakland Regional Center in Michigan. In addition to directing the development of community programs for people with severe disabilities at Macomb Oakland, he has been a foster parent. He has worked closely with attorneys as an expert witness in 11 deinstitutionalization lawsuits.

Julie Racino is Associate Director of the Community Integration Project at Syracuse University's Center on Human Policy. She has had extensive experience in direct service and as an administrator in residential services for people with developmental disabilities.

Lyn Rucker is executive director of Region V Mental Retardation Services in Lincoln, Nebraska. For the last 18 years she has been involved in work with people with developmental disabilities. Since 1972 she has been with Region V and has been instrumental in focusing that region's efforts on integrating people with developmental disabilities into their home communities.

Steven J. Taylor, Ph.D. (**editor**), is Director of the Center on Human Policy and Professor of Special Education at Syracuse University. He is involved in a range of research, training, and advocacy activities related to the integration of people with disabilities in society and has coauthored books and articles on qualitative research methods, institutions, the law, community and school integration, and social policy.

Author Index

Agosta, J., 147
Albin, J. M., 186
Allen, M. L., 39
Arnold, S., 184
Asch, A., 6
Ash, T., 130
Atkinson, T.
see Taylor, S. J., 13
Azrin, N. H., 147, 148, 149, 164

Baer, D. M., 165, 194
Bailey, J. B., 148
Baker, C., 82
Baldwin, G., 147
Balicki, P.
see Callahan, M., 191
Banzhaf, K., 187, 190
Barkley, R., 147
Baroff, G. S., 148
Barrett, B. H., 148
Bartholomew, K., 99
Barton, E. S., 148
Baumgart, D., 138
Baxter, M., 190
Bean, A. W., 148
Becker, W. C., 164
Bellamy, G. T., 164, 186, 187, 189, 193
Belmore, K., 193
Bennis, W. G., 87
Bensberg, G. J., 15, 133
Bercovici, S. M., 10, 134
Berkson, G., 164
Berler, E. S., 148
Bernstein, G. S., 133
Berry, J., 15
Besalel, V. A., 164
Bijou, S. W., 149
Biklen, D., 7, 8, 9, 11, 12, 13, 25, 134
Blatt, B., 8, 9, 10, 104, 134
Boe, R. B., 164
Bogdan, R., 6, 7, 11, 134
Boles, S. M., 187
see also Bellamy, G. T., 186
Bostow, D. E., 148
Bourbeau, P. E., 189
Bowlby, J., 151
Braddock, D., 8, 27, 29, 32
Bradley, V. J., 14
Branston, M. B.
see Brown, L., 141
Brickley, M., 184
Brightman, A., 7
Brody-Hasazi, S., 189
Bronfenbrenner, U., 48
Bronston, W., 31
Brooke, V.
see Wehman, P., 184
Brown, F., 165
Brown, K., 13
Brown, Linda, 42
Brown, L., 32, 121, 130, 141, 186, 189, 192, 193, 194
see also Baumgart, D., 138
Brown, R., 196
Browning, L., 184
Bruininks, R. H., 14, 15, 26, 27, 28
see also Hauber, F. A., 17; Lakin, K. C., 29
Bullis, M. D., 186
Bunyard, P. D., 132

Calhoun, K. D., 148
Callahan, M., 191
Campbell, K., 184

Censoni, B., 39
Center on Human Policy, 8, 9, 28, 87, 207
Certon, N.
see Brown, L., 141
Chadsey-Rusch, J., 195
Cherniss, G., 15
City of Cleburne v. Cleburne Living Center, 12
Cleland, C. C., 164
Cleveland, P.
see Wehman, P., 184
Close, D. W., 30, 147
Cohen, J., 105
Colby, J., 148
Collins, M.
see Bellamy, G. T., 186
Colvin, G. T., 164
Combs, M., 149
Conroy, J. W., 13, 14, 17
Coon, M. E., 130, 164
Corbett, J., 148
Corte, H. E., 148
Crissey, M. S., 28
Crites, L., 192
Cronin, K. A., 164
Cuvo, A. J., 164
Czajkowaki, L. A., 133

Davis, J.
see Ford, A., 131
Dawson, M. J., 147
DeCatanzaro, D., 147
Dewey, J., 46
Dickerson, A.
see Hill, M., 192
Dodd, N.
see Brown, L., 32
Doke, L. A., 148
Donovan, W., 148
Doth, D., 28
Downs, G., 105
Drabman, R. S., 148
Duker, P. C., 147
Dunitz-Johnson, E., 149
Dybwad, G., 33, 81

Ebert, R. S., 133
Efthimiou, J., 17
Egel, A. L., 165
Elder, J., 192
Ellis, W. D., 164
Engelmann, S., 164
Epple, W. A., 27
Epstein, L. H., 148
Ersner-Hershfield, R., 148
Evans, D., 133

Falvey, M., 193
Fanning, J. W., 133
Favell, J. E., 164
Featherstone, H., 7
Feinstein, C. S., 13
Ferdinand, L. R., 17
Ferrara-Parish, P.
see Falvey, M., 193
Finck, K., 189
Finney, M., 94
Fiorelli, J. S., 14, 133
Ford, A., 131, 192, 193
see also Baumgart, D., 138; Brown, L., 130, 189, 194; Nisbet, J., 189, 197; Sweet, M., 193
Foss, G., 186
Foster, S., 8, 14
Foxx, C. L., 149
Foxx, R. M., 148, 149, 164
Fredericks, H. D., 97, 133

Gage, M. A., 133
Galloway, C., 31
Gallup Organization, 11
Garner, J., 190
Gaylord-Ross, R. J., 164
Giambetti, A.
see Taylor, S. J., 13
Gleidman, J., 5
Glenn, L., 85
Goddard, H. H., 15
Gold, M. W., 164, 165, 186, 192
Goldenberg, I. I., 15
Goodall, P.
see Wehman, P., 184
Goodlad, J., 7
Graff, S.

Gottlieb, L., 147
see Sweet, M., 193
Greenspan, S., 194
Gross, A. M., 148
Gruenewald, L., 32
see also Brown, L., 141
Guardanapo, E.
see Callahan, M., 191
Guess, D., 165

Hahn, H., 5
Hall, R. V., 164
Halpern, A. S., 30
Hamre-Nietupski, S., 192
see also Brown, L., 141
Hanley-Maxwell, C., 195
Hansen, C. L., 31
Haring, N. G., 31
Harris, S. L., 148
Hauber, F. A., 14, 15, 17, 28
Heads, T. B., 165
Hearne, P. B., 190
Hemming, H., 17
Hemp, R., 8, 27, 29, 32
Hewitt, F. M., 164
Hibbard, M., 196
Hill, B. K., 14, 27, 28
see also Hauber, F. A., 17; Lakin, K. C., 29
Hill, J., 130
see also Hill, M., 192
Hill, M., 192
see also Wehman, P., 184
Hitzing, W., 26, 31, 32
Holland, J. F., 133
Holvoet, J., 165
Hopkins, B. L., 149
Hops, H., 147, 149
Horner, R. D., 148, 164
Horner, R. H., 97, 164, 187
see also Bellamy, G. T., 186
Howes, R., 8, 27, 29, 32
Hoyt, R., 164
Hughart, L., 147
Humm-Delgado, D., 132
Humphrey, M. J., 110, 111
Hunter, J., 193

Inman, D. P., 164
Intagliata, J., 15
Irvin, L. K., 164
Iwata, B. A., 130

Jacob, G., 50
Jacobson, J. W., 27
Janicki, M. P., 27
Jansen, P. E., 148
Johnson, F.
see Falvey, M., 193
Johnson, Judge F., 26
Johnson, S. M., 148
Johnson, T., 51
Johnson-Dorn, N., 133
Jones, J. R., 149
Jones, P. A., 13
Jones, R., 7

Kaplan, F., 8, 9, 104
Karlan, G., 164
Kazdin, A. E., 165
Keating, R., 11
Keith, K. D., 17
Kerr, M., 149
Kessler, K.
see Brown, L., 186, 190; Nisbet, J., 189
Kiely, D., 149
Kiernan, J., 130
Kindred, M., 105
Knitzer, J., 39
Knoll, J., 8, 9, 12, 13, 39
Koegel, R. L., 165
Korten, D., 96
Krastner, L. S., 11
Kraus, M., 184
Kregel, J., 184, 189
Kudla, J. J., 15
Kupfner, F., 13

Lakin, K. C., 14, 26, 27, 28, 29
see also Hauber, F. A., 17
Lambert, J. L., 164
Landis, S., 88
Larkey, P., 105
Larsen, J. M., 149

Lavender, T., 17
Lemanowicz, J. A., 13, 17
Lichstein, K., 148
Lichter, S.
see Taylor, S. J., 13
Lindley-Southard, B., 133
Lipner, C., 164
Lipton, R., 192
Livi, J., 130
Living Resources Corp., 133
Locke, B. J., 148
Loomis, R.
see Brown, L., 130, 186, 189, 190, 194; Nisbet, J., 189; Sweet, M., 193
Lorimer, W. P., 148
Lovaas, O. I., 148
Lubin, R. A., 17
Lutfiyya, Z., 39
Lutzker, J. R., 148
Lyle, C., 85

MacEachron, A., 184
Mank, D. M., 187
Manning, P. J., 147
Marzilli, R., 148
Mason, W. A., 164
Matherne, P., 148
McBride, H.
see Callahan M., 191
McCarthy, T. J., 15, 133
McCord, W. T., 15, 27
see also Taylor, S. J., 13, 28, 29
McDonald, R. S., 164
McGee, J., 80, 81
McGimsey, J. F., 164
McGowan, B., 39
McNally, J., 8, 10
Mencken, H. L., 104
Messina, R.
see Baumgart, D., 138; Ford, A., 131; Nisbet, J., 197
Meyer, L. H., 97
Michael, D., 106
Mirenda, P., 192, 193
Mitroff, I., 94
Mlinarcik, S.
see Taylor, S. J., 13
Mulick, J., 164
Mulligan, M., 165
Murphy, M. J., 164

Nanus, B., 87
National Commission on Excellence in Education, 7
Neef, N. A., 130
Nelson, D. J., 30
New York Times, 6
Nielsen, G., 148
Nietupski, J., 130, 192
Nisbet, J., 189, 194, 197
see also Baumgart, D., 138; Brown, L., 130, 189, 194; Ford, A., 131; Sweet, M., 193
Noble, J.
see Hill, M., 192

O'Brien, J., 141
Ozolins, A., 8, 10

Page, T. J., 130
Panyan, M., 164
Paolini, M., 110
Parker, R. M., 164
Pelmonter, C.
see Callahan, M., 191
Penrod, D., 105
Pentecost, J.
see Wehman, P., 184
Perske, R., 138
Peterson, C. R., 147
Peterson, L. R., 164
Peterson, R. F., 164
Pezzoli, J. J., 11
Pill, R., 17
Powell, D., 110, 111
President's Panel on Mental Retardation, 104
Prochaska, J., 148
Provencal, G., 55, 59, 60, 133
Pumpian, I.
see Baumgart, D., 138; Brown, L., 141; Falvey, M., 193

Racino, J., 39
Rago, W. V., 164
Rahan, T., 147

Ranieri, L.
see Ford, A., 131
Raynes, N. V., 14, 17
Renzaglia, A., 195
Reppucci, N. D., 11
Revell, G., 184
see also Hill, M., 192
Reynolds, M., 25
Rhodes, L. E., 187
see also Bellamy, G. T., 186
Rhodes, N., 190
Rimmer, B., 148
Rincover, A., 147
Robbins, T., 70
Roberts, M. W., 148
Rogan, P.
see Brown, L., 186, 190
Rojahn, J., 164
Rosen, M., 28, 87
Rosenau, N., 39, 47, 48, 81
Roth, R., 11
Roth, W., 5, 7
Rothman, D. J., 9, 12, 105
Rothman, S. M., 9, 12, 105
Rucker, L., 53, 56, 110, 111
Rudrud, E. H., 133
Rusch, F., 147, 190, 194, 195
Rutherford, K.
see Callahan, M., 191
Ryan, K. M., 186, 192

Sachs, M., 192
Sailor, N., 165
Saitz-Blotner, S., 184
Sajwaj, T. E., 148
Salembier, G., 189
Saunders, R., 165
Schaeffer, B., 148
Scheerenberger, R. C., 14
see also Hauber, F. A., 17
Schell, R. M., 164
Schleien, S. J., 130
Schreibman, L., 148
Schroeder, J.,
see Baumgart, D., 138; Falvey, M., 193; Nisbet, J., 197
Schroeder, S., 164
Scull, A., 13
Searl, S., 27
see also Taylor, S. J., 13, 28, 29
Seltzer, M. M., 11
Seyfarth, J., 189
Seys, D. M., 147
Shaffer, T., 105
Shapiro, S. T., 148
Sheehan, M., 187
Shelton, C. S., 192, 194
Sherman, J. S., 148
Shiraga, B., 188
see also Brown, L., 130, 186, 189, 190, 194; Nisbet, J., 189, 197; Sweet, M., 193
Shores, R., 149
Shoultz, B., 194
Silver, E. J., 17
Silverman, W. P., 17
Simmons, J. Q., 148
Singh, N. N., 147, 148
Sizer, T. R., 7
Skarnulis, E., 40
Skodak-Crissey, M., 87
Slaby, D. A., 149
Slater, M. A., 132
Smith, N., 148
Smith, T. E. C., 11
Smull, M., 192
Sneed, T. J., 149
Snell, M., 186
Solnick, J. V., 147
Solzhenitsyn, A., 77
Sontag, E.
see Brown, L., 32
Sorrell, S., 148
Sowers, J., 189
Sprague, J. R., 164
Stanfield Film Associates, 207
Starr, R., 6
Stokes, T. F., 164, 194
Strain, P., 149
Striefel, S., 164
Strohm, B.
see Brown, L., 186, 190
Strully, C., 138
Strully, J., 45, 138
Sweet, M., 193
see also Baumgart, D., 138;

Sweet, M. ***(continued)***
Brown L., 130, 186, 189, 190, 194; Ford, A., 131; Nisbet, J., 189, 197
Swinson, R. P., 148

Tanner, B., 148
Tarpley, H. D., 164
Tate, B. G., 148
Taylor, B., 184
Taylor, S. J., 7, 13, 27, 28, 29, 39, 134
Terman, L. M., 15
Terrace, H. S., 164
The Association for Persons with Severe Handicaps, 138
Thomas, S., 85
Thvedt, J. E., 164
Tizard, J., 104
Tjosvold, D., 133
Tjosvold, M. M., 133
Tomlinson, S., 16
Touchette, P. E., 148, 164
Turnbull, R., 26
Turner, J.
see Bellamy, G. T., 186

Udvari, A.
see Nisbet, J., 197
U.S. Department of Labor, 193, 196
U.S. Senate, 13, 28

VanDeventer, P.
see Brown, L., 130, 186, 189, 190, 194
Vanier, J., 106
Vilhauer, D. A., 186
Vincent, B., 194
see also Brown, L., 32
Voeltz, L. M., 130
Vogelsberg, R. T., 130, 164

Walker, P., 39
Walls, R. T., 164
Warren, C. A. B., 28
Waters, B., 196
Weeks, M., 164
Wehman, P., 130, 184, 189, 193, 194
see also Hill, M., 192
Wesolowski, M. D., 147, 164
Wetherby, B., 164
Wheeler, J., 130
White, C. C., 14
see also Hauber, F. A., 17
White, G. D., 148
Wieck, C. A., 15
Wiegerink, R., 149
Wilcox, B.
see Bellamy, G. T., 186; Brown, L., 32
Willer, B., 15
Williams, J. A., 165
Williams, W., 130, 164
Wilms, W., 190
Winnenberg, J., 89–90
Winton, A. S. W., 147
Winwood, S., 81
Wisotzek, I. E., 164
Wolfe, M. M., 148
Wolfensberger, W., 85
Wuerch, B. B., 130

York, J.
see Brown, L., 186, 190; Nisbet, J., 197
Young, J., 190
Youngblood, G. S., 15, 133

Zahm, D., 164
Zane, T., 164
Zanella, K.
see Brown, L., 186, 190
Zeiler, M., 148
Zeiter, S., 190
Ziarnik, J. P., 133
Zupnick, S., 147

Subject Index

accountability, 57–59
adaptive devices, and vocational placement, 196–97
administration of services
  and administrative reform, 105–06
  and barriers to integration, 12–13
  in Region V (Nebraska), 117
  see also leadership
adoption, 45
Adoption Assistance and Child Welfare Act (P. L. 96–272), 39
adult family homes, 119
age-appropriateness, 139
agency change and the development of effective services
  agency position within the community and service system, 91–92
  designing a new response, 96–101
  issues of, 101–02
  lessons of, 92–93, 103–04
  revising assumptions, 94–96
  a new social architecture for, 89–90
  a vision for, 88–89
  see also integrated services, development of; leadership
applied behavior analysis, and gentle teaching, 150–55
"area management" system (Region V, Nebraska), 57

Beta Hostels (Attleboro, MA), 94–96
bonding, 148, 149–50, 151–52, 156–63,
  budget development, 122–23

caregiver
  posture of, and gentle teaching, 155–56, 157–58
  see also direct-service provision
cash subsidies, for foster families, 41–42
children
  adoption of, 45
  families for, 37–39
  foster families for, 45–48
  permanency planning for, 39–40
choice making
  and direct-service provision, 139–40
  and self-advocacy, 204
clinical relationship, as barrier to integration, 16–17
College for Living, 206
Columbia County, WI, 52–53
commitment
  and community integration, 55–56
  and leadership, 56, 67–84, 98, 103–04
  proverbs for, 83–84
  renewal of, 88–93
community integration
  and accountability, 57–59
  barriers to, 10–18
  and commitment, 55–56
  and flexibility, 56–57
  making it work, 54–59
  principles of, xv–xviii
  strategies for, 18–21
  see also community participation, vocational integration
community participation
  challenges of, 209–213

community participation *(continued)*
  and community integration, xvi–xvii
  and direct-service provision, 133–34, 138
community resistance, 11
community resources
  use of, and community integration, 20, 124
Community Services for the Developmentally Disabled (Michigan), 42
Comprehensive Employment and Training Act (CETA), 191
Congress, 26
consumer monitoring, 58
  see also self-advocacy
continuum of services, 25–27
  see also residential continuum
coordination of services, and vocational placement, 187–91
costs of services, and discrimination, 6–7
co-workers, 194–95
creativity
  and commitment, 70
  of staff, 117

daily life
  envisioning of, and residential service provision, 130–32, 140–41
Dane County, WI, 44
deinstitutionalization, versus development of quality services, 59–60
Developmentally Disabled Assistance and Bill of Rights Act (1975), 26
Dictionary of Occupational Titles, 193, 196
directo-service provision
  and community participation, 133–34
  principles of, 137–40
  role of, 134–37
  strategies of, 140–44
disability, issues in, 3–18
discriminated-against minority, people with disabilities as, 4–7
discrimination, 6–7

ecological inventories, and vocational training, 192–93
education, and discrimination, 7
educational programs, and vocational placement, 189
Education for all Handicapped Children Act (P. L. 94–142), 7
employers, and vocational placement, 189–91
employment, and self-advocacy, 205
enclaves, 187
evaluation of services, 58–59, 88, 143
  see also rights
external review committees, 58

facility-free service system, 121–22
Fairbury, Nebraska (service system)
  establishment of, 113–14
  selection of site, 114–16
  selection of staff, 116–18
  service models, 118–19
  and quality of life, 118–21
families
  for children, 37–39
  and institutional placement, 8
  and the Nebraska service system, 110
family care
  see foster care
Family Subsidy Act (Michigan), 41–42
Family Support and Resource Center (Dane County, WI), 44
Family Support Program (Wisconsin), 42–45
family supports, 40–45
fiscal responsibility, and integration, 20–21
foster care, 29–30
foster families, 45–48
  payment of, 47–48
  placement of children in, 46–47
  recruitment of, 48
  support of, 47

generic resources/services, use of, 20, 98–100, 124
gentle teaching, 147–78
  and decision making, 165–69
  dimensions of, 156–63
  and interactionalism, 150–56
  responses, 169–77

techniques, 163–65
group homes
as barrier to integration, 14–15
individualized alternatives to, 49–50
operation of, 61–62
and the residential continuum, 29

handicapism, 7–10
homes
definition of, 37
for everyone, 59
versus learning environments, 136–37
as a model of service, 118–19

independence, and interdependence, 135–36
independent living, and the residential continuum, 30
individualized living, 49–53
individualized residential supports, development of, 19, 53–54, 98–99, 111, 124–25, 140–44
see also integrated services
individualized vocational placements, development of, 185–87
institutions, 7–10, 12–13
institutional interests, as barrier to integration, 12–13
integrated/segregated services
versus intensity of services, 31
relative funding for, 32
integration
see community integration, community participation, integrated services, social relationships, vocational integration
integrated services
development of, 121–24
models of, 118–19
and quality of life, 119–121
interactional equity, and gentle teaching, 161–62
interactionalism, 150–56
Intermediate Care Facilities for the Mentally Retarded (ICF/MRs), 28–29
International League of Societies for Persons with Mental Handicap, 19
job creation/modification strategies, 196
job placement, 185–87, 189–91
job-site inventories, 192–93
Job Training Partnership Act (JTPA), 191

Kennedy Foundation, 6

leadership
and commitment, 56, 88–93, 67–84
contributions of, 87
and creativity, 70
and enthusiasm, 72–74
gone awry, 74–76
and ignorance, error, and fallibility, 86–87, 104–07
lessons for, 103–04
and objective clarity, 69–70
and personalism, 76–79
and social activism, 71–72
learning, opportunities for, xviii
learning organization, 97
least restrictive environment (LRE) principle
concept of, 25–27
pitfalls in, 30–33

Macomb Oakland Regional Center, 29, 40, 45–58, 51, 55, 56, 57, 58, 60, 69
Medicaid funds, 13, 28–29
Michigan, 29, 41, 45
Michigan Department of Mental Health, 56
Mills v. Board of Education (1972), 25
minority status, of people with disabilities, 4–7, 21
monitoring
see accountability, evaluation of services

natural routines
utilization of, and direct-service provision, 139
natural supports
utilization of, and direct-service provision, 138
and vocational training, 194–95

Nebraska service system, 56–57, 109–112
neighborhood opposition
see community resistance
New York State Office of Mental Retardation and Developmental Disabilities, 28
nonintrusive interventions, and direct-service provision, 138–39
see also gentle teaching
normalization, and community participation, 211–12
nursing homes, people with developmental disabilities in, 3–4, 28

Of Mice and Men, images of disability in, 5
on-grounds residential facilities, 28
Options for Individuals (Louisville, KY), 97–100
Options in Community Living (Madison, WI), 51–52, 56
Our Voice is New, 207

parents
role of, in services, xviii, 58, 109–112
fears of, 13–14
see also families
partial participation, principle of, 138
payment mechanisms, for job placement, 186–87
Pennhurst State School and Hospital v. Halderman, 26
Pennsylvania ARC v. Pennsylvanit (PARC), 25
People First, 207
permanency planning, 39–40
programming
formal vs. informal, 143
need for, 123–24
Public Law 94–142, 26

quality of life
and community integration, 119–121
defining, 89
and equal opportunity, 20
quality services
development of, versus deinstitutionalization, 59–60

Region V (Nebraska), 49, 50–51, 54, 55, 56, 57, 58–59, 112, 113 (fig.), 114
residential continuum
and the LRE principle, 27–30
problems with, 135–36
Residential, Inc. (Perry County, OH), 88–93
readiness model, and LRE, 32
residential service providers
see direct-service provision
rights
infringement of, and LRE, 33
and quality assurance, 102
Rights Now, 206
rural integration (Fairbury, NE), 113–121

Saunders County Office of Mental Retardation (Nebraska), 58
self-advocacy, 202–08
see also self-determination
self-determination, 19
semi-independent living, and the residential continuum, 30
Seven Counties Services, 45, 46, 55
site-selection laws, 12
social activism, and commitment, 71–72
social relationships
building of, xvii, 94–96, 98–100, 101, 138
and community participation, 210
and job placement, 185
Social Security Act, Title XIX of, 13
social/communication skills, and vocational training, 193–94
Special Olympics, 6
staff
and commitment, 56
and creativity, 117
and the establishment of social

relationships, 94–96, 98–100
ratios, 159–60
selection of, 116–18
roles of, 90, 92
see also caregiver; direct-service provision
stereotypes, 5–6
supervised apartments, 119
supportive living arrangements, 49–54
system design
as barrier to integration, 14–16
and service development, 102–03
systematic instruction, and vocational training, 1955–96

technology, use of, 123

U.S. Department of Health and Human Services, Office of Human Development Services, 191
U.S. Supreme Court, 17, 26

vocational integration, 184–98
community acceptance of, 116
and coordination of services, 187–91
and development of individualized placements, 185–87
and use of instruction and technology, 191–97

Willowbrook case, 31
Wisconsin Department of Health and Social Services, 43, 44
Working Organization for Retarded Children, 55–56
Wyatt v. Stickney (1972), 26

Youngberg v. Romeo, 17

zoning, as barrier to integration, 12